Viewed SIDEWAYS

Viewed SIDEWAYS

WRITINGS
ON CULTURE
AND STYLE IN
CONTEMPORARY
JAPAN

Donald Richie

Stone Bridge Press • Berkeley, California

Published by
Stone Bridge Press
P.O. Box 8208
Berkeley, CA 94707
TEL 510-524-8732 • sbp@stonebridge.com • www.stonebridge.com

See Acknowledgments for publication histories.

Printed in the United States of America.

LIBRARY OF CONGRESS CATALOGING-IN-PUBLICATION DATA
[on file]

Only what is seen sideways sinks deep.
E.M. FORSTER

Contents

IV   On Film

V   The View from Inside

Introductory Note

This is the third collection of my essays on culture and style in contemporary Japan. The first was *A Lateral View* (Japan Times, Ltd., 1987 / Stone Bridge Press, 1992) and the second was *Partial Views* (Japan Times, Ltd., 1995). This third volume, *Viewed Sideways*, contains eleven essays from the earlier collections and twenty-six that have never before been collected. For this edition some of the essays have been edited and expanded or shortened. These thirty-seven essays are intended to offer a cross-section view of Japan's enormous cultural variety.

DONALD RICHIE
Tokyo, Japan
2011

I

*The
Larger
View*

Intimacy and Distance:
On Being a Foreigner in Japan

As Edward Said once wrote: "The more one is able to leave one's cultural home, the more easily is one able to judge it, and the whole world as well, with the spiritual detachment and generosity necessary for true vision. The more easily, too, does one assess oneself and alien cultures with the same combination of intimacy and distance."

I have lived for well over half my life in—from my point of view—just such an alien culture; one, further, considered by both natives and visitors as more alien than most—Japan.

The visitor to mid-twentieth-century Japan, particularly if he was an American romantic, was often accompanied by an urge to intimacy that was tempered by the fact of distance: his voyage was not only inner discovery of what he had not already known, but escape from what he already knew. These differences were rendered dramatic in that so much appeared Western but was revealed as Western only in appearance. He found in the shoe store something he did not know could fit a foot; looking into the carpenter's shop there were very few tools he could recognize; eating a Western meal he discovered that it was mainly Japanese—there were, for a time, even rice cakes in McDonald's.

At the same time there was a new feeling of freedom. The visitor was no longer controlled by his own mores and could disregard Japan's. Exceptions were made for the *gaijin*, who could be expected to know nothing. This freedom included the ultimate liberty of finding everything "other" than himself—just walking down the street he enjoyed the freedom of seeming manifestly different.

In Japan foreigners had been stared at for well over a century. The early accounts all mention it, and until the massive influx of foreigners in the 1980s, they still were. They became used to it and eventually irritation turned to need. No matter what the Japanese truly thought, you were treated like a star. When my wife—tall, blonde, blue eyed—went back to New York, one of the things she said she missed was being stared at on the streets.

Shortly, however, the travelers discover that Japan, at the same time, insists that they keep their distance. It is suggested that they live with their own kind, in expensive ghettos such as Tokyo's Roppongi. The exceptions being made for the foreigner then began to be perceived as limitations. Though the travelers desired intimacy, Japan was gently teaching them to keep their distance. (And, if they were yellow or black instead of white or pink, the lesson would be harsher and the distance greater.)

Another country, says Alastair Reid, an authority on the subject, is another self. One is regarded as different and so one becomes different—two people at once. I was a native of Ohio who knew only the streets of little Lima, and I am also an expatriate who knows best the streets of Tokyo, largest city in the world. Consequently I can compare them. And since the act of comparison is the act of creation, I am able to learn about both.

In the process I am absolved from prejudices of class and caste. I cannot detect them and no one attempts to detect them in me since my foreignness is difference enough. I remain in a state of surprise and this leads to heightened interest and hence perception. Like a child with a puzzle I am forever putting pieces together and saying, Oh. Or *naruhodo*, since I was learning Japanese.

Learning a language does indeed create a different person since words determine facts. When I first arrived I was an intelligence-impaired person since I could not communicate and had to, like a child or an animal, guess from gestures, from intent, from expression.

Language freed me from such elemental means of communication, but it taught me a lesson I would not otherwise have known. While it is humiliating to ideas of self to be reduced to what one says (nothing at all if one did not know Japanese), it teaches that there are avenues other than speech.

Just as seeing a foreign film without subtitles may not impart much about the story but it does teach something about filmmaking, so being in Japan with no knowledge of Japanese language teaches much about the process of communicating.

What I am describing here is what any traveler, expatriate or otherwise, knows, but the degree and the difference depends upon the place and its culture. Japan tends to give a strong jolt because the space between the distance kept and the intimacy implied is greater than in some other countries. Japan is still openly (rather than covertly) xenophobic, but at the same time it has need for the foreigner—or at least his goods. This creates an oscillating dialectic—one that affects the Japanese in regard to foreigners almost as much as it affects foreigners in regard to the Japanese.

From the Japanese point of view, the ideal arrangement is for the visitor to come, do his business, and go home. For one who elects to live here, the fact is cause for interest and concern. How often it is implied that I would do better to go back wherever I came from. This is not unkind, nor even inhospitable. People are reacting as they would were they in a foreign land themselves. Many Japanese want to return to Japan, do not travel well, need *miso* soup, etc. They do not think of others behaving differently in a like situation. "Where are you from?" asks the taxi driver. Told, he asks, "But you go home often, don't you?" Assured that I do, he is mollified.

Given this imposed distance, the intimacy seemingly promised by many Japanese becomes doubly attractive. The promise is, I think, not intended. It is occasioned by a real desire to give the guest pleasure, an inability to say plainly no, and a concern for gain. This means that the foreigner is forever kept up in the air, be it in a business deal or a love affair. Sometimes the emotions in these situations are identical. I heard a frustrated merger specialist ironically complain about a failed deal with a metaphor: "There I was, open like a flower . . ."

And the lone person, the person who does not speak the language well, he who never spent his childhood in the culture—precisely, this newcomer—is most in need of the intimacy that is often dangled before him and is always just around the corner.

That this need often takes sexual form is notorious. Travelers almost by definition screw more (or want to screw more) than other people. Part of it is the freedom ("no one knows me here"), but most of it is the need to affirm self on the most basic level, the emotional. Also, sex is imperialistic since it always implies a top and a bottom, and one of the ways to encompass (and subject) the distant other is through what is often called the act of love but in this context should probably be called the act of sex. When this urge meets the seemingly pliable "native" with her or his "different mores" the result is a kind of infatuation. It can go both ways and often does. But the major consideration is that Japanese have to "live" in their country, and foreigners cannot.

Foreigners, says Alastair Reid, are curable romantics. They retain an illusion from childhood that there might be some place into which they can finally sink to rest: some magic land, some golden age, some significantly other self. Yet the foreigners' own oddness keeps them separate from every encounter. Unless they regard this as something fruitful, they cannot be considered cured.

This is the great lesson of expatriation. In Japan I sit on the lonely heights of my own peculiarities and gaze back at the flat plains of Ohio whose quaint folkways no longer have any power over me, and then turn and gaze at the islands of Japan, whose quaint folkways are equally powerless in that they insist that I am no part of them. This I regard as the best seat in the house. Because from here I can compare, and comparison is the first step toward understanding.

I have learned to regard freedom as more important than belonging. This is what my years of expatriation have taught me. I have not yet graduated, but Japan with its rigorous combination of invitation and exclusion has promised me a degree. For it I have adopted as motto a paragraph quoted by Said from the *Didascalicon of Hugh of St. Victor*: "The man who finds his homeland sweet is still a tender beginner; he to whom every soil is as his native one is already strong; but he is perfect to whom the entire world is as a foreign land."

—*1993*

Japan: A Description

Japan is entered: the event is marked, as when one enters a Shinto shrine, by passing beneath the *torii* gateway. There is an outside; then, there is an inside. And once inside—inside the shrine, inside Japan—the experience begins with a new awareness, a way of looking, a way of seeing.

You must truly observe. Go to the garden and look at the rock, the tree. Ah, nature, you say and turn away—then stop. You have just discovered that rock and tree have been placed there, placed by the hand of man, the Japanese hand. A new thought occurs: nature does not happen, it is wrought. A new rule offers itself: nothing is natural until it has been so created.

This comes as a surprise to us of a different culture. The Japanese view is anthropomorphic—unashamedly, triumphantly so. The gods here are human and their mysteries are mundane. If we occasionally find the Japanese scene mysterious, it is only because we find such simplicity mysterious. In the West, cause and effect this clear tend to be invisible. Look again at the *torii*. The support, the supported—that is all.

Observation, appreciation, and, through these, understanding. Not only in Japan, of course, but everywhere, naturally. But in Japan the invitation to observe is strongest because the apparent is so plain.

Look at the architecture. The floor defines the space; from it the pillars hold the beams; on them the roof contains the whole. Nothing is hidden. Traditionally there is no façade. Take the shrines at Ise. Cut wood, sedge, air—that is all they are made of.

The spatial simplicity extends temporally as well. The shrines have been destroyed and identically rebuilt every twenty years since antiquity. This cycle is an alternative to the Pyramids—a simpler answer to the claims of immortality. Rebuild precisely and time is obliterated. Ise embodies the recipe for infinity: one hundred cubits and two decades. We see what is there, and behind it we glimpse a principle.

Universal principles make up nature, but nature does not reveal those principles in Japan until one has observed nature by shaping it oneself. The garden is not natural until everything in it has been shifted, changed. Flowers are not natural either until so arranged to be. God, man, earth—these are the traditional strata in the flower arrangement, but it is man who is operative, acting as the medium through which earth and heaven meet.

And the arrangement is not only in the branches, the leaves, the flowers. It is also in the spaces in between. Negative space is calculated, too—in the architecture, in the gardens, in the etiquette, in the language itself. The Japanese observe the spaces between the branches, the pillars; they know too when to leave out pronouns and when to be silent.

Negative space has its own weight, and it is through knowing both negative and positive (*yin* and *yang*), the specific gravity of each, that one may understand the complete whole, that seamless garment that is life. There are, one sees, no opposites. The ancient Greeks—Heraclitus—knew this, but we in the Western world have forgotten and are only now recalling. Asia never forgot; Japan always remembered.

If there are no true opposites, then man and nature are properly a part of one another. Seen from the garden, the house is another section of the landscape. The traditional roof is sedge, the stuff that flourishes in the fields. The house itself is wood, and the mats are reed—the outside brought in.

The garden is an extension of the house. The grove outside is an enlargement of the flower arrangement in the alcove. Even now, when land prices make private gardens rare, the impulse continues. The pocket of earth outside the door contains a tiny tree or a flowering bush. Or, if that is impossible, then the alcove in the single matted room contains a budding branch, a solitary bloom.

Even now that sedge and reed are rarely used, the shapes they took continue. Man-made nature is made a part of nature, a continuing symbiosis. Even now, the ideal is that the opposites are one.

The garden is not a wilderness. It is only the romantics who find wildness beautiful, and the Japanese are too pragmatic to be romantic. At the same time, a garden is not a geometrical abstraction. It is only the classicist who would find that attractive, and the Japanese are too much creatures of their feelings to be so cerebrally classic. Rather, a garden is created to recreate (they would say "reveal") nature. Raw nature is simply never there.

Paradigm: In Japan, at the old-fashioned inn, you get up, you go to take your morning bath, and you are invisible. No one greets you. Only when you are washed, dressed, combed, ready—only then comes the morning greeting. Unkempt nature, unkempt you, both are equally just not there. The garden prepared is acknowledged as natural. What was invisible is now revealed and everything in it is now in "natural" alignment.

Thus, too, the materials of nature, once invisible, are now truly seen. Formerly mute, they are now "heard." The rock, the stone, are placed in view; textures (bark, leaf, flower) are suddenly there. From this worked-over nature emerge the natural elements. Wood is carved with the grain so that the natural shape can assert itself. In the way the master sculptor Michelangelo said he worked, the Japanese carpenter finds the shape within the tree. Or, within the rock, for stone too has grain, and this the mason finds, chipping away to reveal the form beneath.

"Made in Japan" is now a slogan well known, and one that we now see has extensions—like silicon chips and transistors. Not the same as carved wood or chiseled stone, but created through a similar impulse. And with such an unformulated national philosophy ("Nature is for use") this is not surprising. Everything is raw material, inanimate and animate as well.

Not only is nature so shaped, but human nature, too, is molded. We of the West may approve of the dwarfed trees, the arranged flowers, the massaged beef, but we are disapproving when people are given the same attentions. Our tradition is against such control. Japan's, however, is not. It welcomes it.

Society is supposed to form. Such is its function. We are (they would say) all of one family, all more or less alike. So we have our duties, our obligations. If we are to live contentedly, if society (our own construct) is to serve, then we must subject ourselves to its guiding pressures.

As the single finger bends the branch, so the social hand inclines the individual. If the unkempt tree is not considered natural, then the equally unkempt life can also play no useful part. So, the Japanese do not struggle against the inevitable. And, as they say, alas, things cannot be helped—even when they can be. This simplified life allows them to follow their pursuits. These may be flower arranging, or Zen, or *kendo* fencing. Or, on the other hand, working at Sony, Toyota, Honda. Or *is* it the other hand?

The support, the supported. The structure of Japanese society is visible; little is hidden. The unit is among those things most apparent. The module: *tatami* mats are all of a size, as are *fusuma* sliding doors and *shoji* paper panes. Mine fits your house, yours fits mine.

Socially, the module unit is the group. It is called the *nakama*. Each individual has many: family, school, club, company. Those inside (*naka*) form the group. This basic unit, the *nakama*, in its myriad forms, makes up all of society. The wilderness, nature unformed and hence invisible, is outside the *nakama* of Japan, and that wilderness includes all nonmembers, amongst them, of course, us, the *gaijin* (foreigners). The West also has its family, its school, its company, but how flaccid, how lax. They lack the Japanese cohesion, the structural density, and at the same time the utter simplicity of design.

Land of the robot? Home of the bee and the ant? Given this functional and pragmatic structure, given this lack of dialectic (no active dichotomies, no good, no bad, no Platonic ideals at all), one might think so. But, no—it is something else.

Let the Westerner sincerely try to live by Japanese customs, says Kurt Singer, Japan's most perspicacious observer, "and he will instantly feel what a cell endowed with the rudiments of human sensibility must be supposed to feel in a well-coordinated body."

Does this not sound familiar? It is something we once all knew, we in the West as well. It is something like a balance between individuals and society. One lives within social limitations, to be sure. And if you do not have limitations, how do you define freedom? In Japan the result is individual conformity: each house and each person is different from all the others yet they are also essentially the same. The hand may shape the flower, but it is still a flower.

If one answer to the ambitions of immortality is to tear down and precisely reconstruct the Ise shrines, then one answer to the problem of the one and the many (a Western dichotomy), one way to reconcile the demands of the individual and those of society, is the Japanese self, one in which the two selves become one.

They are not, as Japan proves, incompatible. The individual and that individual playing his or her social role are the same. Just as the house and garden are the same. The *nakama* dissolves fast enough when not needed—and freezes just as fast when desired. To see Japan then is to apprehend an alternate way of thinking, to entertain thoughts we deem contradictory. Having defined nature to his own satisfaction, the Japanese may now lead what is for him a natural life.

This natural life consists of forming nature, of making reality. Intensely anthropomorphic, the Japanese is, consequently, intensely human. This also means curious, acquisitive, superstitious, conscious of self. There is an old garden concept (still to be seen at, say, Kyoto's Entsu-ji temple) that is called *shakkei*. We translate it as "borrowed scenery."

The garden stops at a hedge. Beyond that hedge, space. Then, in the distance, the mountain, Mount Hiei. It does not belong to the temple, but it is a part of the garden. The hand of the Japanese reaches out and offers (appropriates) that which is most distant. Anything out there can become nature. The world is one, a seamless whole, for those who can see it, for those who can learn to observe, to regard, to understand.

—1984

Japanese Shapes

Man is the only one among the animals to make patterns, and among men the Japanese are among the foremost pattern makers. They are a patterned people who live in a patterned country, a land where habit is exalted to rite; where the exemplar still exists; where there is a model for everything and the ideal is actively sought; where the shape of an idea or an action may be as important as its content; where the configuration of parts depends upon recognized form, and the profile of the country depends upon the shape of living.

The profile is visible—to think of Japan is to think of form. But beneath this, a social pattern also exists. There is a way to pay calls, a way to go shopping, a way to drink tea, a way to arrange flowers, a way to owe money. A formal absolute exists and is aspired to: social form must be satisfied if social chaos is to be avoided. Though other countries also have certain rituals that give the disordered flux of life a kind of order, here these become an art of behavior. It is reflected in the language, a tongue where the cliché is expected; there are formal phrases not only for meeting and for parting but also for begging pardon, for expressing sorrow, for showing anger or surprise or love itself.

This attachment to pattern is expressed in other ways as well. Japan is one of the last countries to still wear costumes. Not only the fireman and the policeman, but also the student and the laborer. There is a suit for hiking, a costume for striking; there is the unmistakable fashion for the gangster and the indubitable ensembles of the fallen woman. In old Japan, the pattern was even more apparent: a fishmonger wore this, a vegetable seller, that; a samurai had his uniform as surely as a geisha had hers.

The country should have resembled one of those picture scrolls of famous gatherings in which everyone is plainly labeled, or one of those formal games—the chess-like *shogi* perhaps—in which each piece is marked, moving in a manner predetermined, recognized, each capable of just so much.

More than the Chinese, more even than the Arabs, the Japanese have felt the need for pattern and, hence, impose it—Confucius with his codes of behavior lives on in Japan, if not in China; the Japanese would perhaps have embraced that rigorous rule-book, the Koran, had they known about it.

Here, however, the triumph of form remains mainly visual. Ritual is disturbed by the human; spontaneity ruins ethics. Japan thus makes most patterns for the eyes and names are remembered only if read. Hearing is fallible; the eye is sure. Japan is the country of calling cards and whole forests of advertising; it is the land of the amateur artist and the camera. Everyone can draw, everyone can take pictures. The visual is not taught, it is known: it is like having perfect pitch.

To make a pattern is to discover one and copy it; a created form presumes an archetype. In Japan one suffers none of the claustro-phobia of the Arab countries (geometrical wildernesses) and none of the dizzying multiplicity of the United States (every man his own creation) because the original model for patterns of Japan was nature itself.

One still sees this from the air, always a good introduction to the patterns of a country. Cultivated Japan is all paddies winding in free-form serpentines between the mountains, or a quilt of checks and triangles in the lowlands—very different from the tidy squares of Germany, or that vast and regular checkerboard of North America.

The Japanese pattern is drawn from nature. The paddy fields assume their shape because mountains are observed and valleys followed, because this is the country where the house was once made to fit into the curve of the landscape and where the farmer used to cut a hole in the roof rather than cut down the tree.

The natural was once seen as the beautiful, and even today, lip service is given to this thought. However, both then and now, the merely natural was never beautiful enough. That nature is grand only when it is natural—Byron's thought—would never have occurred to a Japanese. No, this ideal is closer to the ordered landscape of Byron's grandfather: forests become parks, trees are espaliered, flowers are arranged. One does not go against nature, but one does take advantage of it: we smooth, we embellish. Nature is only the potential—man gives it its shape and its meaning.

Since it is the natural forms that are traditionally most admired—the single rock, the spray of bamboo—it is these that are seen more frequently in Japanese art, delivered from the chaotic context of nature and given meaning through their isolation. There are canons, but they derive from nature. Purple and red do not clash as they might in the West because, since they occur often enough in nature, no law of color can suggest that their proximity is unsatisfactory.

A single branch set at one side of the niche-like *tokonoma* and balanced by nothing is not ill composed because there is a rule that insists that formal balance is not necessarily good. The Japanese garden is not the French: symmetry is something imposed upon nature, not drawn from it; asymmetry is a fine compromise between a complete regularity and an utter chaos.

To think of Japan is to think of form, because these patterns are repeated often and faithfully. Wherever the eye rests they occur. They give the look of a land its consistency, as though a set of rules has been rigorously followed. It is these patterns, these shapes, these forms, these designs endlessly occurring, that mark the country.

Chaos is vanquished; pattern prevails. They make the view more consistent than would otherwise be possible. They create what often identifies art: style.

A pattern exists for everything: for temples, kimono, carpenters' saws, and the new is often in the shape of the old. There is only one way to build a shrine, to sew an *obi*. This traditional rigidity is in the outline, the profile, and is based upon a geometry of stress and repose. In the decoration is individual variation: endless, myriad, protean invention. The shape of a temple bell remains, but the patterned surface varies. Dressed stone, planed wood, decorated cloth or pottery, now the gleaming facets of glass, chrome, plastic—the surface is made visible by its own texture. The profile, austere and timeless, is metamorphosed into the unique, the individual.

Japanese design surprises, both in its extent and in its rightness. It is found in the castle and in the kitchen, and the combination of a nearly unvarying outline and a completely varied surface—a decoration that is all form—creates the kind of sign that is weakly called "good."

Not, however, until recently by the Japanese themselves. Traditional design was never noticed. We, the curious foreigners, are in a better position. On the other hand, if we curious foreigners had never seen and did not know the use of some of our own more lovely objects—the light bulb, the spoon, the toilet bowl—we would possibly find them beautiful. But habit blinds and practical knowledge dims. Japan is still distant enough from us that essence is perceived. Disassociated from function, the object becomes formal rather than practical; it becomes an entity—its visual character is all there is.

Design is a matter of economics, and an unchanging economy creates an unchanging design. Usually this design is the conjunction of the nature of the material and the least possible effort. Japanese design is inseparable from art in that it rarely takes the least effort, but rather, the most. Consequently, Japanese craftsmen are paid almost as much as artists would be.

In pre-modern Japan the economy not only produced the audience for craft, it also maintained it, as well as the standards of craftsmanship itself. So long as the economy remained undisturbed there could be no question of fashion. For two and a half centuries Japan was closed, and even before that there was (except, of course, for the massive cultural importations from China and Korea) little of that great fashion maker, Western influence.

From the age of Shakespeare to the time of Tennyson, through all the French Louises and all the British Georges, Japan isolated itself. Until Meiji, the latter half of the nineteenth century, Japan had no arches, cornerstones, fireplaces, armchairs, or farthingales.

Thus Japan had never had to contend with the old fashioned. It had never seen an entire style wane and then wax again. Since old things continued to be used, except for the minor surface variations (a new way for courtesans to do their hair, a fashionable striped kimono material for Kabuki actors and sumo wrestlers, a popular shade of cinnamon brown we might compare to puce) there was little concept of the structurally old. There were no antique stores, only secondhand stores and pawnshops. Precious old objects existed but always in the context of the present.

These old things showed the same "perfect" shape. They accommodated themselves both to their desired use and also to the natural laws of stress and response. Design followed the Confucian standard in all things: uniformity and authority. It followed that Japan is thus the home of the module unit, the first of the prefab lands. At the same time, however, though the profile is standard, individuality is allowed, even insisted upon in the surface itself. One might say of Japanese design what Aldous Huxley said of the Mayan: "It is florid but invariably austere, a more chaste luxuriance was never imagined."

Although the distinction between outline profile and surface decoration is as artificial and as arbitrary as that between form and content, it is possible to say Japanese design not only permits but insists upon archetypal patterns and that all such patterns show a like division, a like propensity.

This natural affinity everywhere remains. Lewis Mumford has observed that the airplane is called beautiful because it looks like a seagull. In Japan, this affinity is more acknowledged, more displayed, than elsewhere. Thus, one of the reasons for the beauty of Japanese design—its rightness, its fitness—and one of the reasons for the proliferation of Japanese forms, their economy, their enormous presence, is that the Japanese man and woman, artists or not, are among the last to remember the earliest lesson that nature teaches all makers.

—*1962*

Japanese Rhythms

Cultures have their own rhythms: how they divide the day and the nights, when to go fast and when to go slow. Some of the differences are familiar. A well-known temporal gulf exists between the global north and south. The latter has, for example, its famous siesta—night again in the middle of the day. The northern visitor is always surprised at this diurnal difference and is often irritated as well.

Another familiar gulf exists between the East and the West, the Orient and the Occident. We speak of the slower pace, calling it leisurely if we like it, indolent if we don't. These temporal differences are well known. Not so familiar, however, are those cultures that blend the differences and bridge the chasms. Among these, the most spectacular is Japan. Here the rhythms of the West have been rigorously applied and yet, under these, the pulse of old Asia is still felt.

Seen from the outside, the way that the Japanese structure time seems much closer to New York than, say, Kandy or Mandalay. Indeed, most of the Western temporal virtues—efficiency, promptness, get-up-and-go—are being flung in our faces by this seemingly industrious nation.

Yet, viewed from the inside, the older, more purely Asian rhythms persist. There is the new way of arranging the day, and then there is the old. And these two, as with so much else in Japan, coexist—strata in time.

Early to bed, early to rise has been the recipe for business success in the Western world, and this is the image (bright-eyed and bushy-tailed) that many of its inhabitants have of themselves. Thus, the Japanese, taking over this image and making it theirs, now insist that they are a hardworking people and are more flattered than not when referred to as workaholics. Such a role would indeed involve rising at dawn, rushing to the office, putting in long hours, racing home, and going to bed early to rest for the next fulfilling day.

Since this is the official version, it is officially supported. And since everyone has nominally gone home, buses stop running at ten thirty, the subways stop at midnight, and the trains shut down half an hour later. Unlike that of New York and Paris, shameless night-owl abodes, Japanese public transportation does not run all night long.

Yet, the populace is no more off the streets at midnight now than it was in old Tokugawa Japan. The entertainment districts are filled with people long after midnight. These people are not at home resting for the next fulfilling day. They are getting around the night spots by taking taxis.

Nor do the Japanese get up at dawn. Indeed, nowadays, a majority does not get to work until ten o'clock, also the hour when the bazaar at Rangoon opens. To be sure, some attempt an earlier arrival. Being first into the office in the morning supports, and in part creates, the modern idea of the Japanese being very hard workers.

And being the last one out as well. One is supposed to hang around even though one's work may be finished. Being one of the group is considered important and rushing out to conform to an egotistical timetable is bad form. Rather, one subscribes to the group timetable. This has nothing to do with working hard, however; it has to do with mere attendance.

Indeed, as one looks more closely at the manner in which modern Japan structures its business day, one becomes aware of the differences between modern and traditional timekeeping and the manner in which these intermingle.

Once the modern rush to the office is over and the business day is actually begun, the time scheme turns traditional. There are lots of discussions, lots of stopping to drink tea—and nowadays lots of visits to the ubiquitous coffee shop to talk some more. Nor is the talk confined to work in the narrow Western sense of the term. Rather, work is socialized since social talk can serve as work because its larger purpose is the important cementing of personal relations within the working force.

Thus, the amount of time spent at what we in the West would call work is much less than what one might expect. The notorious efficiency of Japan does not depend upon time spent. Rather, it depends upon the absence of intramural conflict (though with lots of intramural competition) and an ideological solidarity that is almost beyond the comprehension of the United States and most of Europe.

This is of use mainly (or merely) in the hours, days, years spent together—in the creation and continuation of the group. This is equally true when the office is finally left. It is often left as a group since no one wishes to break cohesion by leaving first. Then the group divides into sub-groups that then go out on the town, to favorite pubs and bars, to continue the social amelioration that has traditionally been so important to Japan.

Far from early to bed, the upwardly mobile Japanese male is fortunate if he catches the last train home. And often he will stay overnight with an office friend, an event that his wife back home will accept as a part of the normal temporal rhythm of her spouse.

In places where day and night are divided according to the needs of actual work—such as in, I don't know, let's say Chicago— the pattern may be closer to the ideal of which Japan so brags. As it is, Japanese temporal reality is something different—far closer to that of Bangkok or Jakarta, the rest of Asia, places where time is almost by definition something that is spent together.

Yet, for a culture as time-conscious as Japan's (one sees mottoes framed on office walls such as "Time is money"), the amount of real temporal waste is surprising. Here, too, the country shows its ancient Asian roots.

Take the matter of appointments, for example. In the big business world of the West, being punctual is sacrosanct. Again, actuality may be another matter, but all subscribe to the idea that to be on time is to be good.

In Asia, however, this is not so. One is frequently left cooling one's heels in the great capitals of the Orient. And Japan, despite its Western temporal veneer, is no different. If you are meeting a member of your group, then he will wait and you can be late. If you are meeting a nonmember you can also be late because it is not so important that you meet or not.

Spatially, the Japanese are very efficient regarding rendezvous. There are known places to meet. In Tokyo one meets in front of Ginza's Wako Department Store, in front of the Almond Coffee Shop in Roppongi, in front of the statue of the dog Hachiko in Shibuya, a famous beast who loyally waited years for its dead master.

Most waiting Japanese are in the position of Hachiko. It is rare to observe anyone being on time. Those who are on time and are doing the waiting are those in an inferior position (in Japan it is the girls who wait for the boys, and not the other way around), or those who want something from the late arrival. Time is money, indeed, but for all this show of making appointments, Japanese standards of punctuality are closer to those of Samarkand than of Paris or London. Still, one wonders. With time so precious that it must be doled out in little pieces, how then can it be so wantonly wasted?

Well, it is not one's own time that is being wasted. It is the other person's, the he or she kept waiting. In fact, one's own time supply is a bit short. That is why one is late, you see.

We in the West, who make nothing like the fuss about time

that the Japanese do, would be insulted to be kept waiting for, let us say, an hour. Yet many Japanese would wait an hour, standing by the store, coffee shop, or bronze dog.

And is this not perhaps then the largest difference between the time concepts of East and West? Time is not moral in Asia, it cannot be used as a weapon. And it cannot really be used to indicate virtue (hardworking, efficient) or vice (lax, late for appointments).

It is rather a seamless entity, an element like the air in which we live. To live naturally with time, says Asia, is to pay no attention to it. And Japan, despite modernization, still subscribes to this ancient tradition. Dig down, through company minutes and office hours, and there, firm, eternal, is time itself.

—*1984*

Japan: Half a Century of Change

When I came to Japan in a cold January in 1947 the first thing that I noticed was change. It was dramatic. Tokyo, like most Japanese cities, had been nearly destroyed during WWII. People were living in the subway tunnels, there was not enough food, and yet already on this burned plane of black ash was rising the lemon yellow of all the new buildings as the odor of burned wood gave way to the smell of fresh-cut lumber.

Every day I saw roads being made and canals being filled as the new city burgeoned. Watching the carpenters at work—sawing through the new wood—I saw that their tools cut as they were pulled, not pushed as they were back in the United States.

I noticed this with understanding—this was something I recognized. For years I had heard that Japan was a kind of topsy-turvy land where everything was done backwards. This had been among the earliest accountings of the country—a model created by early visitors, which had finally reached the snow-covered plains of Ohio, where I had heard of it. So here was something else I could relate to besides all the change: a paradigm for Japan, a model through which I could grasp the metamorphosing place.

Seemingly different, Japan has always seemed to demand a working model for comprehension, as though the place needed an articulated map, or a working metaphor. Here I was, brand new, and already searching around for one.

My viewpoint was that of unchanging Ohio, from whence I, just twenty-one, had come. Topsy-turvy land fit my needs quite well. When fellow Occupiers, looking at the carpenters sawing backwards, smiled and said, "These people have got a long way to go," I agreed.

That was because these people were by definition trying to catch up with the West. They had been at this for some time now, nearly a century, and taken many a wrong turn. But now, thanks to us, they were finally on the right road.

This is what I thought as I stood at the Ginza crossing looking at the kimono and old army uniforms, hearing the *geta* and watching Hokusai's Fuji being blocked out by all the new buildings. They might lose a view, I philosophized, but they were gaining a city.

This was something we Occupiers could understand. The old Japanese military model had proved faulty and the new American economic model seemed to work a lot better. Finding something familiar in an attitude that estimated everything solely by its practical bearing on current interests, we Occupiers worked hard to help put these reversed folks right. There was land reform, the big business cartels were broken up, democracy was introduced, and individuality was being governmentally promoted.

And as I looked at the city of Tokyo growing taller around me, at the Japanese around growing healthier and wealthier every day, I saw that my topsy-turvy paradigm was itself upside down. I had found them reversed only because I came from the other side of the earth. But if I thought about it, at this very instant the people of Ohio were standing on their heads. And, as for my belief that They were catching up with Us: They already had.

*

I left Japan in 1949 to go back to school at Columbia University, and when I returned to Japan in 1954 the Occupation was three years in the past. Land reform was over, the big business cartels were more or less back in place, democracy was being digested away. I saw so much had changed that I did not recognize the place.

What I saw as new was now even more interestingly mingled with what wasn't. Old Shinto shrines on the top of new high-rises, white-robed acolytes on motorbikes, and ancient *zaibatsu* executives reclined in their new steel-and-glass headquarters.

On the streets I still saw some kimono but this traditional dress was overpowered by copies of Dior's New Look. *Geta* were still seen, and heard, but Western-style shoes predominated, getting ready for the Gucci tsunami to come. And standing on the Ginza crossing I saw that Fuji-san had now entirely disappeared, covered by layer after layer of new buildings. And I remembered my earlier model, the now-vanished topsy-turvy land, as I gazed at the backward people who were rapidly becoming forward.

Looking about, I discovered a new model already in place: Japan, land of contrasts, the new and the old living equitably together. Under the modern veneer, there persevered this ageless core. I found supportive paradigms everywhere.

My neighborhood, little Tansumachi, had its named changed to Roppongi 4-*chome*, and was then flattened to make room for a new high-rise. There went the egg-lady and the chicken-man, there went the fruit-shop boys. And yet when the high-rise was completed, I found that the fruit boys had a new shop in its depths, one now named Boutique des Fruits.

Change within continuity—that is what my new model of the country allowed and accounted for. When the *manga* cartoon craze began and trashy comic books started to proliferate, I was thus able to explain it away by being of the opinion that, after all, Hokusai had himself been a kind of cartoonist, now hadn't he? That there had also been a considerable loss in quality did not disturb me because, probably optimistically looking about at the changed country, I thought that my having Occupied it might have had something to do with its present prosperity.

Nor was I alone in my complacency. Ten years after the Occupation was over, the United States was gazing across the Pacific like a fond parent leaning over a crib. That infant economic nimbleness, now so deplored in what is left of the trade talks, was originally approved by the proud parents.

This perceived Japanese pragmatism, this going for what worked regardless of all other considerations, was, we thought, an American gene happily at work in fecund Japan. The country was our younger sibling—a smart kid with growing pains. And, for so long as it fit, Japan took to the kid-brother role. It fit Dr. Takeo Doi's dictates about *amaeru*—that confident leaning upon another for support. It was also quite economical for the country: the money saved on national defense alone was considerable.

Also, it was a better role than that of big brother, for Japan well remembered (even if it didn't much talk about) just where treating the rest of Asia as little brown brothers had gotten it. Dependent, this sibling now looked up to his protectors. This perceived difference we had all gotten used to in the Occupation. I enjoyed being but rarely contradicted to my face and being accorded what I thought was special treatment.

That I was also being marginalized, and often ghettoized as well (Lovely Roppongi, Home of the Foreigner), did not occur to me. After all, even though that golden age of opportunity, the Allied Occupation, was over, not a few of us still managed to get ahead in Japan almost entirely because of our nationality, our skin color, and because we were the people from whom lessons could still be learned. We were the obvious pragmatic choice for a model, and our favored status would last just as long as did our usefulness.

In 1968 I again left Japan, this time to take up a position in New York. If I had stayed in Ohio I would perhaps have been a salesman in Sill's Shoe Store, but I had come to Japan and so I was returning to my country as Curator of Film at the New York Museum of Modern Art.

*

I saw upon my return to Japan in 1974 that so much further change had occurred that my earlier ideas on the grand role of living tradition in Japan now seemed inadequate. Tradition apparently covered much less territory than I had originally estimated.

An example occurred when I went house hunting. During my first stay the rule for houses had been that the rooms were all Japanese—that is, all *tatami*—except for one Western (hard-floor) room. During my second stay, the rule was all Western except for one Japanese room. And now, during my third stay, all Western, no *tatami*, and in one place I saw that the hot-water heater had been put in the *tokonoma*, the traditional alcove for flower arrangements. Also—further indication of change—it was difficult to find anyone to rent to me. I had to have a sponsor, had to put down a sizable amount as a deposit. It slowly became apparent that I—though a very white American—was no longer looked up to.

Perhaps it had been already noticed that the U.S. model was not as successful as originally expected. And as more and more poor white foreigners came to work in rich Japan—as long-legged L.A. girls came to serve in the clubs, as Ohio boys came to labor as doormen—it finally became impossible to slide by simply by being white. Of a consequence we, native Occupier and newcomer alike, found Japan "changed." The Japanese, we said, were becoming "arrogant."

An interesting word choice because it indicates a change from what was perceived as tractable and compliant. Independence is always viewed as arrogance by those being replaced, and though the United States had not actually intended a postwar colonization of Japan, it still did not like the idea of the natives getting uppity.

And as for change, it was all very well, we thought, so long as it proceeded along the lines of the approved model: the surface changeable, the core inviolate. But now—beginning in the 1970s and growing increasingly more apparent in the following decades—a new model was becoming necessary.

Among the more attractive was one that invoked stratification. Japanese culture was composed of successive layers: the new merely piled on top of the old. The Shinkansen now ran faster than all other trains but the carpenters still pulled their saws. People named their girl children Aya and Misaki and thought the common Hanako unspeakably old fashioned—yet somewhere in the provinces a new Hanako was born.

This geological correlation was attractive but as a working model it somehow reminded of Donald Keene's precise metaphor for the place. The onion: you remove layer after layer and finally you get to its core, which is . . . empty.

Another model was a complicated structural affair in which the country was seen as moving through such polarities as *uchi* and *soto* (inside vs. outside), *ninjo* and *giri* (one's own feelings vs. society's), and one that exhibited many other moving parts as well. This made Japan seem a unique place and was consequently a popular model with the Japanese themselves as well as the interested foreigner. It was a solid stage, however, and impervious to change. Perhaps for that reason I never found much use for this model. It could not prepare us for what was occurring. It lived in the past, and, as was becoming more apparent, as the economy bubbled, Japan lived in an eternal present.

I, who sort of believed in ancestor worship, even if the Japanese did not, was thus surprised when I saw the Shiba Tokugawa tombs razed to make way for the Prince Hotel. And I, who thought that a cozy symbiotic relationship existed between Japan and nature, reacted with alarm when I saw the coastline being concreted over, forests cut down to accommodate golf courses, and national park land given over to developers.

More was to come. Later on I saw that lifetime employment, a Japanese tradition if there ever was one, was there no longer; that the upward-bound escalator—just stay on, don't bother to work, and you will be safely carried to the top of your bureaucratic profession—had stopped; and that the national diet had changed: coffee and toast became the easy-to-make national breakfast with difficult *gohan* and *miso* soup reserved for Sunday, maybe. And finger-licking-good American junk for in between.

And that wasn't all. My former models had all made room for the idea of defenseless little Japan inundated by ruthless Western imports. These poured into the country and thus diluted tradition— that was how my paradigm worked. Now I saw that it was not that way at all.

Japan reached out and dragged in. Anything it wanted it got, anything it didn't was kept out. A discerning shopper, the country willingly opened to what was useful, and snapped shut to what was not. Well, so did Ohio, I supposed, but with nothing like the scale, the openness, the panache. This simplified bivalve exemplar of the country did not have the elegance of former miniatures but it seemed to have the virtue of accuracy, at least for the present. It explained a lot.

For example, the true use of English in the country. For decades now the Japanese had been getting it all wrong. We chuckled over it (We Play for General MacArthur's Erection). Then it occurred to me that this misuse of my language was not funny and further did not, as I then believed, show a contempt for English by ignoring the integrity of the original.

No contempt was involved, and no ignorance either. Writings in ads, on signs, over T-shirts and on shopping bags alike were not intended to be "English." They were Japanese-English and this was not a subdivision of English but a subdivision of Japanese— a language directed only toward an uncritical audience for whom meaning had no importance, though this significance of the newly acquired did.

Tradition was judged by the same rule. If it could be turned into the pragmatically useful it remained. This usually meant becoming a new product. Kimono and *geta* had all but disappeared, yet some remained as new signifiers: a girl in a kimono meant Traditional Type, going about her *ikebana* or her *koto* lesson; a boy in *geta* meant either Traditional Tradesman or Traditional Student Rightist, probably going to Takushoku University. And the despised Hanako was revived as the trendy and self-mocking title for a new magazine, which told all the young people what to buy.

The kimono itself was subsumed in the wrappings of Issey Miyake; the architectural tradition turned into the eclectic Japanesque of Arata Isozaki; Edo-mura became a local tourist draw; and the Japan Travel Bureau began urging a trip to Kyoto as time travel to the picturesque Orient, while I sat and watched my traditional Japan turn into Japanland.

"Trad but mod" said a slogan of the 1980s, and it said this about the new. ("Established in 1988" one read, carved in stone, in 1989.) From abroad poured in the products Japan thought Japan wanted as the traditional was being sliced into bite-sized pieces.

I felt I was living in a museum that was now being swiftly destroyed. The wreckers were at work and—oh, there goes a room I thought never would; oh, there goes a whole wing of what I thought was the permanent display.

And there I was in the shambles without a map, minus even

a model, because eventually my two-cylinder paradigm could not begin to cope with change this great.

*

Then I remembered something that fine scholar and good friend Edward Seidensticker had once written: "The relationship between tradition and change in Japan has always been complicated by the fact that change is itself a tradition."

I had, of course, long been aware of Japanese consciousness of change. For example, the fuss made about the seasons. Japan has four separate and distinct seasons, I was forever being told. Well, so does Ohio, I was tempted to answer, and then I remembered that there we only mentioned the seasons to complain about them, that we rarely celebrated them for their own transient sakes.

Yet even now in contemporary Japan with its vast hydroponic farms and its enormous distribution circuits, flowers and food in season were still made something of, and this seemed so because it gave some excuse for celebrating transience. Certainly the annual cherry-viewing orgies all over the country were such. Particularly, I was told, evanescence is celebrated when the petals are floating to the ground and change was at its most palpable—the death of the blossom. There was even an exclamation for appreciation of natural change: ah, *aware*.

And I remembered my classical readings. For example the famous opening line of Kamo no Chomei's *Record of the Ten-Foot-Square Hut* (here given in Burton Watson's translation): "The river flows unceasingly on, but the water is never the same water as before."

I had thought that in looking at the stream Kamo was affirming the reassuring fact that the body of water was, after all, permanent.

But now I saw that what he was indicating was, instead, the fact that the water itself changed, was always different.

I remembered the shrine at Ise. This single wooden edifice is replaced every twenty years. It is torn down and an identical replica is constructed. This has been going on for centuries. And it had seemed to me obvious that this exemplary structure celebrated tradition. It was the core holding.

But now I was not so certain. Ise surely satisfied the claims of eternity and the hopes of immortality—though in a way quite different from that of, say, the Pyramids. But at the same time it celebrated transience. It accepted change and incorporated it. It did so by accommodating it, by building evanescence into the structure of the Ise shrine itself.

Every culture copes with change but how many, I wondered, had made it a moving part? Lots of nostalgia for the good old days to be sure, lots of bad-mouthing the new bad ones, just like everywhere else, but in addition to this, an accommodation to the evanescent, an acceptance of this fact of life. *Shikata ga nai* (It can't be helped), that bleat which so irritates the foreign resident, could now be seen as a graceful acquiescence to the great principle of change itself. After all, that there is nothing one can do about it really means, Let us rather get on with life.

Change is in Japan put to use in the most pragmatic of manners. It alone is permanent and hence a steady source of power. It is perpetual motion, the dream of the physicists come true. And I saw that during all my decades in the country Japan had not changed in its attitude toward change. It was always hands-on and still is. Any respect for the integrity of any original becomes beside the point when it is change itself that is being accommodated.

For example, the traditional landscape gardener moved this rock over a couple of feet, shifted that bamboo grove back a yard or two, and swiped the view of the mountain in the process. The result was the natural garden, a product of change. *Ikebana*, classical flower arrangement, changes venue and placement, and only then calls itself "living flowers" though they are of course no longer quite that, being cut.

The difference that I thought I had noticed in Japan's attitude toward nature was then but one of degree. When the daimyo built himself a landscape garden his need was aesthetic because such labor-intensive work as this would otherwise not have been so ostentatiously indicative of his social standing. When it is money itself, rather than aesthetics and art appreciation, that satisfies the demands of social standing, however, then forests are cut down for golf courses and ancestral tombs are trashed for hotels. But the difference is only in degree—now, famously, money must make more money. The demand is no longer aesthetic—it is economic. Yet the mechanism is the same. Everything changes. Though there may be amber-like blocks of permanence within this moving magma they remain only because they are for the time being useful. Like now, for example.

The irresistible force has met what has seemed an immovable object. We have in Japan the System, the way things are done, the bloated bureaucracy, the Bank of Japan, the Ministry of Finance, those organizations concerned only with their own propagation. Yet they are now structurally irrelevant. As the pressure for change grows, they will slowly give way. They have already—lifetime employment, the effortless escalator to the top, the golden parachute jump into cushy retirement—all of this is now of the past. And more, much more, will change.

What is important, and what is eventually defining, I decided, is this genius for the harnessing of change. Having decided this I looked at my new, small, metaphor of the country—it lies here in my palm, a whirling gyroscope.

This dynamo might become a model elsewhere, I thought. Not as a slogan ("Japan as Number One" had misled practically everyone)—but as a paradigm. As a system of thought that welcomes and celebrates that very change that so transforms us and our world, that accepts death and taxes as well. If there is no mortality there is no life, let alone aesthetics.

And over the hum of my gyroscope I heard the words of the priest Kenko who now nearly seven hundred years ago wrote: "What if man lingered on . . . how things would then fail to move us. The finest thing in life is its uncertainty."

—1994

The Nourishing Void

In Tokyo for the first time, Roland Barthes looked toward the empty Imperial plaza, the invisible palace, and the woodlands beyond, and wrote in *The Empire of Signs* that while Tokyo does possess a center, this center is empty.

This was stated with an air of surprise. Where he came from, centers were never empty. But he could see why Tokyo's was, and he could understand its consequent function. This empty center was an evaporated nation, subsisting here not in order to radiate power, but to give to the entire urban movement the support of its central emptiness.

The idea of emptiness supporting something is not commonly encountered in the West. But it has long been familiar in Asia. Once remarked upon, it is seen everywhere—both in old scroll paintings and in the modern advertisement. What is all that empty space doing there? Why isn't it filled in?

It is not filled in because it is already filled in with itself. It is a structural support. The emptiness of the scroll defines the tiny person crossing the miniscule bridge. In the advertisement it defines that important small print running across the bottom of the page. In both cases, emptiness plays a positive role. It has its own weight, its own specific gravity, its own presence.

To see the full in the empty can be defined, I think, as a creative act. From nothing, something is created. And Japan has traditionally been elevated by the invention of the fullness that invests the empty. Examples spin out from this central idea. Lots of mud and no money? Then create, like the Chinese and the Koreans, superb pottery. Lots of room and no furniture? Then make an aesthetic of space itself and invent the concept of *ma* to account for it. Lots of time for unemployed samurai? Then elevate manners into a ritual and create a space where temporal routine is so heightened that it becomes transparent—invent the tea ceremony where guests with time on their hands sit and savor the emptiness.

From the tea ceremony came an entire celebration of the empty as reflected in the carefully shabby, the ostentatiously poor, the expensively *maigre*. *Wabi, sabi*—things made of very little, of a striking simplicity: the cracked pot holding the field flower.

Such invention, no matter its resultant chic, is created from want. From nothing something is created because it is necessary. The Japanese woodworker creates in his otherwise empty box an artful disclosing of the very grain of his materials. The Japanese gardener, with only stones and trees at hand, hones out of this emptiness something ideal, which he necessarily calls nature but which is nonetheless his aesthetic.

Emptiness can be a virtue in other ways as well. What else is the Zen *koan* but a riddle constructed to be empty? It is up to you to fill it. As Barthes himself notes: Zen wages a war against the prevarication of meaning.

It does so because meaning fixes fully and for all time just one single meaning. All those overtones that so resounded before this naming are now still. Meaning closes. Emptiness, on the other hand, leaves open, all options still hanging. Meaning, wanting to fill this fruitful emptiness, prevaricates because it opts for the single rather than for the burgeoning multiple.

Emptiness can also be celebrated. Look at the films of Ozu. His world is created of very little: the frames of domestic architecture; a single camera position, low; one form of punctuation only, the straight cut; no plot, simply layered scenes of single, haiku-like cause and effect. Often his scenes are empty. People have not yet entered, or have already left. The camera gazes, in a sleeping, half-dark room, at a common vase holding nothing. And we fill this vessel with the emotions we have been holding, emotions generated by the film itself. We fill the empty scene with meanings just as we fill the empty *koan* with insight.

Meanings flow and disappear as the film fades, as the guests bow at the end of the tea ceremony and go home. Here is the temporal equivalent of a nutritious emptiness—an immortal perishability, an eternal transience. Examples abound: the carefully mended tea bowl, the cherished tarnish of the silver caddy, the haiku that freezes forever a single moment. These are the things created from the stuff of time itself.

Even now, much is made of the cherry blossom—not in full bloom but when the petals begin to flutter down. The transient moment thus symbolized is seized upon and visible perishability is openly prized. Thus transience is traditionally celebrated, just as emptiness is traditionally commemorated. Finding nourishment in the void is truly creative, but you have to have the void before you can find the nourishment. And what if this fruitful void fills up?

Something like this is occurring in modern Japan. As I write, emptiness is draining away. A civilization traditionally predicated upon the virtues of being empty is becoming full. The ideals of poverty have been superseded by the ideals of wealth. Since the end of World War II, this traditionally poverty-stricken country has become progressively more wealthy—that is, the government, not the people themselves. But the people have been easy to lead away from the void of poverty when shown the mountain of things for them to buy.

The empty room is no longer filled with the riches of emptiness. Instead, it now contains the television set, the tape/DVD player, the cassette deck, the deep-freeze, the home computer, the microwave, the answering machine, and much, much more.

There is a glut of time, too—a democratic distribution for

everyone. Stretches of time are no longer creative voids to be filled with contemplation. Time is now to be killed and taxidermized with *pachinko*, or with brand-name shopping, or with karaoke. A nation of creators has become a nation of consumers.

This consumerism is the result of a kind of demoralization. Imagine a nation, the culture of which was predicated on the creative use of want. Now remove the want. If the void no longer nourishes, this is because it is no longer there; nor are the master carpenters or the artist masons, and the tea ceremony and the art of arranging flowers have both been transformed from celebrations of emptiness into big businesses.

As to why this should have occurred in a country famed for wringing nourishment from emptiness, I think that the reason—one of the reasons—is that Japanese culture, perhaps because of its long competitive bias, is one of the most pragmatic.

Everything is for use, hardly anything exists for its own intrinsic self. Nature becomes the garden and flowers become *ikebana*. This surge to create is extremely strong. When there is little to create with, and scant material upon which the searching, pragmatic spirit can exercise itself, *ma* and the tea ceremony come into being. When more material comes to hand, as at present, there is a natural swing toward the methods of consumption—a lesser destination.

As the empty world implodes in the midst of excess, it carries away with it a certain necessary creativity—a special and precious ability that in large part brought into being that fast-receding culture recognized as traditionally Japanese.

The empty center is still there, but it supports less and less. Its immaculate transparency turns opaque. A new Barthes, in Japan for the first time, might not even notice it. And as the emptiness vanishes, a kind of creativity vanishes with it.

—1992

The Coming Collapse of Cultural Internationalization

The Tokyo taxi driver taking me home was talking away. We were having the kind of conversation that Japanese often have with foreigners. What is your country? Are you married? When are you going home?

Then he suddenly said, "Well, I sure hope you people keep it up. Just keep on pushing. That's the only way things are going to get any better for people like me who don't work for the government or for the big companies."

I was startled. Japan can seem so uniform, so bland, phrases so expected coming from faces so neutral. And yet the people are not really like this, as my driver had just let me know.

Japan is not a homogeneous monolith. There is as much individuality here as there is anywhere else. But it is harder to see and that is why the taxi driver surprised me. He suddenly became visible.

The reason that this diversity is difficult to see is that society—and its spokesperson, the government—doesn't want it to be seen. From the early reigns of the warlords right down through the various postwar cabinets, Japanese governments have been parental, authoritarian, dictatorial. All have been concerned with the tasks of maintaining public order, of creating harmony and, as they put it, of avoiding confusion.

There have been correspondingly closed ranks to present undivided fronts and to stifle disagreement. Some of these—the centuries of Tokugawa rule, the decade of the Pacific War cabinet—were police states.

These operated through open coercion. This is a process that became learned. Over centuries, overt pressure becomes unnecessary.

Under the house of Tokugawa, the Japanese people were repeatedly invited to internalize the expectancies of their rulers and to do so for the sake of creating a unified and peaceful state.

Such pressure is to be observed in other countries as well but perhaps only in Japan is it so visible. There are signs of it everywhere—historical remains cropping up through the surface of everyday life.

A simple example is the continuing prevalence of such a can't-be-helped expression as *shikata ga nai*. That, contrarily, it actually can be helped, however, is a thought incapable of expression since there is no such phrase as its lexical opposite, *shikata ga aru*, in the language. There are many other and more complicated examples of pressure, and the result is a cultural internalization that informs the citizens of just where the line of social acceptability is drawn.

When a country internalizes official dictates—making, in Freudian terms, the parental government into a superego—one of the results is a rigidity of opinion. This is at the same time accompanied by a flexibility of application, for otherwise life would become intolerable.

This internalization helps create a great pragmatism and an attitude tolerant of a wide range of behavior, so long as it poses no threat. Everything is case by case, except for the final case. One learns where to draw the line. And my taxi driver had just stepped across it.

This is something that is now occurring much more frequently. To be sure, it is still the rare Japanese who will speak his or her mind outright in public. The brave mayor of Nagasaki is one such exception and he was consequently shot by a rightist—a political extreme sharing authoritarian concerns. Yet the number of people willing to speak out privately does seem to be growing.

There have, indeed, been some periods when ordinary nonofficial Japanese freely spoke their mind, freed of the Tokugawa mind-set.

Film Director Nagisa Oshima has mentioned two of them. One was at the beginning of the Meiji Restoration, just after the fall of the house of Tokugawa in the middle of the nineteenth century, and the other was at the end of the Pacific War in the middle of the twentieth. Both periods fostered freely expressed opinion since all major methods of repression and punishment had broken down.

Yet freedom is difficult to live with. Most societies prefer compromise to chaos, and people like peace. Hence, after both of these periods, governments intent on creating national harmony were again back with their advice and suggested guidelines.

If the Japanese now seem to be individually voicing opinion it is perhaps because the process of cultural internalization is again breaking down. The reason would be that Japan is at present undergoing an era of social change and the old parental/authoritarian model is not able to cope with what is occurring.

Just one of the symptoms is the current rift in the Japan–U.S. relationship. One of the causes is the big-brother-like ways of government and business, the assumption that economic prowess is all, that convenience is a sensible national goal, and that all development is invariably good.

One of the results of this rift, and an indication of the breakdown of internalization, is the growing apprehension, seen in the media and in conversation, that purely economic progress has produced some truly negative results.

There are now Japanese citizen's groups that openly oppose more progress. They are against yet more mercantile-minded world expositions; they openly try to prevent the construction of yet more golf courses; they even buy up land so that it cannot be utilized for development.

It is, to be sure, telling that it is concerned groups that do this rather than concerned individuals. But one of the legacies of a totalitarian repression is the sure knowledge that only a group can counter another group. At the same time, Japan is now experiencing a small but real revolution in the very presence of those groups that disagree with the ways of the major model.

And there certainly remains in the country an old-fashioned element that would still like to expel the foreign and once more slam shut the cultural door. Yet, despite the fact that the door was never really opened (Commodore Matthew Perry merely cracked it), such closure is now impossible. Economically, Japan is a part of the rest of the world. Without trade, the country could not feed even half of its citizens, and one cannot trade from behind closed doors. And so, despite heel digging at the governmental level, Japan will keep on becoming the only thing it can be: a different kind of country.

Much will be lost, but much of that—traditional Japan—has now become so gentrified, so compromised, that one can only question its assumed validity. Patterns of thought, cultural assumptions, and language itself are changing as the internalization process continues to break slowly down.

What Japan is changing into I cannot even guess. One sort of Japan observer insists that though forms change, the spirit is maintained. You tear down the old neighborhood but build it over again in the high-rise that takes its place. Well, yes, but has the spirit been maintained after an operation that extensive? I feel that something basic has been changed.

I also feel that this is the price that change extracts. And current pressures from both outside and inside the country are changing the kind of Japaneseness that has resulted in a people mostly afraid to speak out because the conceptual framework for being afraid is still in place.

Just who these new outspoken Japanese will be is something I can guess even less. From among the young? Yes, I hope so, but looking around me I seem to see mainly productions of a society that pushes docility: *manga*-minded, game-addicted boys and girls who wander around in earphone sets. There are many exceptions I am sure, but these super-dociles form the more visible element.

An inarticulate and uncomplaining general public is the answer to the collective wish of society (any society) and consequently of (all) governments. Here we would have ideal citizens, all of them agreeing and all of them contributing in their passive way to the great ideal of unthinking harmony.

Yet, there are dissenters in the ranks, and I think that these will become more numerous as authoritarian ways are becoming more questioned. A chorus of concerned groups and individual voices— Oshima, the mayor of Nagasaki, my taxi driver—are growing in number and in volume.

—1991

Interpretations of Japan

Perceived as somehow different, Japan has long seemed to require interpretation. It is assumed that the country and its culture is not to be comprehended without some sort of mediation, that before the place can be properly understood a theoretical toolkit is needed—models, metaphors, paradigms.

This seems strange. Few other places are thought to need such explication. Yet, one still hears about mysterious, enigmatic Japan though few have ever referred to, say, mysterious, enigmatic Luxembourg.

There are, to be sure, reasons for this, among these that Japan only relatively recently—some century and a half ago—joined what is sometimes called "the family of nations." Before that it was a hermit empire, closed and by nature unknown. It was perceived as different because it was not a family member. Another reason, however, is that Japan itself early learned to value its singularity; being unique, being difficult to understand—these are qualities of which much can be made during "family" squabbles.

Due to the perceptions of those outside the country and the inclinations of those inside it, there is now an accumulation of well over a century's worth of interpretations—a whole chronology of attempts. A short perusal of these strata indicates some of the shapes that Japan has assumed in the eyes of others and of itself, those levels of "appreciation" upon which apprehension is even now based.

*

A major assumption has always been that each approach presumes a nearer accuracy even though these various interpretations overlap. At the same time prudence is advised. Lafcadio Hearn's early endeavor is cautiously titled *Japan: An Attempt at Interpretation*. Perhaps this initial discretion—an attempt rather than a certainty—is the result of even earlier explanations having been so reckless.

One of the first was discovered after Commodore Perry had "opened up" the country. The contents were carelessly examined and the first paradigm was minted. Japan was to be seen as the opposite to the West. The country was what one of the earlier writers called a topsy-turvy land, one in which everything was upside down, a state to be found either disconcerting or delightful. Here is Mark Twain on the subject: "Their coin is square instead of round; their workmen pull the saw and plane, instead of pushing; they begin dinner with tea and confections and close with the heavy work; they love turnips and disallow potatoes."

In his *Things Japanese*, one of the first serious attempts to describe Japan to the West, Basil Hall Chamberlain has a whole section on "Topsy-turvydom" in which he lists examples and then says, "It was only the other day that a Tokyo lady asked the present writer why foreigners did so many things topsy-turvy, instead of doing them naturally, after the manner of her country-people."

If we see others as upside down then, perforce, we see ourselves as right side up. The ascribed abnormality of others serves to reinforce the idea of our own normality. As Ian Littlewood has reminded us, "Without East there is no West, without natives there are no sahibs." This could, of course, cut two ways. Mark Twain could be affirmed in his assumptions and Chamberlain's Tokyo lady could be affirmed in hers.

Further dualistic anomalies were sought for and found. Japan was shortly discovered to be paradoxical, a country which was a contradiction in terms. The people were quaint, childlike, and polite on one hand, but militaristic, cruel, and treacherous on the other; they were artistic but they were also the yellow peril.

Sir Rutherford Alcock, an early diplomat and theorizer, could summarize his account with "Japan is essentially a country of paradoxes and anomalies. There all—even familiar things—put on new faces and are curiously reversed."

Fifty years later this early attempt at interpretation was still around. Ruth Benedict in her 1946 *Chrysanthemum and the Sword* (a dualistic title) says that "The Japanese are, to the highest degree, both aggressive and unaggressive, both militaristic and aesthetic, both insolent and polite." One hears echoes even later. Peter Tasker in 1987 was writing, "They are the hardest-working hedonists, the lewdest prudes, the most courteous and cruelest and kindest of people."

The success of this particular model was that it was based upon an unquestioned assumption: the duality of all reality, the necessity of "either/or" above "both." This is how most Westerners structure their lives and it is therefore often the paradigm of choice whether it actually fits its subject or not.

That it does not became apparent as later generations of foreign observers looked more closely. Or rather, it fits us all too well. We are, every one of us, creatures of paradox and it is only wishful thinking that finds us consistent. And so, just as Japan was not really to be fully described in presuming to find it upside down, so it was eventually seen as something more than an illustration of rampant paradox.

Yet one paradigm does not succeed another. All the earlier models continue to exist and the new is simply added to the pile. Ruth Benedict offers a sample of this strata, and even an attempt as structurally sophisticated as Roland Barthe's *Empire of Signs* held that contrary to Japan with its elegant *suimono,* "for us in France, clear soup is poor soup."

*

A further refinement came with the next model—one we might place as encountered during the first half of the twentieth century. This retained duality but the emphasis was different. Japan was now Land of Contrasts, a place that naturally, even intentionally, found room for paradox. Old Japan and New Japan were thus harmonized. As I myself described it elsewhere: Old Shinto shrines on the top of new high-rises, white-robed acolytes on motorbikes, and ancient *zaibatsu* executives reclined in their new steel-and-glass headquarters.

Unlike the primitive topsy-turvy paradigm, this one was initially convincing since each part of it was apparent. There really were towering skyscrapers, there actually were cherry-blossomed temples. Further, it was somewhat more benign in intent than had been the insulting topsy-turvy construct. Japan had commanded world respect by winning its war with Russia. This was reflected in admitting difference and refusing to consign blame. However, by focusing our attention solely on these extremes (New and Old), this model left out what was in between, which is most of Japan.

It also taught us to look only for stereotypes. Through these it could then suggest that Japan was a hybrid—interesting perhaps and certainly good at winning wars but not sensible, solid-all-the-way-through, like, say, England or the United States. That there is something dodgy about hybrids is a common Western assumption, be it mixed blood or mixed cultures. They seem to threaten our invented boundaries and hence our definition of ourselves.

One is familiar with this way of thinking, particularly in regards to Asia. It is our aged friend, Orientalism. Edward Said has noted that this construction insists that in order for the West to see itself as rational, humane, superior, it is necessary to create an East that is irrational, undeveloped, inferior. If this cannot be made to entirely apply (as it cannot in the case of Japan), then this part of the East is seen in terms of being upside down, reversed, bifurcated, or shaped in other forms of opposition.

To define by difference rather than similarity is common to us all. For us to become truly human in our own eyes we must have an alien against whom to measure ourselves. A late and notorious attempt to define self through the creation of just such an alien species was that of the then–French prime minister, Edith Cresson, who in 1991, comparing the Japanese to ants, went on to say that "we cannot live like that . . . we want to live like human beings, as we have always lived."

The Japanese are thus not human beings. This indeed is one of the burdens of these various paradigms, though one not usually stated with such clarity. More subtly the proposition of Japan as a land of contrasts provides the same context—though in truth we are all lands of contrast in that none of us maintain the solid-all-the-way-through existence we think we want.

The simplicity of this paradigm and its consequent popularity soon, however, exposed its limited nature. Things were not as simple as a collage-like juxtaposition of old and new suggested. Something else was occurring. A new model had to account for this.

*

Hence the fairly recent concept of continuity within change, an organic model: Japan as a place where the new and old could live equitably together; under all the modern veneer lives on this ageless core. Its appearance cannot be dated but it sounds post–WWII. Japan's talent at winning wars had been exhibited and found wanting. One could explain away the binary model (peaceful/ warlike) by situating them in temporal sequence—something the same but different.

This became for a time the standard model, let us say from 1945 until the fall of the Theory of Japan's Uniqueness at the end of the century. It was often wheeled out, inspected, and approved. Also, it was a favorite of that group of writers now somewhat unkindly called the Chrysanthemum Club. It offered an organic recipe that made differences somehow more "natural," a suggestion found in many volumes. One of the qualities of paradigms is that they reassure—until they reveal themselves as inadequate.

By now—let us generalize and say circa 1975—so many models had accumulated that a name for them became necessary. This the Japanese willingly provided—*Nihonjin-ron,* studies of the uniqueness of being Japanese. Americans wrote them, Englishmen wrote them, everyone wrote them, including of course the Japanese themselves, who had, after all, just as much interest in defining themselves through boundaries as did everyone else.

Some of these were very strange. Japan was somehow feminine, while the West somehow masculine; the Japanese had different brains, or longer intestines; the Westerner is an inventor, the Japanese merely an adapter. One still hears this latter. As Ian Littlewood says, "In our models of culture exchange, the West figures as virile originator, Japan as wily imitator." As though such "imitation" is not general, as though this is not the way that ideas move around the world, as though it is not otherwise known as progress.

Some authors excluded almost as much as they included. Geoffrey Gorer is said to have believed that the most important and most consistent element in being Japanese was an early emphasis upon sphincter control and that this "drastic toilet training" solely lay at the bottom of the value system of Japan. Thus, he gathered, there is no concept of right and wrong, only the concept of doing the right thing at the right time.

Others followed. One (Weston La Barre) found the Japanese "the most compulsive people in the world's ethnological museum." Another (H. M. Spitzer) discovered that Japanese culture as a whole indicates the symptoms of obsessive/compulsive neurosis. Still another (James Clark Moloney) thought that Japanese society was "a potential incubator of paranoid schizophrenia."

Of these and other examples scholar Hiroshi Wagatsuma has cautioned that "Most of what has been and still often is discussed as Japanese psychology or mentality, and frequently as 'national character,' is largely the product of impressionist description, stereotyping, or methodologically inadequate approaches."

But foreigners were not alone in these attempts. They received support from the Japanese themselves who by this time had a *Nihonjin-ron* industry of their own up and running. Here there are myriad examples to choose among. As indication, I will merely mention the most translated, Dr. Takeo Doi, who explained much through such single-engine models as his study of *amaeru* (confident expectation of favor) as the skeleton key to Japanese culture.

There is in all of these attempts a tendency to see similar group behavior as expression of common personality structure. But such similar behavior patterns are often the result of mere conformity to social norms. If one tries to attribute group behavior to any supposed "national character," one falls into psychological reductionism. Which is indeed just what the various *Nihojin-ron* do.

*

Perhaps consequently, there is the need to continually update the necessary model, the permanent desire for a new and improved product. Out of the welter of the *Nihonjin-ron* there emerged, sure enough, a fresh model.

This was purely structural in nature, the country seen as controlled through its own agreed-upon polarities. There was *uchi* and *omote* (back and front, inside vs. outside); there was *ninjo* and *giri* (one's own feelings vs. obligations owed to society); there was *honne* and *tatemae* (the real motive hiding between the stated reason). And there were many other, all of them moving parts in this latest definition. One of the features of this model was that it used Japanese terms to define the Japanese and was hence perceived as being somehow more "fair."

Being structural, it fit in with its times academically (we are now in the 1970s–early 1980s) and with its quasi-scientific phraseology it was seen as intellectually respectable. That it offered the mere skeleton of a society rather than a reflection of that society itself—all bones, no muscles or skin—bothered, for a time, no one.

Eventually, however, as the *Nihonjin-ron* were beginning to lose their adherents, particularly those who were more able to compare real Japanese to the increasingly diagrammatic models held up to them, there rose the need for a newer, more complete model. Back to the drawing board.

*

Interpretations of Japan will yet continue as the country evolves, but with the erosion of the traditional accelerating at such a rate there will eventually be little to mark the "difference" that Japan is traditionally thought to have exhibited, since the country itself will be little different.

It is problematic that any country can ever be truly "defined" by any other, since it remains true that any difference is assumed as a difference from whoever is doing the defining. I have myself in my fifty years learned that if Japan were to rid itself of all those things that are to me puzzling, illogical, distasteful, it would no longer be Japan at all. Perhaps in the future a perusal of these different models and paradigms will create emotions not only of indignation but also of nostalgia.

—*2001*

Crossing the Border: The Japanese Example

Crossing the border: Japan may serve as example because it knows a lot about borders and because it has so many uses for them. And because, unlike those of many other countries, Japan's borders are natural, not agreed-upon terrains but leagues of formerly uncharted sea. An archipelago, like the United Kingdom, it has long distanced itself from its neighbors, something its watery borders have encouraged.

In consequence these borders have seldom been breached. Japan is among the very few Asian nations that did not suffer through the intrusions of Western imperialism—Europe and the United States crossing borders irrespectively.

Japan's borders were breached only twice. In the thirteenth century the Mongols set out to invade Japan but their fleet was stopped by a typhoon and an occupation was averted. This phenomenon was seen as evidence of divine favor and the typhoon was thereafter referred to as *kamikaze*, the "divine wind," a term that was to prove useful on numerous occasions—most recently, describing the activities of suicide bombers during the latter days of World War II.

It was during this war that Japan's borders were again breached. The Allied Powers set out to invade Japan, devastated it, and an occupation resulted. This was the first and so far only time that Japan's boundaries were ignored and its borders broken.

The effect of such an invasion is often decisive. Not only are people killed and dwellings destroyed, but whole cities are ruined, communications systems are broken, and famine and pestilence stalk. The destruction of recognized borders in all fields leads to

social and personal chaos. After all, the borders were there to preserve the very identity that is now threatened.

For Japan, this was the first time it had been invaded. Though
the country had had internal border problems, a massive breach of
this nature had never before occurred. And in addition to the physical damage there was the mental harm that occurs when an idea of
self predicated upon the notion of a state is destroyed. Borders are
there not only to protect but also to define.

Due both to these experiences and the fact that they have
remained very much an island people, the Japanese have traditionally viewed border crossings as something of which to be wary. They
have long regarded their own borders as *boundaries*—not merely
lying adjacent but forming a limiting line.

Indeed, during much of its history Japan remained nominally
closed to outsiders. The government deemed leaving the country an
unlawful act and returning after having somehow successfully left a
criminal one—a national seclusion that is known as *sakoku*. Inside
the country various borders were observed and travelers from one
province to another had to pass through guarded barriers, forts that
contained much the equivalent of immigration and customs services
today.

Borders were also put to work and afflicted not only on peasants
and craftsmen. There was a boundary-based system known as *sankin
kotai* where the daimyo, the lords of the capital, were forced to make
expensive trips back to their own provinces. Since their processions
were seen as ceremonial, they contained large numbers of people
(though members of the immediate family were to be left behind as
government hostages in all but name) and were very expensive. This
had the double advantage of providing work, making money, filling
state coffers, and curbing any thought of political uprising since such
attempts are always expensive. The grand daimyo processions, spill-

ing money, were stopped at each of the many district border forts. Borders were barriers.

And indeed they still are. The 1945 Allied Occupation of Japan had substituted one military government for another and crossing borders, in and out of Japan, became again difficult for the Japanese. This is no longer true but it should be noted that even now the doors into Japan swing only one way. It is easy for the visitor to get out but not to get in. This is something that countries learn. This is why at most immigration barriers everywhere there are separate entry lines for the confident native and for the merely hopeful foreigner.

This is also why there is also so much fuss made about nationality within the country. In Japan there remains a rigid definition. The Japanese are inside the boundary, everyone else is out. Though there are accommodations for Japanese citizenship, these are—like those of all other countries—rigid. There is no accommodation for those who would live and work there without undergoing proper procedures. Even third-generation people whose ancestors came from, say, Korea are routinely denied some of the advantages of citizenship—running for public office, for example.

I myself have spent my entire adult life in Japan, living as a foreign body in the native mixture. Officially I enjoy *eijuken*, permanent residence, a fairly exotic and somewhat in-between category. Before I applied for this I was told that I ought to opt for citizenship because it was so much easier for the bureaucrats to arrange. I could be nominally Japanese in that fashion. With permanent residence I was neither one thing nor another—so I pay taxes but I cannot vote; my borders remain vague.

It is not that Japan is with its history of closed borders more xenophobic than other nations, merely that it is more open about being xenophobic. There is little concern about being observed and found xenophobic—or indeed misogynist, or racist.

Take, for example, the terminology used in referring to foreigners. The standard Japanese term *gaijin* translates, innocently enough, as "person from the outside." Foreigners in Japan, to be sure, find the term loaded with prejudice, but that is their privilege. There are many worse that could be used yet rarely are—*keto* ("red-haired barbarian") for example. And when it comes to bad-mouthing foreigners Americans have little ground to stand on. I remember from Occupation days Eighth Army notices forbidding "fraternization with the indigenous personnel," and few languages can have had terms so unlovely as the standard G.I. for a Japanese person, *gook*, as in: "Hey, that's a good-looking *gook* girl."

Still, tempered though it is in terminology, the truly politically correct, with all of its triumphs and terrors, has never knocked on Japanese doors. And for good reason. Japan is very suspicious of knocked-on doors. This tendency was much strengthened when, in the mid-nineteenth century, American warships appeared with what seemed to be a trade offer but was widely perceived as a bid for imperialistic takeover. With this threat, however, Japan did not, as given its history might have been expected, close its borders and retreat into an even more hermit-like seclusion.

Rather, it compromised and opened its borders, but it did so ever so slightly for the would-be invaders from the West, just a port here or there. But it opened all the way for those Japanese who now needed to go out and learn all that they could about this country that was so politely menacing theirs.

This ploy is a popular one, this one-direction border-crossing convenience. Many countries have found it of use, particularly in Asia—getting in and out of Burma, for example. It is cost effective and considerably slows down invasions, military or mercantile.

It sometimes malfunctions, however. Several years ago Japan, still deep in what it termed "oil shock," occasioned by just one more of Nixon's perfidies, decided to shop elsewhere. Iran was to be the new oil supermarket, and to speed transactions the Japanese government initiated a visa treaty, a tit-for-tat arrangement where I freely enter your country and you freely enter mine. This would, it was thought, allow the Japanese oil people to get in and out of Iran with a minimum of fuss.

Perhaps it did, but the fuss this occasioned in Japan was maximum. While Japan was sending a person or two a month to Tehran, Iran was allowing hundreds to travel weekly to Tokyo. Soon the city was awash with friendly, well-behaved young Iranians, all looking for work.

Naturally they did not find it, though the work was there. After their money had run out these friendly young Iranians found themselves employed mainly by the *yakuza*, who used a number of them for drug running. Thus the authorities could, eventually, after several years, round up and deport as criminals most of these men who had come to Japan to gain a better life. The one-way boundary was reinstated and Japan experimented no more with porous borders.

There are borders other than the corporeal, however. Those, for example, of economic necessity. Perhaps some readers will recall the so-called trade imbalance, a disequilibrium, which for a time remained unchecked, dividing Japan from the rest of the world. Cheaper (and often better) cars and cameras from Japan were bought by too many people in other lands while the Japanese refused to buy in like number the products of the offended nations.

The United States was particularly outraged, claiming that Japan was unfairly excluding products from its populace through wrongful manipulations of Japanese quotas, qualifications, and distribution procedures. Whether this was true or not, Japan waxed wealthy during this period, and the trade imbalance was among the reasons why. This kind of economic boundary was practical.

It was not, however, the kind of boundary that could last long. Shortly the bubble collapsed because cheap production could not be maintained, and other Asian countries could undercut Japanese-product price. The economic borders (some quite imaginatively named: "Japanese structural impediments," "Japanese lack of inter-face," even "Japanese cultural differences") fell and gradually the trade imbalance, the result and the cause of many an economic bar-rier, appeared to right itself.

It is still there; to be sure, it always is; it is one of the qualities of having other nations border yours, but the objects exchanged are now different. Japan, which once purveyed judo, sushi, and Zen to the world, and then turned more palpable with cars and cameras, now began exporting *manga*, *anime*, and the more flashy kinds of pop culture. Since this latter does not make nearly as much money as do cars and cameras, there is no mention of trade barriers. And indeed there are none. Mickey Mouse is welcomed so long as Hello Kitty is reciprocally admitted.

During this decline, however, and all of this closing and open-ing of barriers to the West, Japan had also been busying itself with its borders to the East. This had occurred earlier, to be sure, but never to the extent that Japan's proximity to the rest of Asia might have suggested.

The reason was that Japan first recognized as its major border fissure that of its border with the West, in particular the United States. It was the country with which Japan thought it had to com-pete and, even now, it is the country to which Japan most often com-pares itself, sometimes to its own advantage, sometimes not. The rest of Asia, however, does not have this impediment or this advantage. Cambodia compares itself to Thailand, China compares itself to India, and the borders turn into boundaries, or don't.

When Japan thought of other Asian countries it all too often considered them backward and worthy only of being taken advantage of. Having itself escaped imperialism, Japan, imitating the admired West, turned imperialist, concluding successful wars with China and Russia, taking over Korea and, as it is called, enlarging its borders.

Successful in this, in the first part of the last century it extended its colonial ambitions to, eventually, the rest of Asia. This destruction of other countries' borders was sloganized as the Greater East Asia Co-Prosperity Sphere. It expressed the idea of an economically and politically integrated Asia freed from Western domination and under benevolent Japanese leadership.

At the same time the same phrase was used back home to rationalize Japanese expansionist ambitions on the continent. Claiming that it was saving these unfortunate countries from the perils of Western imperialism, Japan—or at least a part of the Japanese government—was seeking for leverage that would allow an invasion of Japanese people and Japanese money. "Asia for the Asians" was the slogan used.

Members of the sphere, the "New Order," eventually included Japan (along with annexed Korea), China, Manchukuo (the puppet state in Manchuria), French Indochina, and the Dutch East Indies—those countries that had suffered most from the "Old Order," a system of international relations erected by the Western imperialists.

A problem presented by proponents of the plan was Japan's own record in East Asia, which was as self-aggrandizing as that of the Western imperialists. Japan's seizure of Taiwan, Korea, Manchuria—and its more recent efforts to promote an autonomous North China—all constituted a kind of proof that Japan was initiating various economic ties with the peoples it was attempting to subjugate in the name of freedom. In this it was admittedly more civilized than some Western nations, which had used opium to subjugate. It also seemed to offer economic advantage. And some still believe in Japan's sincerity in its stated intentions. For example, Burmese Ba Maw, then head of that country, said that though he deplored the brutal and arrogant behavior often displayed by Japanese soldiers throughout Asia, still, "nothing can ever obliterate the role Japan has played in bringing liberation to countless colonial peoples."

If so, Japan was suitably rewarded. After the war ended (from Japan's view disappointingly) it renounced war entirely. Presumed to be no longer a military threat, it became seen as a place that still, naturally enough, sought economic exchange. Thus what Japan failed to gain through war it has gained through peace. Japan's economy is larger than all the other Asian economies combined.

With all this wartime scrambling over boundaries and postwar cleaning up of borders there are now myriad economic ties with the nations of Asia, and Japan has been able to make the most of occasional relaxations of these, to give aid where it is needed, to cross borders that might otherwise be closed to it.

Some Asian localities—Singapore, Shanghai, Kuala Lumpur—seem in some sense to be modeling themselves on Tokyo. Japan, however, still models itself on America. Some even say that this is but to be expected, its having been a vassal state for these fifty-some years.

Amid this generally peaceful relaxation of Asian boundaries there are exceptions. Even discounting the miserable state of North Korea and the various Muslim insurgencies in Indonesia, Thailand, and elsewhere, there are still some signs of disagreement. Naval authorities in Japan and South Korea search ancient maps in an attempt to find precedent to bolster either Japan's claim to calling the body of water between it and the mainland peninsula the Japan Sea, or Korea's claim that this same body of water ought to be called the Korean Sea, or at least, in Korean, the East Sea.

Having observed so much squabbling over borders—for history is a record of little else—one begins to question just what it is that borders mean. The dictionary offers only limited help: a border is a line or frontier separating political divisions or geographic regions, something that indicates a limit or a boundary.

But borders do more. They not only limit, they also define the area within the borders. Americans who now claim that they are first and foremost Americans are exhibiting that phenomenon. They are defining themselves through their boundaries, having chosen to see self as nationality.

Nonetheless, that nationality, that self, can be defined only through comparison with other nationalities, other selves. Without the rich the poor could not so rightly define their state; without the powers of darkness or the axis of evil the rightness of a particular belief or a particular political strategy could not be made so apparent. There is nothing sinister in this. It is simply that borders define not only "us" but also "them," something other, something different, hopefully opposite, against which we may define ourselves.

Borders thus aid in our predicating who we are since it is only by comparison with a neighbor that we may learn this. Japan is still comparing itself to the continent across the Pacific and not to those other countries nearer at hand. And they, the rest of Asia, are comparing themselves to each other and, increasingly, to Japan as well. This may all end up as stagnant mass-Americanization but at present it is an interestingly roiling batch of emulation and rivalry, of borders physical, political, and metaphorical, of cross-border interactions, of boundaries erected and struck down, and occasionally of exceptional borders as well. "That long frontier from the Atlantic to the Pacific Oceans, guarded only by neighborly respect and honorable obligations"—Winston Churchill was speaking of the U.S.–

Canadian border but indicating a possibility, rare in this world of boundaries though it is.

The example of Japan on which I have predicated this talk does not offer much in the way of possibilities but it does indicate an isolated example of the uses of borders and the employment of boundaries, and some indication as to how we might begin to think of these infuriating, fruitful divisions.

—2004

II

*Culture
and Style*

The Japanese Way of Seeing

Asians have a way of seeing, a manner of viewing, which is all theirs. But then so does everyone else. Each culture has a way of regarding and each is in some measure different from the others.

Look, for example, at the way the Americans view space. They are fond of "wide, open spaces," an uncluttered room is "nicely spacious," an uncluttered head is "spaced out." The assumption is that space is empty—it exists only in order to be filled.

Contrast this with how a traditional Asian regards space. There is an assumption that it is already filled—with itself. It has its own dimensions, its own weight. Old Chinese calligraphy manuals state that true emptiness does not occur until the first mark is put on the paper. Only then does it become truly empty. Space is thus not defined until it can be contrasted.

The differences between Western and Eastern assumptions about space are symptomatic of attitudes toward viewing. And these are sometimes diametrically opposed. Take the assumptions that surround and define Japan's *ikebana*.

While the West makes a floral arrangement structured around shape and color, considering only the effect of flowers and foliage, the traditional Japanese flower arranger believes the space between the branches to be just as important as the space filled by them. The dimensions of this space are calculated and balanced against that occupied by the floral material itself.

If space is full, then what is it full of? It is full of *ma*, an aesthetic term, originally Buddhist (*wu wei* in Chinese), meaning something like "empty" or "space" or even "gap," a problem being that the West has no concept and hence no word, or no word and hence no concept.

Asia does, however, and the Taoist philosopher Lao Tse could write confidently that thirty spokes might meet at the hub but the empty space between them was the essence of the wheel.

How to indicate an emptiness that has weight? Well, look at the hanging scroll—a landscape, let us say. The upper two-thirds are empty; only the lower third holds the scene. Yet the assumption is that the view balances. The two elements (empty/full) are necessary for equilibrium since each weighs the same.

The West, to be sure, believes that empty counts. There is in classical painting a theory of negative space and some painters, such as Poussin, have worked out theories to account for it. But the considerations are different.

The page of an American- or European-printed book traditionally assumes that the bottom of anything is heaviest, because space has no weight and type does. Consequently there is a decidedly empty emptiness left at the bottom. This, as any Western graphics designer will tell you, is to prevent an unwelcome sense of heaviness, since type weighs so much.

Now turn to the Japanese page. Here the space is all at the top, and is positioned there in order to balance with its own considerable weight the type below. The type-filled portion acts (as does the picture in the scroll) as ballast for the heavy space above.

These various readings of space are, in both cultures, what creates the dynamics of the view, whether it be arranged in nature, as in the garden; hung on the wall, as in the scroll; or simply snapped, as in the photograph.

It is this balance of presumed "fulls" and "empties" that enables us to "read" the view, whatever it is. That balance creates a temporal sequence for the spatial image.

At the same time, reading habits determine viewing habits. You are now reading left to right. Perhaps you have never read in any other direction, but in Japan, for example, people read not only from left to right, but also from right to left, and from up to down. There is consequently, perhaps, a different way of seeing, an individual way of reading images, a contrasting manner of interpreting pictorial compositions.

Look at Asia's earliest form of portable view: in Japan the *emaki* hand scroll. It is designed to be viewed in a sequence moving from right to left, unrolling on the former side, rolling up on the latter. This preference for reading right to left continues in the pagination of books. The West may think that Asia reads books backwards, but Asia thinks the same of us.

These various ways of reading affect the idea of pictorial composition. Those found natural and satisfying in the East are found strange in the West, and those that seem proper to native Europeans or Americans seem odd to traditional Asians.

There is a story told of a Japanese publisher who was putting out a local edition of the landscapes of John Constable. However, the plates, sent from England, seemed peculiar to him. He pondered over them for a time and then discovered what he thought was the problem. The original English publisher must have printed them backward.

And so Constable's careful and academic compositions—eye led from left to right, cow leading to hay wain, eye stopped by the big tree on the right—were reversed in the Japanese edition. Eye, guided in from the right, lingered and then slowly departed on the left. Good composition. The tale may be apocryphal but the import is real. Such, indeed, is the way composition in Japan is often read.

I encountered another example of this way of reading some years ago when I was teaching at a Japanese university. In speaking of cinematic composition I used as an example a famous scene from Eisenstein's *October* where soldiers are pushing a cannon up along a diagonal line. My point was that this diagonal, the line beginning at the lower left-hand corner of the frame and rising to the upper right, is in the West read as "ascending" and so the composition consequently spoke of progress, success, endeavor, and so on.

At which point a student asked: But the Bolsheviks did win the revolution, didn't they? He was confused because for him, a traditional-minded young man, that diagonal line had precisely opposite associations. To be sure, Eisenstein had used it to suggest upward-and-onward, but my student was reading it in the Japanese manner. This suggests a steady decline, from the upper right-hand corner down to the lower left. Here the composition indeed (as in, for example, Korin's famous "Iris Screen") spoke of a natural and unavoidable passing on, or away, a flowing outward from action to quiet, a graceful decline, or in the context of my class, military defeat.

Given such diametrically opposed readings of an identical line, it is not surprising to find such differences bolstered by further assumptions, each different from the other. The Japanese reading of the diagonal, for example, would also suggest a presumed accord with nature, a willingness to regard things as proceeding as they must. The Western reading, however, insists upon change, reform and, in this case, revolution.

Reading habits (right to left) also suggest that the right side (beginning) of anything should be given a preference over the left (concluding) side. On the classical stage (Noh, Kyogen, Bunraku, Kabuki), the right-hand side, the *kami* (upper) *te*, is where all important action takes place; the left-hand side, the *shimo* (lower) *te*, is used only for entrances and exits.

Likewise, in the popular *rakugo* (dramatized, humorous storytelling), when the performer is impersonating important people he turns his head stage right, but when impersonating inferior folk, he turns his head stage left. This convention is so well understood that no other indication as to who is speaking is necessary.

Finally, once a scene is filled or emptied, once a composition is constructed and balanced, there is still the consideration that all views are partial since all views are framed. The positioning of this frame—the enclosing ormolu of the painting, the brocade of the scroll, the circumference of the lens, or the lashed frame of the eye—is different in the East and in the West.

The reason is that a frame presumed a viewing position. One's ideas on this position involve a number of assumptions: our relation to the natural world, our position in society, our notions as to who we are, and so on.

For example, the Westerner in Japan is often struck by the fact that all views are partial. The viewer is expected to edit out both the gasoline station and the *pachinko* parlor that flank the celebrated temple gate he wants to take a picture of.

This is something of which Westerners do not think well. They believe that their frames should be wide. They also believe in the integral site, the whole thing, the big picture. The Japanese do not. They will accommodate their frame to almost everything, an aptitude that has led to the observation that the Japanese have a very strong sense of beauty and almost no sense of ugliness.

Whether this is true or not, one Japanese assumption is certainly that things in their fullness are not necessary, and that a frame need not insist upon fullness. The part can stand for the whole in Japanese pictorial aesthetics, just as it does in the haiku where partial attributes (old pond + frog's jump = splash) create a new whole.

It was this way of framing that so excited French painters when first they saw it. Degas was shown a Japanese print in which only a part of the person was delineated. To a painter trained in the frontal fullness of academic Western art, the effect was both startling and liberating. A part can indeed stand for the whole, whether it be the thigh of a Hokusai boatman or half a passerby in a Degas street scene.

At the same time, though ways of seeing are different, they are also complementary—and they more and more affect each other. It is doubtful now that any Japanese consciously reads the diagonal as did my student of years past, and in our age of modern graphics it is doubtful whether any Westerner finds unduly intriguing a stray arm or leg.

At the same time, however, the assumption behind these differences remains. Spaces in the United States are still wide open, even when they are not, and the top of the Japanese page remains as heavy as the bottom. Ways of seeing continue to differ and the world is the richer for this diversity.

—*1993*

Japan and the Image Industry

Though all countries have image cultures, Japan's seems more advanced, or at least more commercial, than many. Its adept use of image in graphics, packaging, advertisement, and all forms of entertainment is unrivaled. Though the reliance on image rather than thought is everywhere a definition of modern culture, no country has carried this to a further extreme than Japan.

*

The word "image" means (dictionary definition) "an imitation, representation, or similitude of any person or thing, sculptured, drawn, painted, or otherwise made perceptible to the sight, a visual representation or reproduction: form, aspect, appearance, cast, likeness, semblance." And we see images, not things. Perception is a function of the mind. This results in our endowing our optical sensations with meaning. An image can (must) be defined.

Some reasons have been suggested for the extreme affinity with this image-making process, shown by both Japan and China. One of these maintains that the nature of its written language predicates this disposition, that the *kanji*—Chinese ideographs—are in themselves images. Each *kanji* character symbolizes a single idea. These are logographs in that one character sometimes represents both the meaning and the sound of an entire word. In other languages, those constructed in the manner of an alphabet, for example, a repertoire of images is neither required nor possible. Here a certain combination creates a formula: d-o-g = dog. This is then translated into an image of the animal name. The same thing occurs in *kanji*, except that there is no middle step. It at once becomes *quan* or *chu'uan* in Chinese and *ken* or *inu* in Japanese. No translation is necessary.

Or, as phrased by Frederik L. Schodt: "The Japanese are predisposed to more visual forms of communication owing to their writing system." The individual ideograph is a simple picture that represents "a tangible object, or an abstract concept, emotion, or action . . . it is, in fact, a form of cartooning."

The popularity in Japan of this form of communication is well known. Called *manga* (a term purportedly coined by the woodprint artist Hokusai in 1814), these pictorial images (published in newspaper, magazine, or book form) tell simple stories in the manner of comic strips everywhere. But only in image-conscious Japan has such a flourishing of "comic culture" become the most significant feature of Japanese mass culture.

It is estimated that 70 percent of people riding public transportation in the country are looking at *manga*, that these make up 40 percent of all publication in Japan, and that in one year alone (1995, height of the *manga* boom), nearly two billion such collections were purchased. That figure equates to fifteen copies for every resident of the country.

The reader scans the image and receives an impression of story line, and a 320-page *manga* takes about twenty minutes to read. This means sixteen pages per minute, or slightly less than four seconds per page. Like a slow but portable TV, the image-propelled *manga* is perused in less than half an hour, then discarded. Each costs the equivalent of about two dollars, a low price by Japanese standards, but adding up to considerable profits for the publishers.

As for content, Schodt has said that "even if they are basically trash . . . they are harmless entertainment," implying no direct reflection of Japanese society. It is difficult, however, to believe that *manga* do not reflect popular culture when they, to an extent, define it. If so, this is a distinction that it shares with that other image-powered entertainment—television. It is, I believe, no accident that the *manga* explosion began in Japan during the mid-1950s, just at the time when the home TV set was becoming a possibility for the majority. It was the images on the tube that created the audience for that portable TV set—the *manga*.

The technical assumptions of both are certainly close. Both insist, as Robert MacNeil has said of American television, that "bite-sized is best, that complexity must be avoided, that the nuances are dispensable, that qualifications impede the simple message, that visual stimulation is a substitute for thought, and that verbal precision is an anachronism." Further, television favors a mood of conciliation and is at its best when substance of any kind is muted. This would be yet another reason for the instant acceptance and reliance upon television in Japan, a country where conciliation is a national stance.

In discourses conducted through visual imagery rather than words, a one-sided conversation made up of images is created—a fast conversation, allowing little time for reflection. The average length of a TV shot is under four seconds. What viewers watch are millions of pictures of short duration and dynamic variety. As Neil Postman has observed: "It is in the nature of the medium that it must suppress the content of ideas in order to accommodate the requirements of visual interest."

This, of course, does not trouble the viewer. Indeed, it speeds him onward.

After all, words need to be understood while images merely need to be recognized. In an image culture words become irrelevant. As the American action-star Bruce Willis stated upon reading an unfavorable review of one of his films, "These [reviews] are only for people who read. . . . the printed word has become a dinosaur."

At the same time, however, something is occurring that does

indeed affect individuals and, consequently, society and thus the culture itself. In all countries, as Ernst Cassirer saw, "physical reality seems to recede in proportion as man's symbolic activity advances. Instead of dealing with the things themselves, man is in a sense constantly conversing with himself . . . he cannot see or know anything except by the interposition of [an] artificial medium."

When a diversion is omnipresent, as TV is in Japan, its effects are certain. One understands this when it is learned that (George Trow reporting) "a child will have seen nearly four thousand hours of television before he or she ever sees a school. This is twice as much time as that child will spend in his or her college classroom," and these American figures are certainly applicable to the Japanese experience as well.

That image culture is destruction to print culture, however, is not the point. The form in which ideas are expressed will affect what these ideas are. The point is that there is now such a massive audience for images that a highly profitable industry has evolved. By its nature, this industry will seek to create an even more extensive image culture.

An example is the continuing rise of the computer game and the various simulacra to which these have given rise. We step here from the "real" to the "virtual" image, but there is a real difference only in effect. An image is always read as an image. The difference becomes one of degree. Among recent developments has been the appearance of the virtually real person.

An example is a seventeen-year-old female high-school student named Shiori Fujisaki. She originally appeared as a character in a video game named "Tokimeki Memorial," the goal of which was to get Shiori to go out on a date and fall in love with you. Packaged on compact discs, she was available to anyone who had a computer, but responded differently to different stimuli.

The idea was to make her heart icon beat more rapidly, since *tokimeki* means "throbbing heart." The user plays until Shiori (who has a limited but decided vocabulary) can be brought to say "I Love You." Then the game ends. But it can end even before these words are spoken. The suitor can give up. Those who play say that rejection is much easier to take from a machine.

One game developer, twenty-five-year-old Yukio Watanabe, said that with games he could do things that were too difficult in real life—like telling a girl that he liked her. Another young man, Shingo Hagiwara, twenty-one, is famous for having fallen in love with Shiori himself. He has bought all the calendars, posters, mugs, and watches carrying her image. When she appears in "personal appearances" via video screen, he attends. He has, as he says, given his heart to a virtual girl.

In the first months after her appearance Shiori had sold over a million copies of herself and, with that kind of success, there are plans to make virtual reality "idols"—entertainers who are nothing more than computer graphics. Quasi-girls, without the encumbrances of stories, plots, personalities, they will be able to sing and dance and never tire. They are, by definition, a cheap and easy date.

Among those already on the market is Jenny. Child of a Japanese mother and an Arab father, Jenny is fluent in both Japanese and English and is skilled at singing and dancing. Another new idol is Kyoko, already out on compact disc. She has a radio program as well and her voice is heard on selected CDs. Both are popular and have been welcomed by the press.

The *Asahi Shimbun* greeted these simulated creatures in an editorial praising their lingual prowess and expressing confidence that Japanese research and development would result in even more lifelike creations. Idols could make "live" appearances. The "handshake session" might be difficult but science would find a way. Also "she will not be choosy about her work, even if she has to take on two or three assignments at the same time, and her 'personal' appearances on big outdoor screens and the sale of her image for use in television commercials would help offset the cost of her development."

The image industry is being fueled by strong investments and ambitious entrepreneurs. Witness the remarkable success of the virtual pet named Tamagotchi. It is a compact portable computer game shaped like an egg and the user "parents" feed and care for it by pushing its buttons. The enclosed instructions read: "You take care of Tamagotchi, that mysterious small animal on the liquid crystal screen. The special feature is that Tamagotchi will grow up in diverse ways, depending on how you raise it."

The computer image of an egg hatches five seconds after a button is pushed. The creature has a life expectancy of a week or so and during this time constantly calls for attention with a beeping sound. The owner is required to feed it, to dispose of its excrement, to play with it, and to discipline it. Its appearance and character are affected by the degree of care it receives. If not fed it may die of starvation; if ignored it turns delinquent. There are ways to reprogram it and there are ways to satisfyingly kill it. Its success was instant and within its first year millions of units were sold.

That Tamagotchi became a craze is perhaps indicative of something other than simple popularity. In Japan, more than in some countries, everyone is supposed to look (though not be) the same. If a new fashion is evolved (*chapatsu*—dyed brownish hair—loose socks on girls, Burberry scarves, and *puri-cura*—print club—tiny photo stickers of one's friends) and you don't have it, you're out. But even if you have it, there are more crazes inside crazes—it is only the white Tamagotchi that really counts, all other colors are somehow inferior.

Why has the Japanese image industry had such an extraordinary success? I have indicated some of the reasons but there is another factor as well: aesthetics.

Many years ago a Japanese aesthetician noticed something regarding images. "If," he wrote, "there is a painting that is lifelike and that is good for that reason, that work has followed the laws of life. If there is a painting which is not lifelike and which is good for that reason, then that work has followed the laws of painting."

This was written by Tosa Mitsuoki in the seventeenth century, and in this idea he clearly separates the separate identities of not only object and image but also the means of rendering it. He also expresses an awareness of the differences involved in the creation of images. To imagine is to form a notion or an idea, a mental image. This is the image-making process in the mind. In response to stimulus—words for example—a mental image is constructed for the individual doing the imagining.

To create an image is both to amplify and to short-circuit this process. Mitsuoki thus distinguished between two kinds of images. Those that mirror the object and those that mirror the mechanisms of the means through which the image is made. This latter concern is one that has been one of the richest sources of Japanese aesthetics—respecting the artistic means. This would retain the grain of the wood, the strata of the stone, the limitations of black ink on white paper, the syllable count of haiku and *waka*. These are "good" because they have followed rules other than the "laws of life."

In doing so they also short-circuit the image-making process in that the discipline imagines for the viewer and presents an image that is not concerned with the laws of life. Images that respect pen and brush, woodblock printing, computer graphics, the laws of virtual reality, are in this respect the same and have in Japan a long history.

It is upon this base that the image industry of Japan firmly rests.

It is also from here that the industry grows. It imagines for us and presents us with an image that is not intended for any single individual but for everyone. In this way, the industry markets. It also editorializes because its standard image precludes all others and insists upon a single, standardized model. It is this that it sells.

—*1996*

Traditional Japanese Design

Entre le bon sens et le bon goût, il y a la différence de la cause à son effet.
(Between good sense and good taste there is the same difference as between cause and effect.)

JEAN DE LA BRUYÈRE (1645–96)

Precisely—despite its having been said by the French and we are talking about the Japanese. Still, in aesthetic matters the world over, taste is the observation of deserved worth and that should define the matter, except that we are not all agreed as to what good sense consists of.

Some cultures say one thing, some say another. The Japanese traditionally say that we have been given a standard to use. It is there, handy, daily. This is nature itself, things as they are. Nature makes good sense, the only sense, really, and it should be our model. We are to regard it, to learn from it.

This observation makes such sense that one would have expected it to apply to everyone everywhere, but this is not so. Indeed, as the eminent Japanese aesthetician, Makoto Ueda, has said, "In premodern Japanese aesthetics the distance between art and nature was considerably shorter than in its Western counterparts."

Elsewhere—Europe, even sometimes in China—nature as guide was there but its role was restricted to mimesis, realistic reproduction. In Japan this was not enough. It was as though here there was an agreement that the nature of nature could not be presented through literal description. It could only be suggested and the more subtle the suggestion (think of haiku), the more tasteful the work of art.

Here Japanese arts and crafts (a distinction the premodern Japanese did not themselves observe) imitated the means of nature rather than its results. One of the means was simplicity. There is nothing ornate about nature; every branch, twig, and leaf structurally counts. Showing structure, emphasizing texture—even boldly displaying an almost ostentatious lack of artifice—this was what the Japanese learned to do. Such simplicity would come to particularly create a number of aesthetic categories.

The result—a prerequisite for taste—was that this simplicity was found beautiful. And though Japan coined a word for aesthetics only late in the nineteenth century, it takes beauty seriously indeed—so seriously that one might say a word was not needed for its study until the modern world had already begun its process of uglification.

There is thus beauty to be found in texture and grain, in naked structure, also in the precise stroke of the inked brush, the perfect judo throw, the rightness of the placing of a single flower. This beauty is both the expression and the result of an awareness that comes from an open regard of nature and an accompanying discipline, which is one of the reasons that the arts are rarely casual in Japan.

But such a subjective term as "beauty" (even under a rubric as generous as "good sense equals good taste") needs to be codified. Though Japan is much more interested in (and better at) synthesis than analysis, some means of cataloguing are necessary if one is to understand (and explain) the aesthetic impulse. It is thus that Japanese good taste was early divided into a number of tastes—five of which have here been chosen. All share qualities in common, despite their differences.

One might consider one of them. This is that courtly taste for grace and refinement, which we call elegance. Natural to its roots, elegance flowers—and these graceful blooms have been given names: *yugen, iki, furyu.*

Let us examine this last—*furyu*. Historically one associates its initial appearance with Ashikaga Yoshimasa, who ruled from 1449 to 1473. It was he who helped define the quality. Just what this quality is, however, is open to some interpretation. The dictionary (offering "elegant, tasteful, refined, graceful, artistic, aesthetic") is of no help and, in any event, English has no precise equivalent. The example of Yoshimasa himself, however, gives some of idea of the meaning of the term.

He had led a full and active political life and was sick of it. The fifteenth century in Japan was just one civil war after another. So, if the shogun could not make peace he could at least make some kind of order. Yoshimasa therefore cultivated the unostentatious, the subdued, the meditative—more important elements of *furyu* than elegance and refinement.

He had learned that anything perfect arouses the acquisitive instinct. Therefore all of his buildings, his gardens, his vases and plates were made (with a wonderful natural grace, it is true) of the plainest materials, the materials of nature itself.

In Western terms we may substitute the basic black Chanel suit, full of *furyu*, or it would be if it were made of less expensive fabric; native African pottery, refined over generations but made of the same common earth, has the quality; so does the music of Erik Satie, composed as it is of common harmonies cunningly juxtaposed, the most unadorned melody sculpted with style.

Japanese *furyu* has something else in addition. When objects exhibiting it are brought together they create a special kind of atmosphere, the essence of which is a sort of assured serenity. Listening to Satie while wearing a Chanel suit and looking at a Bantu pot only faintly suggests this quality. One will simply have to imagine what it was like to exist beautifully in an environment composed of nothing but the most elegant simplicity.

The resulting craze for the natural, an ostentatious rush for the unostentatious that developed following Yoshimasa's aristocratic example, might be partially explained in that the concept of *furyu* agrees so well with both the basic Buddhist doctrine that this man-made world is delusion, and the equally strong Japanese belief that the only way to live in this world is to subject oneself to its natural immutable laws.

This thought is no stranger to the West. For example, the seventeenth-century English poet Edmund Waller compares his beloved to a rose and then, in fine Japanese fashion, tells the flower to be his messenger, to go and die before her eyes "that she / The common fate of all things rare / May read in thee." For, "How small a part of time they share / That are so wondrous sweet and fair!"

A Japanese would have instantly understood. The poem by no means issues an invitation to "gather ye rosebuds while ye may." Rather, it acknowledges the transience of all things—and it is also an attempt to find beauty and consolation in this acknowledgment.

Many people everywhere spend their whole lives trying to escape the knowledge that one day they and all of theirs will be no more. Only a few poets look at the fact, and the Japanese, I believe, are the only people to celebrate it. This celebration takes many forms but the most common would be looking into a mirror, seeing one more gray hair, discerning one more wrinkle, and then saying to oneself: "Good, all is well with the world—things are proceeding as they must."

This attitude (so the opposite of going to the beauty parlor) also gives pleasure—the pleasure that one experiences upon discovering a corroboration of this great and natural law of change in one's own personal face. This attitude extends to the outside world as well and a disassociated and satisfied melancholy is appreciated. Cherry blossoms are to be preferred not when they are at their fullest but afterwards, when the air is thick with their falling petals, and with the unavoidable reminder that they too have had their day and must rightly perish.

Immortality, in that it is considered at all, is to be found through nature's way. The form is kept though the contents evaporate. Permanence through materials (granite, marble, the Pyramids) is seldom attempted. Rather, the claims of immortality were honored in another way. Here the paradigm would be the shrine of Ise, made of common wood, razed every twenty years, and at the same time identically rebuilt in a neighboring plot. *Yugen*, *wabi*, *sabi*, all indicate a quality that finds permanence only in its frankly expiring examples.

*

This would lead us to a prime quality of the Japanese notion of beauty. Not only should the aesthetic be natural, it should also be impermanent. This appreciation of the evanescent could also, as Makoto Ueda reminds us, "be considered a variation of elegance, for exquisite beauty is fragile and apt easily to perish."

This one finds in such a concept as *aware* and its elaboration, *mono no aware*. (There have been various valiant attempts to translate this into English, a language that has no way to do so. Perhaps Ueda's paraphrase will give some idea: "a deep, empathetic appreciation of the ephemeral beauty manifest in nature and human life, and therefore usually tinged with a hint of sadness [though] under certain circumstances it can be accompanied by admiration, awe, or even joy.")

The concept is important to traditional Japanese aesthetics (Murasaki Shikibu uses the term over a thousand times in the *Tale of Genji*) and from it sprouts such related aesthetic categories as *wabi*, *sabi*, *yugen*, and many others.

One might, thus, call attention to the very fact of such a categorization of aesthetics. In the West one cannot too successfully accomplish this—though Plato, Hegel, Kant, and many others attempted to. These aestheticians are forced to use such imprecise terms as "soul" and "spirit" and "the ineffable." In Japan, however, a language sometimes seemingly more vague than most, there is apparently no problem. Aesthetic categories thrive. And categories within categories. One of these might be mentioned both because it is sometimes overlooked and also because it gives some insight into the Japanese aesthetic sense at work.

Within the tastes themselves there operates another system of categorization. It is this that describes what we will have to call the "mood" of whatever it is: flower arrangement, the manner of holding a tea bowl, the quality of writing itself, kimono pattern, tatami binding, a way of walking or even standing, other forms of creation and comportment. It is used to convey emotional states and is an agreed-upon tripartite system of categorization (*shin-gyo-so*) that the early aestheticians hoped would cover all such moods and their reflections.

The first term is *shin*, which covers things formal, slow, symmetrical, imposing. The third is *so* and is applied to things informal, fast, asymmetrical, relaxed. The second is *gyo* and it describes everything in between the extremes of the other two.

It works this way: The Washington Monument is *shin*. It is symmetrical, formal, correct, official, imposing, and at the same time almost elaborately beautiful. *So* is the contrary, and though we have no public monuments in this style (all of them being *shin* by definition of being monuments), a Frank Lloyd Wright house might serve as an indication. It is asymmetrical, informal, relaxed, and is at the same time both simple and beautiful.

Or, this tripartite system of categorization can also explain mood in terms of strength and warmth. Thus dogs are *so* but cats are *shin*. In the same way Alain Delon is very *shin* though Jean-Paul Belmondo is quite *so*. Or Mozart is a very engaging aspect of *so* tempered with *shin*, while in Beethoven we have *shin* tempered with *so*, and Brahms is all *gyo*.

There are numerous other applications. In Japan they serve to describe the differing moods of calligraphy and ink paintings—the way we in the West might contrast formal, informal, and hastily cursive handwriting. Another distinction was observed by flower master Sofu Teshigahara when he said that *shin* is a traditional *tokonoma* alcove, floored with *tatami* mats, its main post lacquered, and all of its proportions exact and formal, but that *gyo* is a *tokonoma* floored with wood, its grain still showing, and its post perhaps a natural tree trunk. He said he had never heard of a *tokonoma* in the *so* manner, as they are simply not made that way, but surely the rudimentary *tokonoma* of some rustic tea-ceremony hut somewhere might theoretically approach *so* in its informality.

There are also a number of combinations that are applied to varying intermediary degrees of the three moods. There is the *so* of *shin*, the *so* of *gyo*, and the *so* of *so*, for example. Hemingway would probably be the *so* of *gyo*, while Faulkner would perhaps be the *so* of *shin*. There are nine such combinations in all—so like the nine postures of the Amida Buddha—and the collective Japanese word for this process is *santai kyushi* (three bodies, nine forms).

All of this aesthetic terminology might seem pettifogging to the Westerner though a quick look into the more recondite pages of Emily Post will remind us of like constructions. Actually formulations like the *shin-gyo-so* triptych serve the same purpose of some of hers. They serve as shorthand in the discussion of a complicated art.

The Japanese of the fifteenth century—like those of the twenty-first and all centuries in between—delighted in such rules. When people gathered and talked about such things the atmosphere perhaps resembled some chic New York or Paris opening with recently acquired apparel being showed off and much connoisseur-talk about the merits of this or that—whether the pot or the bowl or the *ikebana* showed the *shin* of *shin* or merely the *gyo* of *shin*. Still, the emotion called for, the real reason for the party, is familiar. It is the pursuit of beauty.

*

On such an occasion a standard of taste is agreed upon. Good taste is thus a shared discovery that fast deepens into a conviction. It may have its origin in the unpeopled world of nature itself but it soon enters good society.

In Japan, particularly from the seventeenth century on, Yoshimasa's private if courtly formulations became those of moneyed folk at large. The quality of *iki*, for example, is based upon this social agreement. As Ueda has pointed out both *iki* and *sui* are not only aesthetic terms, they also represent moral ideals. "Aesthetically both pointed toward an urbane, chic, bourgeois type of beauty with undertones of sensuality. Morally they envisioned the tasteful life of a person who was wealthy but not attached to money, who enjoyed sensual pleasure but was never carried away by carnal desires . . ."

Shuzo Kuki, a man who wrote a whole book on the subject, said that "the intoxication of the so-called *amour-passion* of Stendhal is truly contrary to *iki*." Closer was Verlaine who did not wish for color, "only for its shades." At the same time Kuki wondered if the pictures of Constantin Guys, Degas, and van Dongen, all painters of a contemporary aesthetic in the Paris he knew, were really "endowed with nuances of *iki*." The negative is implied but this is less important than that he thought to ask the question.

All of this has now had its day. *Iki* turns into whatever is found "cool," nature is put on the back burner, and method becomes media. Hence, then, the value of looking back along the long corridors of history and glimpsing a world where beauty was sought, where its qualities could be classified, and where a word for aesthetics was not necessary. Our five tastes, like Miyamoto Musashi's five rings, indicate a method and still something of a hope. Though it does not seem likely, Jean de la Bruyère's dictum yet holds. To enjoy good taste we only have to decide, for ourselves, what good sense is.

—*2001*

Signs and Symbols

Visitors to Japan soon notice a vast number of signs and symbols around them. They seem everywhere; almost every available surface carries a message but travelers have little hope of deciphering them.

Even if they could be read, however, tourists would probably pay them no more attention than they give signs and symbols in their own country. Still, they are obviously a functional part of the environment and they clearly proclaim. In addition, they are often beautiful. The visitor admires the pleasing abstract shape and the skill with which many are executed. This enjoyment is proper in that traditionally signs and symbols in Japan are also meant to be aesthetically pleasing. Still, the illiterate visitor is missing much.

To be sure, some signs are universal. Red is for negative direction, green for permissive, yellow for warning. This the visitor understands, as well as the use of red to signify hot and blue to show cold. Moreover, since Japan uses universal pictographs, the tourist can figure out which toilet to use. Most other messages, however, remain opaque, though to the Japanese the meaning is so transparent that they seem not even to notice.

If visitors stay for a time, however, they begin to discriminate among the messages. As a child learns, they will start by sorting the signs into groups or classes, and the first among these will probably be according to shape. Traffic signs, for example, are usually distinguished not only by written message but also by their form. In the United States this is standardized: stop signs are octagonal, yield signs are equilateral triangles, warning signs are diamond shaped. Japan has an analogous shape vocabulary that one readily learns.

Much more difficult is the text. The Japanese written language is a complex of ideograms and syllable signs. It is comprised of Chinese characters (*kanji*) and two syllabi. The first, *hiragana*, is used for phonetic renderings of native Japanese words, and the second, *katakana*, is usually used for words transliterated from other languages.

A Chinese character usually represents a whole idea. It is thus a complete word in itself, a system that reduces the need for sentence structure. In a language depending on an alphabet, a sentence is needed to convey a thought of any complexity. In *kanji* country, however, it is the character itself that often stands for all, and is all that is necessary. Centuries of using this system have developed in people an extraordinary ability not only to read the characters themselves, but also to understand the nuances and overtones that surround and color each character.

We follow a somewhat similar process, for example, when we read "The Pause that Refreshes" and helplessly visualize a big, frosted bottle. It could be argued, however, that when the Japanese read the character 酒 (the *kanji* for *sake*), associations of conviviality, warmth, solace, and enjoyment emerge more strongly than when we read the word "whiskey."

Our word is a combination of alphabetic letters (like every other word we possess) while the Chinese characters stand more strongly for the thing itself.

Just as the Japanese are alive to the nuances of the word, they are also aware of the way the word is written. In the West, unless we work in publishing or printing, we are no longer likely to be sensitive to the effects of different fonts and styles of typography. We know the bold lettering of news headlines and the fancy script of wedding invitations, but few other, and the fact that virtually all of our communications are mechanically or electronically printed has blinded us to the subtler nuances of handwritten styles. In Japan, however, calligraphy remains important.

The effectiveness of any sign or symbol depends on the nexus of associations surrounding it. A symbol reminds us of all the attributes we associate with what it represents, and much more is conveyed when the writing itself gives resonance to the basic sense.

An example from our own culture makes this clear. If in the United States we come across *Ye Olde English Tearoome* we know what is being sold besides tea. Both the affectations of Edwardian script and Elizabethan spelling indicate gentility, also a certain respect for the past, for age. Certainly the atmosphere will be both more respectful and more contrived than an establishment that simply proclaims "EATS." All of these complicated overtones we hear at a glance, as it were. The full message is understood without our thinking about it. We receive the message the proprietors have directed at us. We have an instant index of the place.

In Japan the process is similar. The reading and interpretation, however, allow for more complicated apprehensions. The reason for this is Japan's many styles of script, each with its own associations.

To begin with, Japanese distinguish among four major categories of written scripts. The first of these, *reisho*, evolved from China before the Han dynasty and derives from the lettering used for inscriptions carved in stone or on seals. (There is another similar form as well, also stiffly Chinese: *tensho*.) The second written category, dating from late Han, is called *kaisho*. It is the calligraphic style from which the Japanese developed *katakana*. The third is *gyosho*, the style in which most Japanese now write. The fourth is the fluid *sosho*, from which came *hiragana* (or, as it was once called, *hentaigana*). It is so loose that it is often difficult to read and the Japanese say that anything more flowing than *sosho* is illegible.

These differences in style will become clearer if the illustration below is studied. The *kanji* involved is *tsuki* or "moon" and this pronunciation is indicated phonetically in the *hiragana* printed form at the extreme right of the diagram. The pair of *katakana* separated vertically by a dot indicate two other pronunciations (and meanings) also carried by this character. First is *getsu*, as in *getsuyobi*, the word for "Monday." (English has something similar. It has "moon" and also a form of the word "moon" in Monday.) The second group of *katakana* indicates another meaning and pronunciation: *gatsu*, the suffix used in naming the months—*ichigatsu, nigatsu, sangatsu* (January, February, March), etc. This then is what the character means.

Reisho   Kaisho   Gyosho   Sosho   Printed Forms

The various scripts, however, indicate or create further nuances. To explain this, let us pretend that there are four restaurants, each calling itself Tsuki and each using this character in its advertising. What kind of atmosphere would one expect to find if each used a different style of lettering as per our diagram?

To Japanese the *reisho* characters could only indicate a Chinese restaurant or else a place with very old associations, either actual or assumed. The feeling might be a bit like that of our Olde Tearoome, old China being to Japan as old England is to the United States. The second restaurant, its name in *kaisho* script, would not tell us much since this is a style widely used for many signs. The nuances might be understood as "traditional," or as "everyday." In either case, however, there would be an association with Tokyo and the culture implied by this "new" capital.

With signs in *gyosho* or *sosho*, however, the customer's thoughts would turn to the "old" capital, Kyoto, and its softer, mellower moods. A shop sign in *gyosho* indicates a degree of refinement, a kind of delicacy that could be feminine. *Sosho*, which many Japanese find difficult to read, can also indicate self-conscious elegance—perhaps something with an artistic flavor.

While all of this might seem sufficiently recondite to the Westerner, it is only the beginning. Each of these styles has subdivisions. There is, for example, the script style called *edo-moji*. This is associated with Tokyo in the eighteenth century when it was still called Edo. It consists of sub-styles called *kantei, yose, joruri, kago,* and *kaku-moji*.

From each of these styles, then, other styles are derived. *Kantei*, for example, produces the *kabuki-moji*, a style associated only with that drama, and the *sumo* or *chikara-moji* is connected mainly with sumo wrestling. In addition, there is the popular Edo style called *hige-* (or "whiskered") *moji*, in which individual bristle strokes are visible.

A cursive script, near *gyosho* in feeling, the "whiskered" style, though intended to appear spontaneous and free, is in fact rigidly stylized. The passage of the brush must leave seven distinct bristle marks, in the narrow parts of the character it must show five, and as it leaves the paper it must show three. This seven-five-three formula, derived from China, is thought to be an auspicious combination and is applied to many occasions, such as the necessary shrine visits of young children at these three ages.

Again, all of this is arcane to the Western visitor (and, it might be added, has become remote to the Japanese resident as well. Yet there is still a wealth of nuance, a treasury of shared and accepted associations that all Japanese have derived from their signs and symbols.

The process is less complicated than it sounds because no

conscious thought is involved in this kind of reading. Such nuances are felt at once or not at all. Since associations are involved—"feeling" rather than "thoughts"—putting them into words makes them sound more rigid than they actually are.

Japan's proliferation of signs and symbols is overwhelmingly evident in commercial advertising. The viewing audience is not only the potential customer but virtually everyone else as well—the whole society and (if we consider commercial votive tables) the gods themselves. Advertising in Japan is not only a public art, it is also a major cultural force.

Underlying this art of advertising is the traditional art of calligraphy.

Whether the medium is black ink or neon tubing, the aesthetics of calligraphy can move foreigners almost as deeply as the Japanese. It is the beauty of the forms as much as their meaning that is appreciated. Among Japanese, an individual is still judged by the way the characters are formed. Letters from strangers are read not only for what they say but also for the way they are written. Bad writing still means a bad, or at least weak, person, and a good, clear, even, elegant hand is still considered a requisite. Aesthetic qualifications become moral qualifications and beauty becomes honesty.

For how long, one wonders? In the age of electronic communication, no one any longer writes by hand. You write through the keyboard. The wonderful world of signs and symbols in Japan is showing signs of strain. In the United States the youngest generation no longer needs to spell because spell check takes care of everything. Even simple arithmetic is no longer necessary since everyone has a calculator. In Japan is it likely that the arcane rules of communication will survive?

—*1974*

The Tongue of Fashion

We express ourselves in various ways: deeds, words, gestures. The expression is presentational: we show who we are, or who we wish to be taken for. There are many systems of such expression, some well known, others known scarcely at all. Spoken and written language is a well-studied system of expression. Other forms of expression are scarcely studied at all. Among these is clothing as a system of expressing feeling and thought. Yet, as a means of self-presentation it is one of the most common forms of gestural language. The paragraph formed by the complete ensemble speaks plainly about the wearer and is so intended and the language is rarely studied.

In Japan, a land where the emblematic is visible and where signs and signals are noticeably displayed, the language of dress is more codified than in many countries. It is consequently better known and more consciously used. Kunio Yanagita, the early folklorist, said that "clothing is the most direct indication of a people's general frame of mind," and this observation is shared by a majority of Japanese—or used to be when the traditional Japanese costume was the only form of sartorial expression. Indeed, it said much about the country and its people.

The kimono comes in only two sizes—male and female. It is almost never designed to fit the wearer. Rather, the wearer is designed to fit it. The assumption is that we Japanese are all alike—except for the important difference of gender. Tailoring as a form of uniqueness is not valued in this land where the truly unique is so often unwelcome. Rather, since harmony is our goal in all things, we show our happy similarity in our national costume.

To be sure, there is room for minor variation. A young girl

shows she is young by wearing a bright kimono, and an older woman shows she is older by wearing only subdued colors. Traditionally the wealthy but otherwise unprivileged merchant indicated his state by having his plain kimono lined with the most expensive of materials. And in general, both kimono pattern and hairstyle indicated the social position of the wearer. A geisha would look quite different from the married woman of good family.

The kimono, like all forms of dress, also shows much more than it ostensibly presents. The language of clothing, like any other language, is filled with nuance. Thus, the kimono defines the wearer in more senses than one. Though not shaped to the body, it encircles and confines it, holds and supports it, as do few other forms of dress.

In contrast to the Arab kaftan or the Persian chador, which have no contact with the body at all, which merely cover it, the kimono delineates the wearer. It is, particularly in the woman's costume, so tight and so supported by layers of inner kimono, that it is like a molded shell.

What is molded, however, are not the breasts, the hips, the behind, those areas emphasized in the West, but the torso itself. The result is a costume so tight that it hobbles the wearer and prevents any actions other than walking, standing, sitting, kneeling—a repertoire of movements that, given the possibilities of the human body, is quite limited. The inescapable suggestion is that something this tight and constricting must enclose—like the lobster's shell—something soft and fluid.

In this sense the kimono can be seen as a metaphor for the idea that the Japanese have of themselves. We are a people whose social consciousness is at least as strong as our individual consciousness: we live in a rigid, conforming society and both our strong social self and the equally strong social rules we obey are necessary because we would not otherwise know who we are. Like the lobster, we are defined not by an inner core but by an outward armor, which is both social and sartorial. These—our ideas, our clothes—are informed from the outside. We so express our social self because, to an extent, that is all there is.

At the same time, however, the social contract has many escape clauses and the kimono itself has myriad possibilities for individual expression. Our emotions, our vagrant fears and wishes, can all be expressed so long as we show these only within the context of our society and its laws—these are thus visible within the context of the kimono, our national costume.

A standard costume is like an accepted idea. It is self-evident. One does not examine its meaning until one has ceased to believe in it. In the same way, when the meaning of the kimono was not apparent any longer, it ceased to be widely worn. Now we see that— a truism—those who still wear kimono also still entertain old-fashioned ideas. At the same time there lingers, naturally enough, an air of the respectable about the kimono. The well-brought-up girl has one and wears it on the proper occasions (wedding, tea ceremony or flower arrangement lessons, New Year's visits), though the rest of the time she may be in jeans. She is showing that she is a decent girl but that she also has modern ideas. She is not suggesting, I think, that she is just dressing up, that the real her is different. Though these might be the thoughts of an American girl gotten up in old-fashioned gear (white, lacy, with veil and train) for an American wedding, the Japanese girl is stating that she is both modern and respectable (mod but trad) at the same time.

Hers is one solution (sometimes in kimono, sometimes in jeans) to a communication problem the Japanese have had for some time now. How do you indicate sartorially who you are when the vehicle for so doing is disappearing?

When Japan began modernizing itself over a hundred years ago many were the mistakes—bustles worn backwards and the like. The Japanese were not prepared to properly read the lexicon of Western dress. As might have been expected, the Japanese choice was initially for Western clothing too formal for either the occasion or the person. Hats, gloves, sticks—elements known to have had originally aristocratic nuances—were used by all Japanese men who could afford them. The women likewise were always too dressed up. One still sees remnants of this early reading in even informal imperial court customs, and Japanese abroad usually appear, given foreign standards, overdressed. That a Japanese in Western clothes always looks as if he or she is off to a wedding or a funeral is an old observation but one still, to an extent, valid.

One can understand the reasons. The rigidity of the kimono was being sought in the rigidity of foreign formal dress. Overdressing for an occasion, which is what all formal dress consists of, means by definition a presentation of the social self. The clothing is much like the conversation on such occasions: social, that is, impersonal.

The language of dress in the West is now nothing if not personal. Fashion has become a system of dialects. Individuality is sought for, if not always achieved, and social dress (as in formal dress) has all but disappeared. The Japanese, having scrapped their own native costume and having proved understandably maladroit in handling the various nuances of Western formal dress, are now handed a new problem of how to present the social self when the West offers only highly individualized clothing styles.

To an extent, however, modern Japanese have the choice made for them by fashion itself—the linguistic equivalent of which might be free speech, but the true aim of which is to make everyone for a season speak alike. The Japanese problem, its quest for clothing expressing a social norm, is solved so long as everyone appears more or less the same, even though the clothing itself may have originally carried highly personal nuances.

Take jeans, for example. These have now become the uniform of the young in all countries. Being a uniform, this means that the young are all saying the same thing. Though the fashion (as fashion) was originally radical in the United States (we are not going to dress up, we are going back to our agrarian roots, we are egalitarian, etc.) and even to an extent revolutionary (down with formal clothing, down with elitist thought, down with civilization), jeans have now become the equivalent of an accepted idea. Now called Levi's, acknowledging the merchandizing skill of an early jeans maker, their use is commonly accepted. If called upon to be defended the users may answer that jeans are cheap, easy to wash, do not need ironing, and everyone else wears them.

Once in Japan, jeans became the uniform for the young. Originally they came carrying the message of youthful revolt. In time, however, jeans (always bought a size too small and given to shrinkage besides) became the kimono equivalent. Physically they encase snugly, and their metaphysical message has become socially conciliatory—if everyone says the same thing, then no one says anything.

Not that this has not occurred in other countries. And not that other countries do not likewise seek the safety and security of the unexceptionable social costume. In Japan, however, the results are so much more visible and state so plainly that we are conforming; we are rocking no boats. Also given the admitted difficulties that the Japanese encounter in their "reading" of modern fashion, their mistakes are often instructive.

Take, for example, the emblazoned T-shirt. In the United States, where the fashion started, wearing a Coca-Cola sloganed T-shirt meant precisely that one would not subscribe to those institutionalized habits that accompany habitual Coca-Cola drinking.

The intent was ironic, as in so much American fashion. If one wore a Yale or a Harvard T-shirt, not only did one not go to these institutions of higher learning, but also one was expressing an ironic scorn for the qualities they presumably inculcated. Wearing surplus U.S. Army gear meant you were anti–Vietnam War and hence anti-army.

In Japan, however, Coca-Cola wearers love Coca-Cola. It is a sign of modernity. The boy with Yale or Harvard on his chest would really like to attend these universities. To be this cosmopolitan is to be progressive. Surplus army uniforms (always U.S., never Japanese) mean merely being in some obscure sense "with it."

And as for the emblazoned messages, since no one can read them or, reading them, understand them, the mere fact one is wearing English indicates a contemporary and progressive frame of mind. Some of these consequently fashionable items are, it is true, startling. "If It Moves Suck It" might be fitting on the chest of a sardonic American college boy but not when (where I saw it) decorating the bosom of an innocent Japanese high school girl. The mock come-on or put-down built into the American youth context is here entirely missing.

Yet, even when the ostensible message is misunderstood, the under-message ("We are among the new knowledgeables, we are with it") is there. Printed T-shirts everywhere mean I'm okay, you're okay. In Japan the printed foreign word (divorced of all meaning though it must be) announced by its very presence that "I am not an old fogey, I am not a stick in the mud. Rather, I am cultured." Foreign words—English in Japan right now—have the same *éclat* that French on the menu used to have in America.

Often the difference between Japanese and American use of the same object or attitude lies mainly in the interpretation given it. An example is the brief career of the too-big look, clothes purposely several sizes too large, pants or skirt bunched at the belt, coat or blouse sleeves extending down over the hands, shoulders sagging. The avatar was the Diane Keaton character in Woody Allen's 1977 film, *Annie Hall.*

The message, consistent with the character of the heroine, was that the girl in the too-large man's suit was really saying that try as she may for a man's role in this man's world, it was just "too big" for her. When the fashion was imported into Japan, however, the message had no social relevance whatever—Japanese women were still far from having the confidence to attempt such a role.

Something analogous, however, did occur. Though too-big as a foreign fashion had been taken over unexamined, it was shortly tailored to fit Japanese needs. Too-big outfits began to appear, but only on the men (or the boys). There were a number of these fashion-conscious adolescents in their bunched trousers and sagging coats that were, in the West, only associated with fashion-conscious girls.

Yet, in Japan, this edited version of the American message made perfect sense. Japanese male youngsters cannot "fill father's pants." Both the costume and the social responsibilities it suggests are "too much" for the wearer. The outfit is a parody of Papa's best suit and its use means that Sonny cannot live up to his inherited responsibilities.

Although sometimes the messages of fashion thus coincide, most often they do not. Take, for example, the American ensemble that consisted of such unfashionable materials as georgette and velveteen cut in a deliberately old-fashioned manner—yoke neck, puffed sleeves, often accompanied by hair in a bun and sometimes granny-glasses. The message is that we are so serious that we do not care about fashion (though this ensemble, in fact, for a time became fashionable), and we in our own way care for and have indeed found the true virtues: those of our grandparents if not our parents. Further, we are sober and recognize worth and are honest enough to proclaim this in how we look.

Such a complicated sartorial metaphor is not legible in Japan where, in any event, the different strata of historical costume in the West are not recognized. At the same time, however, since fashion is fashion, this proto-hippy granny look was for a time everywhere in the larger Japanese cities.

Here again, however, some changes were made. Since Japan has never had a fashion that has been downgraded (and, as we have seen, even the kimono is at certain times and places proper, and hence fashionable still), there is no need for irony. The Japanese see the unfashionable look therefore as simply a continuation of one of their own fashions: the velveteen little-girl dress first encountered as a late-nineteenth-century import, which has, indeed, never gone out of fashion.

Styles of the 1930s (to which the proto-hippy American look is most beholden) are not recognized as such and, in any event, the implied nostalgia cannot be felt. Therefore, the American unfashionable look is treated as a logical extension of Japan's own little-girl look. This says that I am innocent and nubile, of good family and am firmly aware of my own cuteness—I am something for you to admire and think fondly of. Consequently granny glasses and puff sleeves as a fashion fit well with angle-length party skirts and hair ribbons. Kate Greenaway is laid full length on top of Clyde's Bonnie.

Not only does the Japanese read Western fashion differently (jeans), creatively (the too-big suit on the boy), and wrongly (the ugly look as cute), they are also not at all "at home" with Western fashions and never have been. The only Western dress to which they have thoroughly accustomed themselves and that they wear naturally is the institutionalized costume.

We foreigners are in our various countries used to this only in specialized professions—nurses, stewardesses, etc. And, typically, the wearers are usually female. In Japan, however, the institutional costume is everywhere. All Japanese cooks wear a "cook suit," white, with a big puffed hat; most young Japanese students wear the black serge, high-collar, Prussian schoolboy suit; day-laborers concoct typical and usually identical outfits; even the ordinary man off for a day of skiing or hiking fits himself out in full sports ensembles. The conclusion is inescapable: the Japanese is truly at home in Western dress only if it is some form of livery.

Alison Lurie has written that to wear livery is to be "editorialized or censored," which is quite true. But it is, at the same time, also to be defined. It is this, the need for definition (at the cost, to be sure, of editorialization and censorship), which seems to be so felt by modern Japanese.

One cannot wear jeans forever and so the logical progress is therefore into identical dark business suits, invariable white shirts, and forever sober neckties, with company badges in the lapels. To be defined is (in Japanese terms) to know who you are socially, and even sociologically. This is of prime importance. Thus everyone "says" the same thing, and this "conversation" uses only the safest of clichés. If "who I am" is the sartorial message the world over, then clothes can also answer the even more pressing question, "Who am I?" The Japanese response to this is: I am what I appear to be, I am the role and the function I am dressed for.

There are thus within the purely Japanese context no problems of ambiguity, dishonesty, irony, or intention vs. interpretation (terms Alison Lurie has used in speaking of a possible vocabulary for dress). Likewise, since the costume that even the young must eventually opt for is so unequivocal that there is no room for eloquence, wit, or even any but the most rudimentary information. Unexampled similarity remains the ideal of Japanese dress, though the unavailability of the kimono, that most strictly Japanese of garments, is still sadly felt.

—*1981*

Japan the Incongruous

Among the current attractions offered the West by Japan is the image of a modern culture that seems to critique our own, to playfully question it and, at the same time, to query our own way of seeing them—to seem to position this image as incongruous.

This is the latest in a long list. The West has long felt that Japan needs some kind of definition, that differences were to be identified and maintained, that some set of characteristics could be discovered, those that could be recognized as belonging uniquely to it alone, constituting its individual personality.

Such narrow longings soon infected Japan itself. Identification became a craving. Japanese could be heard speaking of their unique island mentality, could be seen writing such efforts as *Nihonjin-ron*, serious papers about their difference from everyone else. Shortly the brain capacity was found larger and the bowels longer, both reasons for exclusivity. But first I must define my term—why incongruity?

A common example: here we find a country where printed visiting cards (the ubiquitous *meshi*) are given the scrutiny of scripture, but where both tenderer and recipient may be wearing T-shirts lettered in foreign tongues that they are unable to read and anyway don't want to.

Something we recognize (our language, English) is keeping close company with something we don't (theirs, Japanese). Since we know the nexus of our familiar things and find that these assumptions are being ignored, we read the resulting enjambment as out of place, out of keeping, absurd, and, nowadays, amusing.

This current amused delight at Japan's cultural mix was not, however, always evident. Things incongruous are also things in disagreement. We detect ambivalence, something having either or both contrary qualities; we detect ambiguity, something capable of more than one meaning, of doubtful classification, of uncertain issue. Historically this once upset us in the West because it seemed to question our assumptions, to deny them.

Samurai, it is said, incongruously used to shield themselves with their fans when walking under the telegraph lines that were increasingly appearing in their country. They did this to protect against the lethal electricity, which was thought to be dripping from the wires.

We foreign observers back then did not find this amusing. Rather, we found it benighted, unenlightened and, further, something of an insult to our own obvious superiority—it was we, after all, who had provided the wires. Incongruity was perceived as criticism.

It no longer is. If we now regard Japan's observed incongruity as amusing it is because we no longer hold these assumptions, we have ceased to believe in them. Now we would side with the samurai because we can equate the dangerously dripping electricity with the ruinous downpour of television and other electrical products in our own culture.

The perhaps apocryphal story of the enterprising Japanese storekeeper who sought to intensify the Christian spirit of Christmas by displaying a crucified Santa Claus would have excited Western criticism a century ago. Not now. We live in critical times and it delights the critical to see an agreed-upon order stood on its head—such incongruity seems to indicate simple truth.

Japan has long offered this service. For well over a century the West called it "the land of topsy-turvy." It gave the idea of an ordered place where the assumptions of rank were very different and where the rank of order was not ours. By contrast our own order was then validated. They were topsy-turvy, not us.

Japan, of course, was innocent of any such intention. It did not know it was seen as upside-down and would not have understood the reason it was so regarded. The reason was that it chose (or, as we now maintain, was forced to choose) an imitation of Western culture—a culture in many ways different from its traditional own, and thus a fertile ground for a resulting incongruity.

When the American ships appeared in the middle of the nineteenth century a number of demands were made: treaties, trade, etc. Japan, long regarded as closed, was to open up; a profit was to be made. But during the time when Japan had been pretty much left alone by the rest of the world, an entire traditional culture had matured, one that is still remembered as "Japanese."

Confronted with a dilemma, Japan, one of the more pragmatic of nations, decided to join rather than oppose, and to imitate rather than confront. New Japan copied itself on what it understood of the West. Naturally, entertaining anomalies resulted—things strange and difficult to identify or classify. Many are the stories of sartorial mix-ups—derbies worn with kimono, bustles worn in the front rather than the back—and much was the foreign amusement.

The Japanese in their new finery responded with a kind of dress code. Things Japanese were to be kept separate from things Western. One could not wear shoes with a formal *haori* coat. One ate either *washoku* (Japanese food) or *yoshoku* (foreign food). One lived in a *washitsu tatami* room or a *yoshitsu* Western room. This distinction continued for well over a century—but it no longer does.

This is because the erosion of traditional Japanese culture is almost complete. What remains is largely fossilized, yet this culture was millennia deep and so the run off of a few centuries still reveals native shapes here and there. Japan's attitude regarding religion still maintains, the structure of the language remains as it was—masses of loan words, but no articles; a pronounced neglect of pronouns— all of which is traditional.

And in this age of fusion in which we live, accommodations have been reached. Perhaps consequently that defensive wall that the Japanese erected between our things and their things has been breached. That double-layered fashion, the Japanesque, was invented and this summer's pop item is nylon summer kimono, loudly colored *yukata*, worn with high heels and the *obi* all wrong. No one can tell the difference anymore and no one wants to because no one cares.

As we look at the country it is now perceived by us as being much more like us. Differences may remain apparent but these are no longer seen as criticisms of our ways. Rather, they are seen as affirmations, all the more delightful in that we of the West do not take them seriously. They are like Hello Kitty: opaque but harmless, probably autistic but endearingly and mysteriously (no mouth) mute.

Among the other reasons for this gradual Western appreciation of Japan-encountered incongruity is that we are no longer so sure of ourselves and question many received ideas and previous assumptions—Orientalism, colonialism, imperialism are all being questioned. Most history has now turned into revisionist history. Incongruities, once seen as implied criticism, are now viewed as ideas with which we tend to agree.

Another reason for Western enthusiasm for what is seen as Japanese incongruity is that inevitable evolution (at present called postmodernism) that breaks down agreed-upon categorizations. One of the symptoms is the collapse of the barrier that in the West once separated "high" from "low" culture. Now it is quite permissible to mix: Bach and Bix Beiderbecke are no longer to be viewed as opposites. Fusion is an idea in music as well as in fashion and cooking. The resulting blend partakes of the merger, and many are the commercial examples of this, particularly in Japan because this country separated high from low only in its own traditional culture, and encouraged other cultures to promiscuously mix their levels once they came to Japan. Also it takes its mixtures a step further than does the still-cautious West. It is now possible to mix Bach with Guy Lombardo—Japan does it regularly.

Along with the West's fairly recent tolerance for incongruities, which were once read all the way from disrespect to rank insult, comes a new lenience in which some formerly ignored categories are now acknowledged and applauded: toys, games, plastic culture, *manga, anime*. Among these have been new appraisals of sensibilities common everywhere but discovered in abundance in Japan: the elevation of kitsch, the acceptance of cute, and the employment of camp.

Kitsch, from German for "trash," is anything that claims to have an aesthetic purpose but is in itself tawdry and tasteless. The West often equates it with cheap, sentimental objects for the common market—the Manneken Pis is an example. Also it is used to indicate something that inappropriately solicits our attention or admiration: the Lord's Prayer written on the head of a pin, a model of the Eiffel Tower built entirely of toothpicks.

In the West, along with our disillusion with accepted worth has now come an appreciation of the uselessly artificial, beginning with model ships in bottles and ending with Andy Warhol. We have thus become accustomed to see Japan as an extended mall of such—wallpaper colored to look like marble, plastic sushi as table decoration, a tissue box in the shape of Mount Fuji, the emerging Kleenex as smoke—such kitsch items are found amusing, refreshing. Tokyo has a whole street of such cheap, sentimental *komono* in Harajuku; many Japanese admire the ingenuity and patience needed to construct an Eiffel Tower entirely from toothpicks, and plastic food has a commercial place, acting as a menu.

Aligned to the fad for kitsch is the cult of the cute—*kawaii* in

Japanese. It has long been prominent in Japan. It associates cuteness with smallness and/or infancy, as in the various *komono* kitsch items so beloved of the Japanese young.

Some Japanese observers have said that the attraction of the *kawaii* is rooted in Japan's "harmony-loving" culture, that it suggests a quality on which all can (or should) agree. Whatever; it is ubiquitous in modern Japan. Ultraman, Atom Boy, Hello Kitty are everywhere. Further such *kawaii* fabrications are used in locations that in Western culture would be considered incongruously frivolous: commercial airlines with Pokémon characters on their sides, military advertisements with a beaming Doraemon, government publications with Mickey and Minnie (visiting kitsch), and so on.

This may be because the cute is nonthreatening, it is uncomplicated, its appreciation requires almost no thought. Formerly such an infatuation with the cute would seem to have upheld General Douglas MacArthur's much-resented observation that Japan was a nation of twelve-year-olds. But now all of us are twelve years old.

Americans (and increasingly Japanese) dress like children—play clothes, sun suits, hip-hop garb. They talk rap, and pidgin-English is preferred communication now that a traditional trust in words is mostly lost. And over it all, magic wings of *manga* and *anime kawaii* sweep the world.

Akin to kitsch in its pretensions and *kawaii* in its frivolity is the sensibility of camp. It has been variously defined: a love of the artificial, the exaggerated, an attitude consistently aesthetic, a victory of style over content and aesthetics over morality. One of its aims is to dethrone the serious, to be frivolous about the solemn, but solemn about the frivolous. It slights content to elevate style; whenever there is any development of character, camp is reduced and being becomes role-playing.

We now find Japan incongruous and appealing in the same way

that we find Disneyland delightfully incompatible with everyday reality. And we then read into these various artifacts in Japan intentions that are not theirs but which we find nonetheless.

Hello Kitty, without a thought in her head, is seen by us as somehow knowing, the affectless Haruki Murakami is made into a personification of cult cool, *kawaii* is seen a certification of a proper frivolity. All of these readings reflect more of the unrest of the West than of any social Japanese relevance. In fact, in Japan few of these attributes are read in the current Western manner.

Yet, though Japan may be the kingdom of kitsch, it doesn't know it. It never distinguished between our high and low culture (a brand name is a brand name), and though Japan is the country of camp it does not, cannot, recognize it. The T-shirt with *Life Sucks* on it is not voicing an opinion, or even an attitude. It is making a fashion statement.

It cannot do anything else. This is because Japan (maybe the campiest place in the universe) remains innocent of a devastating quality that has so shaped the contemporary West. I speak of irony, which the dictionary defines as "an incongruity between what actually happens and what might be expected to happen, especially when this disparity seems absurd."

Or, to put it another way, irony is that line we observe between the face and the mask. In it we see the absurd difference. But what then in a place where the mask is the social face, where the very real face is rarely compared to its social equivalent, where the resultant absurd is tolerated, institutionalized, where to act is to be? There is no irony because there is no comparison.

At least this is what the Westerner sees when he looks; this is what it seems to be from his (my) point of view. When we enthuse over the apparent mindlessness of Hello Kitty and celebrate its cute stupidity, we are still intruding our perceptions since the local attractions of Hello Kitty are different—she (always a "she" in Japan, a land ignorant of political correctness) is *kawaii* and that is that because everyone has agreed that that is that.

The need for an agreed-upon definition, Japan the beautiful, Japan the ambiguous, Japan the incongruous, has little to do with Japan as such and much to do with the needs of those bothering to define. If we savor rather than scorn Hello Kitty it is because we are still condescending, though now in a different manner.

—*2006*

Pink Box: Inside Japanese Sex Clubs

The proliferation of playlands in Japan never fails to impress the visitor. You can go to Anne of Green Gables Land; or Hans Christian Andersen's hometown; or Niigata's Russian Village, with trained seals all the way from Lake Baikal; or the real resting place of Jesus Christ in Shingomura, Aomori—turns out it was his brother Iskiri who was crucified; or Hello Kitty Land and, of course, Mickey Mouse's imitation of the United States—all of them fantasies, all of them imitations of something else.

Just as substantial and just as varied are the Japanese playlands devoted to sex. Here the visitor is entertained by imitation nurses, waitresses, elevator women, girls in traditional kimono, in Chinese costumes, or girls dressed as brides still in their veils. For the more adventuresome there are girls in body stockings all ready to be ripped, girls in police uniforms with handcuffs ready, girls under black light, girls in pink boxes. There is even a Sexual Harassment Land—a popular venue, so advertised. And there is a like menu of boys in all postures and positions, ready for the female patron or for another male.

Unlike similar practitioners on the anonymous backstreets of big cities in Europe or America, the Japanese playland brings with it its own environment. The bride can have her own chapel while awaiting her ravisher; the policewomen are in their specially constructed police stations with bars and doors that lock; there is a fake movie theater if you want to make out with a stranger at the cinema; and the schoolgirl can be found in a mock-up of a train car where she can be freely felt up and more.

This last environment will, if examined, give some indication of the role that such sexual playlands play in Japan and indicates why they are so popular. This fake train car embodies the agreed-upon fantasy of fondling women in the train or the subway. So apparently common is this urge that the practitioner has been given a name. He is a *chikan*.

The idea is that the unknown but attractive women will be so embarrassed by the public nature of the *chikan*'s attentions that she will endure them until he completes his survey. He, having asserted his virility and bested the woman, strides off into anonymity.

In actual fact, this scenario is mostly fantasy. Women know how to defend themselves, and the cops are wise to the ways of these *frotteurs*. Perhaps that is the reason then that one of the most popular of the environmental playgrounds are these fake train cars, fully detailed (even with signs warning against *chikan* activity), where young women impersonate school girls (uniforms, bare legs, book bags) and stand complacently while the customer has at least a part of his way. The fantasy here finds its own reality.

Venues with decor this elaborate are called image clubs, and they come in many flavors. The sets are detailed and inhabitants are often elaborately costumed. Elevator girls, airline stewardesses, hospital nurses wear convincing work attire often with the appropriate logo. A lot of hard work has gone into making believable what is, after all, fantasy. But this is what the sex clubs of Japan are selling. No less than *manga*, no less than *anime*, they are entirely concerned with fleshing out a fantasy—a capricious or fantastic idea, a conceit.

If you look up the term in the dictionary you get: "Fantasy—an imagined event or sequence of mental images, such as a daydream, usually fulfilling a wish or psychological need." So what psychological needs do pink boxes suggest?

Well, some concern group identity. Maybe that is the reason for all the costumes. Japan, many have noted, is home of the defining garment. Traditionally the kimono you wore and the way you did your hair defined your social status. Now your occupations do—not only uniforms on school students, but also puffy hats and aprons on cooks and full alpine gear when you climb the nearest hill. You are what you wear.

Another psychological concern might be about emotional security. Our safest time was when we are little, and so it is little we are encouraged to once more become upon visiting our pink-boxed playland. Our cute servers wear little-girl costumes. They look like *anime* characters, and they often behave in the same chirpy and juvenile way. Like the girls on the pages of *manga* they are always ready for a little rowdy playtime, the more infantile the better.

In the sex saunas (hygienically labeled soaplands in Japan) infantilism is also encouraged, though here it is the patron who is supposed to be emotionally retrograde. The soapland lady is fantasized as more mature and the customer as less. He is thus firmly guided through his erotic experience. "And now the left one. There we go. Aren't we having a good time?"

Men put up with and even encourage such treatment because they too are concerned with emotional security. They often enter the soapland or the image club or the happening bar as a group. There they are initially engaged more or less en masse, and boys are encouraged to be boys. Comfortable with his peers, thoroughly male-bonded, the individual is so secure that he can let it all hang out. Just us boys together.

In this the sexual playlands of Japan are nothing new. Boys have been boys for centuries. And (like everywhere else) Japan has always had its red-light districts and its licensed quarters. The difference, however, is the spirit in which things were undertaken. A hundred years ago there was (compared to the West) a playtime feeling to the brothels. Jokes, laughter, folks having a good time, lots of humor—so much so that there was a name for it, that spirit of *asobi* that you can still smile over in the *shunga*, those traditional erotic woodblock prints.

In the West laughter in the whorehouse must be a rare commodity. Commercial sex can be a sobering affair. In Japan, however, where everyone is dressed up (or down) and giggling, laughter is an indication of what a good time we are having. And any establishment that wants to stay in business had better create a fun atmosphere.

One of the reasons that this is possible is that buying a person for sexual purposes carries little stigma. Perhaps in the West it is still felt as somehow not right, but Japan's religions are not so sexually uptight as those of the rest of the world, and its stigmas are different.

This being so, sex as consumerism is right up there with cameras, transistors, and new cars. Since the purchase power is high, so is the competition. There has to be a new wrinkle every night. One establishment starts *demai*, home delivery service; another suggests a Russian-roulette-like innovation, *nama-shaku,* fellatio without a condom; yet another offers a new Internet information service describing all the various enticements in all the various playlands in this enormous labyrinth of Japanese pink boxes.

All of this requires a huge superstructure and a whole army backstage. Options are everywhere, and these take hard work. Is your girl going to wear black hose, or flesh colored, or "sparkly"? This means that all three kinds must be purchased and stored. And all the girls carry timers. These have to be bought by someone and held in readiness.

And there has to be endless rules and regulations. These are usually posted in the places of action and must help create the schoolroom ambience so necessary if you are going to go back to childhood. But the rules are for the girls as well as for the customers. Nothing is left to chance.

One of the reasons for all this care is that sex play is a very big business. Japan's sex industry has been estimated as a ¥4 trillion business. Just how this figure was arrived at and how it compares with those of other countries is not apparent, but it is very large—indeed, it is almost equivalent to the national defense budget.

It is so huge that its operations must be run like all big businesses—through rigorous administration. The administrators are largely the Japanese mafia, usually termed *yakuza*. It is they, sitting in offices, using email, wearing ties, who control their teeming empire.

And teeming it is. A patron not uncommonly pays the equivalent of two or three hundred dollars for his pink box encounter. The girls, however, usually receive merely an hourly fee, except bonuses for valor beyond the call of duty. If she swallows the produce from a *nama-shaku*, it is said, she gets half the amount the donor paid. Otherwise, the boss gets to keep the major proceeds.

His financial clout may account for his political power. Tokyo, for example, is the only large city in the world that does not have all-night transportation. Rails and subways shut down shortly after midnight. Following the pattern of New York or London or Paris would alleviate the late citizen but such reform never occurs. And this, it is said, is because inconvenienced people on the loose in night-town usually become customers—either at a proper playland or at subsidiaries such as peeking parlors (*nozokibeya*) or telephone clubs where they can wait for hours until someone calls and talks dirty.

The women employed are, however, not (apparently) enslaved. Though less fortunate women from Korea, China, and Thailand are routinely mistreated (locked up, passports withheld), Japanese women are more commonly "recruited" (certain streets are alive with these "recruiters" following women about) and brought more or less willingly into the fold.

If buying a sexual partner carries small stigma, then selling yourself as one does not carry the weight it would in other countries—so long as you are out of the marriage market and do not care about gossipy neighbors. And the motives for such prostitution seem simple. Half the women recently polled said they just wanted enough to buy a Gucci bag.

Here we see that consumerism is a two-way street. The customer pays to be with the sex worker and then the sex worker goes out and becomes a customer at Louis Vuitton or Fendi or Prada or elsewhere. The demands of national economy are satisfied and the buying public is at the same time entertained, reassured, and given a very good time. Would that all economies worked this well.

—2007

III

On
Expression

The Presentational Urge as Theater

Most countries experience some kind of presentational imperative, an urge toward that form of ritual that we call theater. At the same time each country has its own ritualistic needs and consequently its own theatrical codifications. In any comparison among these I feel that Japan would rank high, that as a culture it experiences a strong need for ritual and hence exhibits a wide range of its theatrical manifestations.

Among the various origin myths I think only the Japanese offers a paradigm for theater. The circumstances are related in the *Kojiki,* Japan's earliest "history."

Amaterasu Omikami has in a fit of pique retired into her cave. Since she is the Great Divinity Illuminating Heaven, this leaves the world in darkness. She is lured out again by the feigned merrymaking, dancing, and the like performed by the other deities. Curious, she peers from her shelter and is drawn forth to again illuminate her world. It is a presentation, a performance, which is the salvation of the land. In Japan the theatrical paradigm is in place from the very first.

Japan is certainly not alone in creating such myths as this, but I think it is very nearly the only culture to so plainly label its solar myth as performance. The goddess is fooled, the merrymaking is feigned—it is all false—and this is approved. While it is not unusual for the legends of other cultures to include some kind of performance (Judas kissing Jesus is a dumb show for the centurions), it is unusual that this be approved—given the blessing, as it were, of both Shinto church and Yamato state.

Not only has Japan early expressed a theatrical urge, it has also continued to manifest this in much of its culture. A familiar example is traditional Japanese architecture. Though much influenced by that of Korea and China, this way of making a building is—as many have noted—rather like making a stage. The reference is to the native Japanese house, which many earlier observers saw as a performing area. It is raised off the ground, like a stage, it has no fourth wall (indeed it has no walls at all), and its interior divisions can, like stage sets, be moved about at will.

Admittedly one cannot make too much of this because such structures share much directly with domestic architecture elsewhere, but inside this theatrical house is a smaller theater that might be unique to Japan. This is the *tokonoma*, an alcove in the main room of the traditional house that serves as a place of presentation—nowadays mainly of a flower arrangement or a scroll, or both in some kind of artful juxtaposition.

To be sure there are Eastern antecedents, and the West has something like this in its furniture of display, the whatnot, the china closet, and so on. In Japan, however, the theatrical analogy is stronger. Not only are there featured players—the scroll, the flower arrangement, sometimes the valuable vase as well—but there are also frequent changes of bill as the seasons pass.

The *tokonoma* as stage has thus built into it the spatial and temporal considerations that limit and define the theater itself. It might thus be used as indication of theatrical urge in Japan.

Another might be the way in which domestic nature is presented. The Japanese garden is well known, indeed nearly notorious, for being actually a contrived spectacle.

That stone is moved over three feet, and this bamboo stand is moved back five. The pebbles or sand are brought in at much expense and the view of the distant mountain is purloined and called borrowed scenery. This then is the "natural" garden.

One might argue that European and Middle Eastern gardens are even more constructed, with their balanced symmetry and their geometrical intentions. And so they are, but the inventors and admirers of these gardens never called them natural and this is just what the Japanese assume theirs to be.

Nature has been presented. Tidied up, stylized, it has been made, as the old garden manuals have it, to express nature better than nature itself does. It is presumed that the integrity of any original does not exist. As in any dramatic presentation the only integrity is that of performance.

Not only does nature in the form of the Japanese garden become spectacle (as in, for example, the garden at Ryoanji), but it also becomes the theatrical experience itself, as in the Edo tour gardens where vistas are disclosed, scenes hidden and then revealed in a manner reminiscent of the revolving stage.

Even more theatrical is the art of *ikebana*. Here the stage is prepared (the *tokonoma* or its modern equivalent), the presentation has its rules (never mind that these "living flowers" are now dead) and—as in naturalist theater—the aim is to make the real more real than reality itself.

One could find many more examples of a pure presentational urge in Japan but, leaving unmentioned many, we might turn to one of the most recent and most spectacular. This is the annexation of an entire theatrical world. The paradigm is, of course, Disneyland, which is not Japanese at all, but the success of the concept and the ingenious ways in which it has been nationalized would indicate to what an extent the concept satisfies the Japanese theatrical urge. One is more than familiar with the principle. The area (city, country, "It's a Small World" itself) is miniaturized and made portable. In the process it is simplified and domesticated. Finally it is displayed.

It will be seen that the Disney imperative, like so many post-modern ideas, shares much with traditional Japan. It is not therefore surprising that more theatrical elements of Disneyland have already been made a part of present-day Japanese culture. To indicate but a few of these alternate performance worlds that have appeared in the last five years:

Japan created its first small world in Sasebo's Holland Village, an island-built replica of Deshima, home of the first foreigners, and it was here that the Japanese could visit a part of his own culture. So popular was this venture that the parent company later opened up Huis Ten Bosch, an enormous 152 hectares of canals, windmills, tulips, and wooden shoes. There are "European-style" hotels and those who wish can buy an on-site Dutch house and live the life of the Nederlandisch burgher without ever having left Japan. Also there is, naturally, none of the dingy danger of, say, Amsterdam. The original Dutchman could from his island view Japan as spectacle, now the Japanese can view Holland as spectacle from the comfort and safety of their own land. During its first year Huis Ten Bosch had nearly four million well-paying customers.

Shortly, Ashibetsu in Hokkaido—having lost its coal-mining industry—decided to go into the theme-park business. Canada World opened—Japan's largest lavender field, a complete St. Edward's Island–like Anne of Green Gables Land, and seven resident Canadians quilting, playing the fiddle, and chopping wood.

In Niigata's Russian Village one can, without the difficulty and danger of actually visiting Russia, see the Suzdal Cathedral, eat pirozhki, drink borsch, and enjoy a folk song and dance troupe and the talents of performing seals direct from Lake Baikal.

There is Nixe Castle in Noboribetsu, a full-scale replica of the castle and hometown of Hans Christian Andersen; Shuzenji's Britain Land, a slice of 17th-century British countryside complete with homes and shops. In Kure there is Portopia Land, which includes all of Portugal's Costa del Sol in some form or other.

Plus a number of New Zealand Villages in Hiroshima, Yamaguchi, and Shikoku, which specialize in sheep shows, an exotic entertainment in non-mutton-eating Japan, and in addition the Edomura in Tochigi, Hello Kitty Land, Yomiuri Land, Wild Blue Yokohama, and the Chiba Hawaiian Center (with wave machine), etc.

Then, for those in a hurry, there is the newly opened Tobu World Square where you can see 1/25-scale models of over a hundred of the world's most famous buildings all at once. The Taj Mahal is next to the Empire State Building, which is next to Saint Peter's, which is next to the Eiffel Tower, and so on. All are complete down to the smallest visible detail—they were made by the Toho Eizo Bijutsu, the people who gave us Godzilla—and they offer the world at a glance.

Though the onlooker at these spectacles may be reminded of Dr. Johnson's maxim that nothing is more hopeless than a scheme of merriment, the financial success of these various artificial foreign lands within the safe confines of Yamato has proved their viability for the Japanese.

It also says something about the Japanese audience for such spirited theatrical recreations, and about the presentational urge itself. A part of its imperative is certainly acquisition, whether this be the reappearance of the Sun Goddess, the distant mountain view, or Anne of Green Gables Land.

But a part, the part that concerns us, is that vital need for ritual, which has resulted in a culture that is, I believe, distinguished by what I have called the presentational urge.

—1994

Some Loose Pages on Japanese Narration

Narration, says the dictionary, is the act of telling a story or offering an account of something. It is also, continues the entry, the voiced soundtrack of a film when given by a commentator who does not appear. This definition applies just about everywhere but it does have regional interpretations—one of these is the Japanese.

The rest of the world is familiar with some of them. The haiku, for example, narrates an unusually short close-up view of a discovered connection. Here is an example from Yosa Buson (1716–83): "Ah, it cuts deep—/ to step on my dead wife's comb, / here where we slept." This is a narrated perception and we are free to identify the narrator with Buson, but the effect of the verse does not insist upon this.

Rather, the effect is universalized rather than personalized. This is accomplished through a studied simplicity. The verse includes only the moving parts of the experience: the "bedroom," the comb, the misstep and—connection—the pain of loss.

In the West, the customs of narration would, I think, insist on further elaboration or presentation or explanation. Japanese narrational habit, however, allows a kind of structural nudity. Shown is only that which is considered essential. This effect might be compared with the abbreviated final entries of Tanizaki's *Diary of a Mad Old Man*, or with the exclusion of not only romance but also marriage at the end of Ozu's *An Autumn Afternoon*.

*

An early distinction—it goes back to Aristotle—is that between narrative and drama. The former is told, recounted by a narrator; the latter is shown, enacted by characters in the narrative itself. Film may appear to be enactment but the medium itself is narration; cinema seems to lie between narrative and drama, between mediation and enactment. Or, between the presentational, offering an apparent interpretation, and the representational, feigning to offer no such interpretation and often passing as "reality" itself. Or, between "telling" and "showing."

Just as narration is often thought only to tell, and enacted drama only to show, so in films it is said that the editing of film tells (mediates, presents) while the film itself can only show. In all of these notions, however, some kind of storyteller is assumed, someone must make the choices through which both narrative and drama proceed.

Japanese narration avails itself of all possibilities but one can, I think, detect a kind of Japaneseness in a Mizoguchi sequence (I am thinking of *Taki no shiraito*) that keeps the camera so far away that details are invisible, which continues the scene for so long that interest shifts from story to how the story is being enacted—a sequence that shows everything and explains nothing.

*

"Besides picturing a dramatic fiction enacted before it, the movie camera enacts the fiction of a perceiving eye, an apprehending consciousness. The dramatic fiction imitates an action; the camera imitates a gaze, a point of view, an act of perception and of consciousness." Thus acutely observes Gilberto Perez.

What kind of eye is this? In most films, it sees only the characters or other devices that seek to impose the priorities of the plot. The camera is thus thought to be an empowered observer who can go everywhere and do anything in order to see what needs to be shown. Sometimes this can be a point-of-view shot of one of the characters, but often it is the shot seemingly motivated only by dramatic necessity, the best possible view of what it is necessary that we see. The concerns of plot and of character are considered paramount.

There are other possibilities, however. Rather than a "dramatic" camera serving the action, giving best views, there can be a "narrative" camera giving us its own view of the action. Its way of seeing can be discrepant with what occurs in front of it—its presence is indeed established by that discrepancy.

The lovers kiss and the camera does not move closer, but moves further away, or looks somewhere else. Its moves are not those demanded by the emotions being acted out, by the best possible view of the osculation. A result is no longer emotional identification but critical detachment. Or, the camera pays attention to things other than those having some bearing on the main action. Everything is put in the foreground while drama requires background and foreground, perspective. Or, a shot showing something dramatically significant is held longer than is necessary for the making of a dramatic point. We consequently find the point reduced, or questioned. Doubt enters. We wonder why we are being forced to look, to consider. In all these examples a different way of seeing is being suggested. We detect the presence of a narrator.

Japanese narrative no more than any other resists its literal narrators. Even something as nominally realistic as Kurosawa's *Ikiru* has one: that voice-over narration that tells you that Kenji Watanabe is, first, ill, and then, dead. It also has its visual narrators as well. Just who, in Ozu's *Early Spring*, is not showing the courtship and the wedding, and just who is insisting upon those long and pregnant scenes with "nothing" in them (notably that vase in the darkened room)? It is someone polite, even compassionate, someone who never hurries his actors off the screen, but respects the empty set once they have done so. This is a narrator who is teaching the audience how to act, as well as how to think and how to feel.

*

Who is telling/showing us this? Is it Ozu himself? In films we often assume that it is an auteur, someone whose consistency is recognizable. But this auteur is no more narrator than Vladimir Nabokov is Humbert Humbert—and no less. The visual narrator is a construct, an assumption.

What kind of assumption is involved? Alfred Hitchcock sometimes favors a didactic presenter who gives advance notice. A telephone is shown to us. It is going to ring. It does. Chekhov made fun of such intentional simplicities in his remarks about Dostoevsky's knife—once shown it must eventually be seen in use. There are lots of Japanese Hitchcocks but there are also many more anonymous narrators. I am thinking of Kore'eda, of Suwa, or of—in his way—Kitano.

Maybe the aesthetic difference is a reflection of the social. Japanese people mostly do not insist; they wish to appear polite, they wish to give the respect they hope to themselves deserve. The intelligence of the Japanese audience is occasionally respected as well. It is assumed intelligent enough to put together what the narrator tells it.

*

In the conventional narrative of any culture (Japanese or otherwise) the moving (panning, dollying, craning) camera always seems to have a mind of its own, seems to know where it is going. It gets to the next location before the actors do and then waits for them. Or they come from one direction and it comes from another and they meet as precisely as though planned. This camera always seems to know more than they do. And more than the audience does as well. But what or who is this intelligent camera? It is not point-of-view in any accepted sense. It is a somehow informed and invisible spirit that conditions our view, the presence of which we do not usually acknowledge. Yet it complicates the apprehension of what we see. It renders it suspicious, frivolous, arbitrary. The only honest record would be that of a camera that never moves and hence does not declare.

We sometimes find this in the Japanese film. Ozu, Mizoguchi— they are often mentioned when the subject comes up. But this could be because the West has long found an uninteresting shot slow.

*

Japanese films are so long, and so slow—thus the traditional Western complaint. This is often followed by the objection that they are (consequently) boring. Well, in the first place, boredom is merely an expression of the limitations of those feeling this emotion. And, in the second, length and tempo are felt only in relation to those lengths and those tempi to which the spectator is accustomed. No traditional Japanese ever said that the day-long Kabuki play *Chushingura* was too long or too slow, though by Western standards it would be thought both. No complaints about Ozu either—even at his most leisurely.

Perhaps another reason for such lack of complaint is the manner in which both are narrated. The play and the film are constructed of various scenes that inform each other. Scenes are left out at will (in that all productions of *Chushingura* are "different") and the spectator is expected to bridge any gap that is discovered.

(The West used to have something analogous. In Anglo-Saxon

countries each new film version of *Robin Hood* could leave out
scenes, characters, since it was assumed that the basic story was so
well known that any child could fill in the holes. This is no longer
true—it is no longer true of *Chushingura* either.)

Such a narration also assumes patience, forbearance as well. All
Japanese narrators are trustworthy (no Humberts among them), and
even when not (the couple writing the diaries that make up Tanizaki's *The Key*) we know their reasons and consequently go along
with them.

A slow tempo and more-than-ordinary length is no problem when you trust the narrator. Also, there is another attraction.
When you watch nothing for a long time you notice everything.
You become like an attentive child. You no longer assign meaning to
movement. Movement itself is enough.

*

A problem sometimes mentioned in Western criticism of Japanese
film is that the structure is unexpected. These films begin somewhere
past the beginning and they do not properly end, they merely stop.
The critics complain that Imamura's *Murderous Instincts* did not give
enough character background, that Naruse's *Flowing* did not see the
characters through to the conclusion.

Indeed, Japanese structural expectations are different. *Chushingura* divides itself into two; so does Kurosawa's *High and Low*. And
the order of the emotions is different. Musical programs are sometimes by Western standards indigestible. The FM radio plays "La
Poupée Valsante" *after* a rendition of *Le Sacre du Printemps*.

There are reasons. The last is an attempt at the aesthetic concept of *aji*. A red seal is seen at the bottom right-hand corner of
an India-ink monochrome scroll. This dot of red is to distinguish

the blackness and the whiteness. Perhaps it does so, but it is problematical whether the charm of Poldini's waltzing doll sufficiently contrasts with the muscle of Stravinsky.

*

The filmmaker presents his spectator with a picture. If it is a series of close-ups, tightly edited to form a message, that is one thing. If it is a single shot, taken from far away and lasting a long time, that is another. In the first, instructions have been given; in the second, they must be discovered. In which of these examples is the intelligence of the spectator being respected? Why, in the second, to be sure.

Perhaps that is why, in the West, such shots are found usually only in films intended for smaller audiences, art house patrons. One does not find Theo Angelopoulos or Bela Tarr in the big chain theaters. In Japan, however, the films of Ozu and Mizoguchi were made for the big chain theaters. Was it that the directors thought that they could trust the intelligence of the Japanese audience, and that producers let them do as they wanted?

Maybe. An audience that could look squarely at a haiku and put it together was likely to be able to ferret out details in the long-lasting long shot. Or maybe not. An audience that was used to filling in story-line lacunae in *Chushingura,* and lots of other narratives as well, would be naturally adept at filling in the spaces.

*

So, who narrates? And in Japan one may also ask *what* narrates. Structure is nominally ignored, one thing suggests another; association is all. As one page follows another with no superimposed narrative assumed, we read what appears to be a spontaneous flow.

This is a favorite form. It is called *zuihitsu*, a term often translated as "following the brush." The writer does not worry about imposing a structure—lets the brush take care of it. The brush (or the pen or the computer) is the narrator. This does not mean that there is no narration, merely that there is no narrational order—no cause and effect, no beginning, middle, and end, no conclusions.

It is this that I am imitating in these loose pages, to give the idea of the extremes of Japanese narration.

—*2005*

Notes on the Noh

It is not impossible to read the Noh as literature, but it is difficult. It requires the kind of imagination essential to anyone who sits in silence and reads a score. It also requires a like amount of skill. Going to the Noh in Japan is like going to chamber music recitals elsewhere. Some have the text open on their laps. Since the language is obscure, the delivery slow, the syllables drawn out, many Japanese could not otherwise understand much. Even with the texts, as with the score of a Schoenberg quartet, one must study it both before and after performance for the subtleties to become apparent. The pleasure lies in tracing the allusions, in understanding apparent ambiguities, in discovering the richness of the association.

The text of the Noh is a collection of poems, some by the author of the play, some not; it is a repository of popular songs of the day; language and often action turns on the pun, the pillow word, the invented portmanteaux, pivot words, conceits. Reading Noh is like reading late Joyce. Each word must be savored, weighed, calculated, and then put into context; it is this context, not the word itself, that creates the image. Noh defies translation. Properly Noh should include two pages of commentary for every two lines of text. When the earth-bound angel dances for her feathered robe and sings for the heavens in *Hagoromo*, she does more than just that. What we are given is a created cosmography in which float bits of T'ang poetry, pieces of earlier Japanese, traditional refrains, and transient songs of the day. The language turns, convolutes, devours itself.

A kind of analogy would be Middleton, Webster, Ford, or, in Shakespeare, the echoing lines of *Measure for Measure*, the subjective rant of Thersites in *Troilus and Cressida*. The language of Noh is like music of the Elizabethan period, like the parade of reminiscences—controlled but not seeming so—in *The Cries of London*, like their canons and rounds, cunning, lapidary. The Noh is mannerist drama.

Yet the Noh text is terse. It is concerned with the drama, with its description. Since bare action is as important to the Noh as is the bare stage, there are no encrusted couplets, no jeweled stanzas. A line may have five ambiguities but will contain not one simile. Instead, the scene is laid with adjectives, and we recognize the style: it is that of Greek poetry. The "autumn-winded pine-tree," and the "wine-dark sea" have a common ancestry.

Both are nature poetry. In Noh, natural forces, natural surroundings, are everything—it is animistic theater, the drama of Shinto. Demons come from rocks and ogres from trees, the angel descends from a pine grove, and the stage is peopled by the dead. And nature is there not only in the images of the language but in others as well. The backing of the stage is a single great pine, always the same yet always new—as constant as a ground-bass by Purcell, but as varied as the chorus that embroiders the scene.

The costume is always the kimono but such a kimono as never walked the earth. Of indeterminate period, a synthesized garment, it is a landscape all by itself. It is pure spider web, rich earth brown and silver skeins; or it is autumn incarnate: red, orange, with a touch of dying green. It is a flaming maple tree or spring's young cherry blossom. The costume is a vista made animate and each slow turn, each upraised arm, reveals new views. The simple props of the Noh—the fan, the rosary, the traveling hat—are indications. The costumes of the Noh, however, are the images of the play itself. And the talk is of clothes as well—sleeves get wet, trains trail, *obi* slide, and hats, hair, headdresses are all reflected in the text itself.

The Noh stage is a square, raised platform and the audience is at the front and to the right. Like the reconstructed Elizabethan stage, like the boxing ring, it is a viewing platform. It is the plateau that holds the action toward which all attention is directed. This as it should be because Noh, like the Elizabethan theater and unlike ours, is a theater of action.

To read the Noh is to think of drama but to see it is to think of ballet—and it was those first seeing it who called it the "dance-drama of Japan." The costumes are theatrical in a way we have lost but for the dance; the movements like the rituals we retain only in the ballet. The careful, creeping movements, heel-toe, the abrupt wheelings on the stage, the stamps, the sudden falling on the knees—these we would call dance though what the Noh calls dance is more purely formal—a *numéro* embedded in the text, accompanied by the chorus, and rendered in English only by the stage direction, "She dances."

And this translation must suffice for that moment when the forces of the play are drawn into a knot, that incandescent moment when words no longer serve, when action must reveal the story, the plot. The kneeling second-actor—a classical fall guy—has asked all the questions. The standing first-actor—facing the audience, masked, once human but now monster, demon, angel, thing—has answered every one. The final question, and the dance. She—he, it—will now show, will now demonstrate, will now repeat the action, as in that moment in therapy when the patient realizes he must live again, and this time live through the forgotten, the refused, the evaded experience. At one remove, no longer what she was, faced with the absolute—that peopled world outside the stage—she lifts one foot, then the other, turns and the final revelation has begun.

A long, drawn-out, hour-long accelerando, ending in the incandescence of dance; a gradual, almost imperceptible movement from *molto largo* to *prestissimo*: this is the tempo of the Noh. To try and watch the tempo grow is like trying to watch the movement of the hour hands of the clock, like trying to watch flowers open. Yet, there are seconds when you realize that before your eyes this tempo has changed. It seems faster, you think. It really does. Then: It *is* faster. Then: It is much faster than even I had thought. Midway through most Noh plays the tempo catches you and what had seemed a uniform (dignified, serene, dull, boring) flow is now revealed—after it is accomplished—as an incredibly subtle metamorphosis from dead stop to as fast as possible. And, at the height, somewhere past the middle of the play, comes the dance, the roaring, swooping, pounding, crushing dance of the demon or the ogre, the ecstasies of the mad ghost, or the quick dance of sorrow or bereavement, the dance of the spirits, of the dead. And this dance, the heart of the Noh, occurs at the precise moment when truth is recognized, when shame is thrown off, when the first-actor, the protagonist, appears as he really is.

The opening of the Noh is on the level of our theater. It is slower but it is, in its own way, realistic. We are in a mountain pass, or in a forest, or by a sea shore. The second-actor—as truly our representative as ever was the audience in *The Knight of the Burning Pestle*—comes forward and speaks our language. I am called so-and-so, I come from such-and-such, I am here to tell you a story. Him we recognize. He is one of us. Then comes out a being who initially also looks like one of us but is not. This we know from the mask, from the walk, from the beauty of the landscape on his back. This is not one of us and the story of the play tells us why. Our questions are only partially answered, or they are evaded, or are cunningly returned with ambivalence. We circle warily around the truth. We guess but dare not ask.

Then the being disappears; the actor is changing robes—into ones even more magnificent—and we and the second-actor (us) ponder. In some old plays we are at this point distracted by a comic interlude, like the nineteenth-century European concert audience receiving its restorative in the shape of a delicacy by Hummel between the movement of a grand symphony by Spohr or Cherubini. In others, we are not. Modern Noh performances more rarely pause. Then the being reappears. It no longer creeps upon the stage. It strides with little steps. It races with almost no movement at all. It looms and we are confronted. A ghost, an ogre, the spirit of a mother searching for her child, a soldier killed in his prime a hundred years before. Words fail us and this radiant being, too, no longer speaks. The dance begins.

Though the text is written the music is not, or at least not in the same way. The score is noted but lies in the memory of the performers. It is said to be always identical from performance to performance and, given the Japanese their reverence, it probably is—perhaps with changes so minute that one's great-grandfather would be reassured though Zeami ("father of the Noh") would find it unrecognizable.

It is a music of richness and complication. Like all the music of Japan, however, it is not absolute. It does not, cannot, exist by itself. There are no suites from *Shunkan*, no dramatic fragments from *Kumasaka*. The songs may be abstracted, studied, and performed, but only if the text is retained completely. The music exists to punctuate the word.

A dry, percussive music, it is extended *recitativo secco*, and it has been said to be of no more musical interest than that. But, in the context of the play, just as dance carries the action, so music carries the words. Though at first all seems arbitrary, chaos is shortly vanquished and form emerges. Amid the taps and clicks of the hand-held drums, the banging of the big floor-drum, the grunts and groans of actors, chorus, and musicians, the flute is the single voice that sings throughout, it sustains emotion and its skirlings and filigree become the dance.

Music is to Noh what Wagner had in mind, but a Wagner

without paraphernalia, without *leitmotiv*, without those bass cymbals that sound only twice during the four-evening performance of *The Ring.* The world of the Noh is very near the world of *Pelléas et Mélisande.* Reading the Noh text is like reading Maeterlinck, and just as the oboe becomes Mélisande, so the Noh flute becomes the voice of the protagonist when he no longer speaks.

The drums thump on, their sound and that of the stamping actor all confused, the sound of earth, the sound of man, the sound of death. And over it, amid the waving and kimonoed arms, like a bird let loose, the flute spirals upward with the dance. It is the voice of the angel, the voice of the demon too. It is the sound of heaven, the sound of any afterlife, the sound of truth disclosed.

The costume transfigures: the mask substitutes. Its function is apparent when we see that the second-actor, the other actor, wears none. There is no need. He has a face, is human, is alive. But not the first-actor, the protagonist, though the opening mask, the mask of the first half, looks alive—as in those moments of emotion when the mask bends down and we seem to see it weep, when the mask turns up and we seem to see it smile. It seems to move, this mask, to counterfeit our nature, but we know which face is real. It is that of the second-actor, he who kneels by the side of the pillar and attempts to turn this face into a mask: no smiles, no frowns, eyes as though painted on the face, nose a bulge, mouth a line.

His face is alive, is real, but it is the mask that draws us. At first we think of the actor behind it. It must be difficult to see, to breathe. Perhaps this is why he moves so slowly—he cannot find his way about the stage. But, just as in the doll theater it is said that the faces of those who hold the puppets soon fade, that we no longer see them, that they no longer disturb us, with the Noh the invisible actor becomes truly invisible: we forget him, that face behind the mask. The mystery is undisturbed and we believe in it because we are not shown. The mask is necessary. It is because the second-actor has a face like ours that we do not believe in him. We believe in what we do not recognize. We believe in the mystery.

Noh drama is a rite. But, whatever its Shinto derivatives and Buddhist associations, it is a rite no more esoteric than listening again to a Mozart quartet or rereading Proust. It is repetition that offers dignity and no rite can exist without repetition. This is the ritual of Noh-goers. They go because they have already gone. They own the texts, they are enthusiasts, *aficionadi*. There is no other audience for Noh. Not one in a thousand Japanese have ever seen it. The average Japanese may know its name just as the average American may know Mozart's, but those who have seen the Noh and those who have heard K. 590 are in a like minority.

For this reason the Noh has long been in the hands of "amateurs," unofficial artists who keep it alive. Gagaku music and Bugaku dance belong to the Imperial Household, while the Bunraku doll-drama and the Kabuki are protected by one of the largest of Japan's entertainment industries. Noh, however, is "unofficial," in that a few old families and organizations perform it, as though for their own amusement and enlightenment, and few people come to the performances. Everyone except the *iemoto*, the grand master, has some other job, the one that makes a living. Thus Noh is like the amateur string quartet, like the living-room performance in someone's house. Except that the performance is not amateur. It is professional with a rigor that few professional performances know.

No one has ever made a mistake on the Noh stage, no one has ever forgotten a line; there are no stumbling entrances, no halting exits. When the amateur appears on the stage he is without error. Just as the archery expert, who may sell insurance all week long, visits the master on the appointed day and never fails to hit the bull's-eye, so the performances of the Noh are devoid of the incompetence

that has made "amateur" a bad word in our language. Noh is a dilet-
tante theater only if the word is correctly understood. Both performance and appreciation are based on love, respect, enthusiasm. The
ritual of the Noh is like the ritual of a party but the party is formal,
meaningful, elegant.

The actor is, in all Japanese drama, the most important element.
The Kabuki audience goes to see so-and-so in something or other.
It thinks in terms, as we do in opera and ballet, of the prima donna,
the premiere ballerina. The Noh audience does not usually go to see
a famous actor in a famous role, but the role of actor is no less important. It is the actor (any actor) who communicates the Noh experience. Without him (the protagonist) there is no Noh. It is in a way a
one-person drama, a dramatic monologue, all soliloquy.

This is seen in the formalization of the drama itself. At first the
stage is empty. Then, from a small side door comes the orchestra,
three or four men, followed by the chorus, four or five men. They
enter unostentatiously, making themselves small, like members
of the audience arriving late. Then from the opposite of the stage
comes the second-actor. Equally unobtrusive, he is merely observed,
already on the veranda leading to the stage. There he is, already in
place, walking more or less as you and I walk, if more slowly.

But the music is building and we turn to gaze at the brocade
curtain at the end of the veranda. This is where *he* will appear. The
curtain is still, the stage is empty of movement. We wait. Nothing happens. The suspense that only silence and stillness can build
grows. Then, suddenly, the curtain is jerked away and there stands the
masked first-actor. He appears as though in a kind of transformation. First there was nothing, then, there he is. He is already super-
natural. Slowly, very slowly, he makes his way onto the stage and the
play begins. At his second entrance, halfway through the play, after
the outer kimono change and the implied inner transformation, the

curtain is again whipped up and the disclosed angel, ghost, monster, swarms upon stage—again transformed, again new.

It is this first-actor who dances, who moves, who "sings" if movement and speech may be called song. And behind this being, behind this mask, stands the actor controlling the play, controlling the audience. Because he is masked, because he is both priest and god, he compels an attention that the merely human never commands. We look at him because we cannot look away. Though his movements may initially irritate (so slow, so seemingly aimless, so apparently meticulous but so arbitrary), our eyes again and again return, as though unwillingly, to this expressionless face, this mask that mirrors expression.

He holds us. At the same time, we hold him. Were it not for this mutual rapport, Noh would become a pantomime in pretty clothes. This is what occurs when Noh is filmed—the rapport is lost. To a lesser extent this also occurs when opera or drama is filmed. But opera has musical commentary and drama has implied logic. In the Noh there is nothing—just an ambiguous story, a text that is fragmentary, even arbitrary; the music is a part of the stage decor. There exists only that bond between the mind of the actor and the mind of the audience. There is nothing else. Noh is naked theater.

Zeami has something to say about this. "Sometimes spectators of the Noh say that the moments of 'no action' are most enjoyable. This is one of the actor's secret arts. When we examine why such moments are enjoyable, we find that this is due to an underlying spiritual strength of the actor that unremittingly holds the attention. He does not relax when the dancing or singing comes to an end but maintains an unwavering inner strength."

The West has nothing like this unless it be the boxing match where the two fighters exist as naturally as fish in this human sea of spotlights, roarings, shouts, and exclamations, held and sustained by the thousands of eyes that have made their focal point these two fighting bodies. Two boxers boxing together in an empty room would not be boxing, they would not even be able to fight. This kind of bond is the most important fact of Noh and it is toward this that the text, music, decor, costume, all work. The essence of Noh is that which makes performer and audience one—that which welds together priest and congregation, which unites the lynching mob. It is this that the actor must create and then maintain.

Before he goes on, the actor waits in the room on the other side of the brocade curtain. His mask is placed over his face and he sits before a mirror, looking at himself. He is preparing. Is he losing himself in the character he imagines? Or is he observing the effect he makes, the better to step outside himself and present it? Both are possible. Either he becomes the spirit or else he sees the spirit in his outer form and seeks to most effectively present it. He becomes, or he controls. He loses himself completely or else so completely controls himself that presentation becomes possible.

The term "Noh" could mean "accomplishment" or "skill" and "talent." It derives from a verb meaning "to be able," or "to have power." Zeami spoke of the Noh as meaning "elegant imitation," the music and singing were to "open the ear of the mind," while the dancing was to "open the eyes of the emotions." He wrote that "first of all, be a perfect image of the being you are impersonating, then you will also become like him in action." He speaks of the skin, flesh, and bone of a performance and condemns the actor who is content with skin alone. When a Noh performance is "perfect" (a word Zeami often uses) it captivates by impressing with a sense of strength coming from the bones, a sense of security from the flesh, and a sense of beauty from the skin.

Acting then is "a psychic force that is capable of excellence resulting from a lifelong effort of training and a careful choosing of right from wrong." Above all, when imitating, "it is important to adjust the act of imitation according to the nature of the thing," which means that the actor must know what the thing is.

If an actor tries to show an old man merely by bending his knees and back, he is creating an ugly figure, lacking in both strength and beauty. Rather, the old man is required to flower, and by "flower" Zeami means that something which arouses and captures the interest. This is accomplished by the actor's responding correctly to the state of his audience. In any event this audience must be taken by surprise—one must "bewitch the audience." The actor must maintain that state of balance between himself and the audience, whether he portrays an old man, a woman, or a young warrior, and this state is described as being like "a flower blooming on an old tree."

The bond between actor and audience is a bout. The actor retires, after the play is over, exhausted. He has been a god, or else he has stood beside and controlled a god. Whichever, he must rest, he must lie down, he must sleep. Like the boxer he had his first bout with the mirror and, like the boxer, he returns battered, having endured not merely the blows but the consciousness of other wills beating against and finally with his own.

The text is closed, the costumes folded, the stage empty—but to those who have seen Noh, even to look upon the empty stage is to remember that naked will, disguised as a god, standing there, demanding and receiving. The experience is religious and, like all religious experiences, it is also aesthetic. Like any sacrificial act, like the high mass, like boxing, it is also cleansing. Though tragedy has not stalked the stage, the effect is still cathartic. By becoming one with something not oneself, one is cleaned, made new, and (if only for the moment) made whole.

—*1966*

The Kyogen

The Noh is usually about gods and spirits. It is idealistic drama peering deeply into the mysteries of the spirit. Kyogen is always about human beings, and even its gods are obviously mortal. It has no use for that ideal face, the mask; it does not need music because there is no mystery to suggest; nor is it slow, stately, or poetic, the language is vernacular and the tempo is like life, or faster. Kyogen is satyr-play, anti-masque, it is Pyramus and Thisbe to Noh's Theseus and Hippolyta. Happening in the kitchen, near the warm hearth, leaving the stately if chilly main hall to the deities, it is resolutely, resoundingly human.

It was indeed human frailty that created Kyogen since it was originally intended to obviate the sublime and unavoidable boredom of the Noh. Though its ancestry is plebeian, though that of the Noh is aristocratic, an alliance was arranged between the two houses and the marriage still holds. Even now a Kyogen is usually sandwiched between two Noh plays, or even between the halves of a single Noh drama; even now the marriage shows what all successful marriages must: a dazzling contrast.

The Noh concludes, the last wraith slides away and the Kyogen begins. The carpenters appear, they open their mouths, and we fall from the clouds and land with a bump, just as does one of their gods in one of their plays. Moved by the Noh, transfigured, our eyes still wet with its beauty, we—the audience—are suddenly part of a comic plot when, bounced back into reality by the Kyogen folk, we discover that we too have two hands and a nose like everyone else, and that those funny people in front of us are ourselves.

And we are hilarious because one of the surprising things about the Kyogen is that it's so very funny—not to read perhaps, but then the text of a Labiche farce or a Keaton film, or even a Molière play, is not that funny to read. Comedy, unlike tragedy, lies in the doing.

The Kyogen doings are based on a slender repertoire of situations. A lord has a stupid servant who cannot tell a fan from an umbrella, or who inadvertently gives away to his mistress his master's philanderings, or who drinks up all the sake and fills back the bottles with water and then tries to fool the master into thinking he is getting drunk. He is joined by a large cast of comic characters, each as distinctive as himself, each as sublimely stupid, as gloriously sly, as eternally innocent.

For it is our foibles that Kyogen celebrates, just as the Noh illuminates our aspirations. Comic situations are as limited as tragic and it is their scarcity that links the great and presumably opposed houses of tears and laughter, enabling great minds to flip the plots over like flapjacks and to show us that Hamlet and Don Quixote are really first cousins.

Not then, for the Kyogen actor, the brocades of the Noh, those great, living landscapes. Instead, he wears domestic colors—brown, gray, all in checks and squares. Clean, neat, starched, and common, he is nonetheless ready to run and fall down. And when he races off at the end of the play, it is not, one feels, to that mirrored room of the Noh actor for communion with the mysterious self. No, it is straight for the kitchen and the warm fire and a cup of hot sake taken with smacking lips.

He is a real professional, the Kyogen actor. He delivers fast, is always on his feet, a true stand-up comic. He bubbles over, he aspirates and yet—sharing with the greatest of comedians—he is never coarse. Zeami, the man who invented Japanese dramaturgy, speaks straight from the fourteenth century when he says that Kyogen should "kindle the mind to laughter," but that "neither in speech nor gesture should there be anything low. The jokes and repartee, how-ever funny they may be, should not introduce the vulgar."

Hence, perhaps, the warmth, the charm. In Kyogen one senses that the actor, knowing perfectly well that he is impersonating a comic, also feels that both breeding and goodwill insist that he hide this fact. He is never a wise guy. He is observing what Zeami himself was probably only observing when he laid down the law that there should be a "tinge of unreality in reality," a "refinement and concen-tration of all conflicting qualities into one dominant note." This note seems to sound in the ears of only the greatest of comedians: you, a human, must impersonate a human.

And the Kyogen is sublimely human—if I can put it that way. It celebrates foibles in the way that melodrama celebrates goodness, and that tragedy celebrates devotion. Mistakes, error, sloth, and all the appetites—this is the stuff of which Kyogen is made. The mirror that it holds up is not the mirror of the Noh, the self alone, com-muning, but a minutely detailed picture of the world as it is, crowded and crawling, like a barnyard by Breugel.

This vision is half the world and it knows it. It is one pole of the human experience, just as Noh is the other. The resulting stress is what makes the combination so right. The way we would want it to be, the way of aspiration, this is the Noh. The way we are, the way to acceptance, this is the Kyogen. Both roads lead to wisdom.

The Kyogen actor with his air of amusement, the savoring smile of a loving artist enjoying his comic role—this is a look that says, I know that I am human, only human, with all of my foibles, but this I can accept—the change of seasons, my aching back. This is how things are—my world of Kyogen is your world as well.

—1969

TV: The Presentational Image

Television, when it presents only itself, presents itself only as television. The convention of theater and film is that something else is being presented—life itself. These are borrowed by television when telling a story, but mostly it is not concerned with story: it is a day-long, night-long variety show. This being so, presentation in television is direct. The person doing the talking looks directly at us, the watchers. There is no convention to insist that we are looking at something other than what we are. Someone in front of the television camera is talking to us, making a presentation—the only reality is the ostensible.

If we are being addressed this directly by commentator, salesperson, interviewer, interviewee, we are, in a way, also addressing them. These people are doing it for us, the watchers, and our opinion of them is for various reasons valuable. They want to appear at their best both because they want to sell us something or influence us in some other way and because, since they are in the public eye, they want only good opinions. Various are the ways in their attempt to obtain these.

We are familiar with some of these: carefully chosen words, an implied flattery, attempts to create enthusiasm, a certain unnatural naturalness. We are not, however, so familiar (nor are they) with less conscious means—those through which they, perhaps unknowingly, imply and we, often equally unknowingly, infer. These would include what is said without using words—the speech of the stance, the face, the hands. It would also include their ideas on the medium of television and how to use it.

Such ideas vary in various countries since assumptions upon

which behavior rests vary from one culture to another. This being so, something is revealed about assumptions, beliefs, and generally agreed-upon ideas. Those to be seen in Japan are common to that country and there are many of them. Let us begin with one presentational notion, which is, so far as I know, unique to Japan.

This consists of the commentator at one side of the screen and his assistant at the other. The commentator is always male and usually middle aged. The assistant is invariably female, usually young and often pretty. He comments on the news or whatever the subject of the program is, and she assists. But her assistance is so minimal that, to our eyes, she might as well not be there at all.

Not for her the "equal" participation of the American "anchor person." Rather, she merely nods soberly at the camera when he makes a pronouncement, often says *So desu ne* ("Isn't that just true though?") when he makes a point. She will sometimes add a bit of information on her own but this, upon examination, turns out to be merely a rephrasing of what he himself has just said.

To people of other cultures watching these two, the effect is unsettling. We are used to double commentators but usually each commentator actually comments. In this format—and it is one very common on Japanese television—the pretty girl is not only redundant, she seems quite unnecessary. This is because we fail to comprehend her function. Yet, she is believed to have an important one.

A commentator is, by definition, giving his opinion. In the West this is quite enough—one man's opinion is as good as another's, etc. In Japan, however, to give an opinion is to appear opinionated, and this is a fault in a society where dissenting opinion is at least officially unvoiced, and where a consensus of opinion is an invariable goal.

These two qualities are hopefully ensured by this near-mute, if attractive, young lady. Her nods and monosyllables of agreement indicate that her superior is not alone in his opinion, that therefore he is not merely opinionated. Rather, he is stating a truth, since more than one person agrees with what he says. At the same time the assistant introduces harmony. It would be unthinkable of her to disagree with him or even offer a conflicting opinion of her down. This sought-for harmony is found in her indicating that we all (and it is *us* that she is so earnestly nodding at) agree, and that the wished-for consensus is, in fact, already up in place.

One can trace this strange duo back to radio and other earlier forms of entertainment. In the Bunraku doll-drama, the various voices of characters and commentator (all delivered by a single male narrator) are mutually supportive. In the Noh drama, the chorus affirms the dialogue and comments upon it. I can think of no instance where such commentary is not supportive, which means that I can think of no example where irony or any other "deeper" meaning is even suggested. Nor should it be, since the intention is a straight presentation with a context that seeks to make us regard the ostensible (and only that) as the real. This is as true, in Japan, of ancient drama as it is of modern television. It is, however, only radio and television that has made the assenting voice female, thereby implying that women in Japan have a male-supportive role.

That women are somehow the weaker sex and are therefore naturally subservient is a typical message and appears in many forms through many different media. The Japanese example is noticeable mainly because it is so unquestioned. And in television this message is strongest delivered by the commercials. Here, by implication, the woman can only be the daughter, the homemaking wife, or the mother. In these roles she is identified almost entirely as a consumer. When young she eats chocolate and tries out new face creams; married, she is careful about underarm odor; about the house she smiles over the virtues of detergents and vacuum sweepers; and as a mother she forces various foods on her surprised and delighted children.

In this, of course, Japanese television is little different from television in any consumer society. The difference is the directness with which this is done. In the ostensibly democratic and egalitarian United States the commentator's helper would be laughed (if somewhat nervously) off the screen since any such overt suggestions (there are covert suggestions aplenty) that woman's place is in the home would no longer help sell the product. As always in Japan, however, the intention is so open, so unveiled, so innocent of any irony, that the message emerges with an often-startling clarity.

Take, for example, the "togetherness" that is being pushed by TV commercials now that the "prime selling target" has moved from wife and kids and become the family as a unit. Also, in accounting for the success of this maneuver, it should be understood that to be a family man is a progressive social stance to take. It means that one is unwilling to sacrifice one's family (and by extension one's self) to demands of an all-powerful employing company. In this regard one's private concerns now come before one's social responsibilities. This mini-revolution is actually meaningless because, in practice, it means that the husband merely devotes more leisure time to his family and may, occasionally, attempt to avoid working at the company on Sundays. But the idea of such a revolution is attractive.

One of the symptoms is the wide use of the English "my" in various slogans such as "My Car / My Family." It is symptomatic that it is the English "my" that is used and not the Japanese *watakushi no*. The one, being a foreign word, is as yet free from the unwelcome egotistical nuances that surround the Japanese.

Another symptom is the "happy family" that now finds its way into TV commercials. Here father, mother, and kids are all gathered at the family table while mother introduces them to this or that new product. The juvenile glee is so extreme that even father is carried away by it and compliments his wife on her buying prowess. *Sasuga* ("Isn't that just like her,") he says, smacking his lips. She simpers her pleasure and the children grimace and look at each other knowingly—everything is okay with Mom and Dad.

Messages are rife in this vignette. Among things suggested are: buying the right things is the true secret of a happy home life; through shopping the woman is fulfilling herself in her roles of mother and wife—just look at the smiles on those kids' faces, and just look at the playful hug her husband is giving her.

There are some perhaps unintended messages as well. The one that strikes most strongly is the apparent lunacy of the family. They behave like manic-depressives in an upward phase—all those roguish smiles and frenetic laughs over what is, after all, only a recent breakfast food or a new laundry soap. It is the behavior of the mouse family in the animated cartoons. There is something inhuman about these excesses.

In some other countries TV watchers are already familiar with this type of crazy family. Indeed, they were reacting to the message with a degree of cynicism. When the sponsors discovered this, the family was promptly removed. In Japan, however, the viewer is usually immune to cynicism (being Japanese) and the happy family is taken at face value. These people are happy with their new product, new products make for happiness—these are the only messages read.

(That the sell is very hard indeed is apparent. But in Japan there is only hard sell, no soft. The reason is that, in a culture where the ostensible is always the real, any attempt at soft sell—and there have been some—results in an unfortunate side effect: the sponsor doesn't really believe in his product; he is sneaky in its presentation; if it is good enough to buy why doesn't he just say so?)

More important than this simple reading, however, is what the reading affirms. In being happy with the new product the family has reached yet further agreement, even higher harmony. No dissent, no confrontation will rend this happy group. And by behaving like a demented mouse-family this social unit has, furthermore, shown that they are unexceptionable, that they are Mr. and Mrs. Status Quo with all their little Quos, that they are, in fact, no threat. I am no threat—this message is so clear, so incessant, and so accounts for the tone of Japanese television, that one might wish to examine the phenomenon in some detail.

In that case one might begin by noticing that the adults in Japanese TV commercials are often really children. They cock their heads like precocious youngsters, they use the gestures of the school child, they smile and laugh in the most uninhibited manner (one markedly in contrast to the smiles and laughter of the true Japanese adult), and they cajole in a way truly typical of the spoiled Japanese child. Further, the disembodied voices in these commercials—those we listen to while looking at the products—are plainly adults imitating children. Further, the music accompanying all this is often reminiscent of the jaunty marches associated in Japan with kindergartens.

Perhaps behind all of this is some inchoate urge to return to the golden age of undisciplined, permissive, Japanese childhood, but the primary implication would be that we are all as harmless as children. Look at us: we makes fools of ourselves, we invite you to laugh at us, we are fatuous to a degree—and yet, since we are so harmless, your laughter cannot but be indulgent, your hand cannot but reach into your pocket, your fingers cannot but open up the billfold. And if you don't want to, then there is no harm done because, you see, we have not really asked.

This is, in a way, soft sell with a vengeance. These monstrous children are, in a truly childlike manner, having it both ways at once. It is in this manner that their message reaches the consumer who, not having been really, truly asked, can feel all the more free to do just what has been suggested. The happy family has merely offered an example of unexceptionable, nonthreatening togetherness.

Look how unexceptionable I am. This is a message that demotes the threat of another person looking into your living room. If the actors in TV commercials purposely imitate children, then those non-pros on talk shows, amateur hours, endless "personal" interviews, indicate that the child-play is based upon something very real.

Notice the hands of the ordinary citizen when he or she appears on television—and bear in mind that in Japan the ordinary citizen is brought to appear on the tube with a frequency greater, I would guess, than most other countries. Where are the hands? They are folded in front, one gripping the other, in the lap if sitting, at the crotch if standing. This is the "good" position.

On foreign TV, particularly American, non-pros often seek to make something of their personalities by waving the hands about more than ordinarily. They suddenly become "expressive." Likewise, the stance—if they are standing—differs from that of the non-pro Japanese facing the TV camera. The foreigner often assumes a "natural" stance in which the pelvis is expressively tilted—just a hint of aggression. If Americans stood as does the opposite Japanese number, feet together, hands safely in front, something like the school child at attention, then these would be read as indication of embarrassment, someone immature and, at any rate, without "an outgoing personality."

In Japan, conversely, the gesticulating foreigners are seen as egotistical (a bad thing), ill-mannered, and quite capable of disturbing an implied social harmony. On the other hand the Japanese are seen as standing in well-mannered identical positions (well-mannered because they are identical), no one calling undue attention to possible danger areas (the hands, the pelvis), all individualistic tendencies properly sacrificed to attain a goal of unexceptionable "good manners."

(Apparent contradictions to these observations are, I think, only apparent. That Japanese TV dramas, as differentiated from the commercials, are filled with antisocial violence does not indicate that such a display is condoned. Rather, it indicates a concern for the natural violence that hands firmly in the lap keep successfully under control. Thus the display is part titillation and part horrible example. In any event, those exhibiting this degree of individuality are always reformed, or put into prison, or killed. In the same way, the fact that in the Japanese home drama the housewife is revealed to be a mass of suffering, given to multiple love affairs, to abortions and suicide, indicates no further degree of reality about real Japanese housewives. Rather, it represents an opposite extreme, both ends being equally far from the middle: the real Japanese woman. In any event, both violence and tear-jerking are illustrations of those fantasies entertained by the sponsors and by TV producers, not by the audience.)

The pervading juvenility of most Japanese TV is the result of its conciliatory intentions. Bland, inane fatuity is a small price to pay when the presumed result is something as grand as complete uniformity and utter consistency. I am not, please note, saying that the Japanese are really like this. I am saying that the image they project on television, the image they choose to present, is this.

One sees it in other situations as well. (Japanese formal behavior, so relentlessly conciliatory, seems absurd to foreigners who do not understand its reasons.) These are always those where a degree of presentation is called for. We are unexceptionable, we are no threat, we are—just look—nice and good. An evening of Japanese television, in which this single intention is tirelessly presented, makes one wonder just how the myth of Japanese inscrutability ever got started.

Could anything be simpler, or more simple-minded, than this open, naked display?

What we are seeing, however, is only what has been selected. People on the tube (amateur, pro, the newscaster, his producer) select this image. Just as Americans choose to present a type that is more individual, more argumentative, more "vital" than anyone you are apt to find on an American street corner, so the Japanese have chosen an image carefully lacking in any obvious individuality, one given wholeheartedly to assent, but equally "vital" in that the goal of the presentation is a uniform front. That safety could be identified with childishness and security with inanity are natural consequences of the presentational aim. Here too, as in the various home dramas, we are dealing in part with hopeful fantasy, since no people could ever be as bland, as unexceptional, as those on Japanese TV. Unlike the fantasy in the dramas, however, this behavior is accepted as "real." One presents one's image as into a reflecting mirror—and that mirror is the audience.

—1980

Outcast Samurai Dancer

The *kawaramono*, those vagrants by the river's edge, the *hinin*, something not quite human, the outcast—the actor, the dancer—have been so perceived and so excluded not only in Japan, but any place where an aristocratic order needed a perceived pariah class against which to define itself. The ruling shogunate, the daimyo, the samurai all found the outcast necessary.

The shogunate had its dancers in Shinto *kagura* and in court Noh drama, but these mirrored only ideology, liturgical ambitions, and doctrines of salvation. They did not define the forces of a perceived chaos and, in various forms, damnation, against which they formed the bulwark.

The actor/dancer outcast was given the task of personifying darkness since it was the sacred *kagura*, and the noble Noh, that represented light. *Yami,* the place of darkness, this was where the dancers danced, danced for *yami no kamisama*, the faceless unknown god of darkness. No matter how sunny the occasion, the village *matsuri* had its *omikoshi*, that massive float borne by the happy revelers. And inside this festive ark was that small black box where the faceless god—so far from the multifold deities of Shinto, from the embracing visage of the Buddha himself—reveled in the chaotic bounding about, the disorderly shouting, the certain confusions of the dark.

Yami no butoh: this was the first name taken by the remarkable movement that reinstated the former outcast into civil society, something that occurred only when its leaders—the aristocrats, the military—had no more need for definition since they themselves were no more. After WWII the high were brought low. Naturally, the low itself, no longer stigmatized, now, climbing to the surface, sought expression.

Butoh expressed generations of *kawaramono*, of *hinin*, of *burakumin*, millions of individuals who were marginalized and suppressed during centuries of stigmatization. It suddenly embodied its own stigma, exposed it, paraded it, in the same fashion as other hidden groups in the social revolutions of the final decades of the last century. Its vocabulary of movement proclaimed its origins.

*

Tatsumi Hijikata, one of those who crafted Butoh, once said that it must begin not from the kneeling posture of the well-born, legs tucked neatly beneath, but from the squat of the farmer, ass suspended between heaven and earth. This squat, at once relaxed and vigilant, has a low center of gravity, as though to better recoil into action. It is anchored in the ground. It does not aspire. It reaffirms.

Before Butoh had fully emerged, the Western ballet was in Japan already taking the place of prewar and wartime aristocratic dance. Among the first of the noted ballet dancers to visit the country was *première danseur* André Eglevsky. He was met at the airport by a bouquet-laden Japanese *première danseuse*, Momoko Tani, who was taken aback when the foreign dancer asked her how she managed on such short, little legs. Eglevsky, famously outspoken, was not malicious, merely curious.

How indeed? Western ballet, like the Japanese Noh, is about aspiring. The ballerina augments her height in toe shoes, she stretches, practices elevations. With the help of her partner, she performs gravity-defying leaps. Hers are the ambitions of civil society made manifest. Upwards and onwards. Beneath her the common ground is spurned.

Imagine though another kind of dance, in all ways the mirror image of ballet. Butoh is earthbound. Dancers emerge from it and return to it, not reaching for the sky but grasping for the ground. It does not aspire, it affirms. And the dancers are not the sky colors of the ballet, they are the colors of the earth: blacks, browns, tans, and the bleached white of bones.

White, in Japan the color of death, is also the color (or lack of color) of the corpse. The land of Yami is also the land of the dead. Here the dead are imitated, the actors' white shroud-like loincloths dragging. In later Butoh (not Hijikata's but that of the Dairakuda-kan and other like troupes) the dead, zombie-like, crowd the stage, lolling red tongues and rolling red eyes. The return of the corpses, the revenge of the dead—as though centuries of stigma has opened all those graves.

*

Butoh is like a peasant's revolt. Indeed, though a part of the inspiration (that of Kazuo Ono) came from Harold Kreuzberg, Mary Wigam, and the nascent modern dance of Europe, another part came from the ancient peasant land of Tohoku. Here, in the far north, where farmers have traditionally lived in poverty, Hijikata spent a youth watching peasants planting rice seedlings in the mud, patiently coaxing food from the naked earth. The life was hard and in times of famine peasants revolted. In Japan the result was always the same. The petition was duly received by the daimyo's representative and its claims often met, but the samurai's sword flashed. The farmer's representative was then executed for his impudence.

Or not. There came a time when the samurai were redundant. Modernity at the doorstep, the Meiji officials ordered first the abolition of the top-knot, then the abolition of the sword, finally the abolition of the samurai themselves. And even before that, as the Tokugawa Shogunate unraveled, the samurai were being laid off. Those losing their jobs were called *ronin*, masterless warriors, homeless. In one of the finer ironies of Japanese history, they in their turn had become outcasts. Gone were their armor, their helmets—they even, when they could, sold their swords. We last see them slinking away, naked.

*

Class covers—a lack of it uncovers. Rulers button themselves up, corset themselves with power. The ruled are, by definition, unbuttoned, powerless, naked. In Japan the peasantry wears few clothes. In the summer farmers traditionally wore only the *fundoshi* loincloth. The ocean fishermen did not wear even that. It is this world that the Butoh recreates, a place where the body is exposed, and if clothed it is covered only in the fabric of the skin. Ideally, Butoh should be performed completely naked, genitals punctuating the landscape of the body. That it is not so performed is because the daimyo lives on in the public morals, offices, and the police department—and not only in Japan.

Peasant sex is not dalliance. It is procreation. In the ancient days of the Tachikawa-ryu there was mass copulation in the rice paddy. The coming crop was fertilized by analogy. Rice shoots, new babies, one dependent upon the other. This is something that Butoh remembers. The stage picture of forms intertwined, of bodies colliding, even something of the gibberings of the offspring of uncle and niece, of brother and sister—these are distant views of the days when sex meant birth.

*

An early performance, held at the crematorium at Shinanomachi. Typical—a charnel house, daily filled with bones. And here, on the improvised stage, not a Japanese peasant but a French renegade. Hijikata had chosen to dramatize a work by Jean Genet, *Notre Dame des Fleurs*. In order to present his story of transgression he had chosen a foreign exemplar so that it would be the better understood. But he did so in the style of Tohoku. A live chicken was, toward the end, beheaded on the stage. Perhaps this was to titillate Tokyo. More likely it was in homage to the hungry snow country.

Yukio Mishima was in this early audience—an aristocrat savoring the peasant feast and at the same time both a sensitive observer of the uses of power and a sympathetic partaker of stigma. He knew what these *kawaramono* felt and yet at the same time he emulated the oppressor. Sun and steel, the will to build the body into the required shape, the mindless worship of the power of mere masculinity. This double regard ushers Butoh into the city. A modern samurai opens the door and lets in the peasantry—outcast samurai dancer.

The *kawaramono* did not have to worry about becoming commercialized. Theirs was a talent no one wanted. However, in no time at all, Kabuki was spawned from this very river bank (the Kamogawa in Kyoto) and its mad message assured a popularity. Now themselves popular, the nonpeople started to make money and consequently tailored their arts in order to make even more. They still do.

So does Butoh and hence it runs the risk of becoming decorative, of covering its origins with the cosmetic of commerce. It is only through continual transgression that Butoh can remain a faithful reflection. It must continually remind of its pariah status, even though we are paying money to share this status. Originally there was no audience, only performers. Now though, we who buy the tickets need something against which to define ourselves. In our complaisant midst we find Butoh necessary. Or else—the idea circling endlessly—we would not know who we are.

—*2003*

Retro Dancing

Rock 'n' roll, an American commercial amalgam of white "country music" and black "rhythm," is now a memory in the land of its origin. With a twelve-bar blues chord structure, it incorporated a blues-type singing style and, after Elvis Presley had initiated rockabilly, a stronger beat, more heavily emphasized, with lyrics on themes perceived as violent, punctuated by cries and moans. Accompanying this, a choreography including tight jeans and/or black leather, hopefully macho footwear, and pelvic thrusts emphasizing the sexual aspects of the music.

Originally a product of 1950s United States, it seemed to deny the status quo and took the "forbidden" sounds of black blues to a white audience. The early practitioners were Amos Milburn, Matt Lucas, Curtis Ousley, Charlie Feathers, Roy Brown, and the more commercialized Eddie Cochran, Gene Vincent, Chuck Berry, Little Richard, Jerry Lee Lewis, and Bill Haley and His Comets—the latter usually given credit for ushering in the style with "Rock Around the Clock."

Elvis Presley, the singer who did most to commercialize the style, came into prominence in 1954. He mixed country music with rock 'n' roll, developed an innovative singing style, more explicit lyrics about love and sex, and a suggestive manner of moving. Presley was a white man who sounded black, or at least sounded like what white people thought black sounded like.

"Don't Be Cruel," "Heartbreak Hotel," "Hound Dog"—these early Presley songs, accompanied by the singer's typical delivery, and his trademark pelvic thrusts (early national TV programs never showed the singer from the waist down) rendered the sentiments not only explicit but also safe.

Presley, as pale as white bread, displayed the anodyne looks of the boy next door, and thus rendered the forbidden respectable. The primal sexual power with which whites sometimes decorate their image of blacks was thus sanitized and made socially acceptable. Women, young ones in particular, and always white (Presley had few black fans), bought the records, saw the movies, and flocked to the concerts all prepared to scream at the erotic gyrations.

Rockabilly, having descended from rock 'n' roll, then gave birth to rock, the 1960s sound, highly amplified, very strong beat patterns, dignified as "Progressive Rock" after 1967. Presley died and with him the remains of his style. Punk rock, yet more aggressive, emerged and gone were the stylistic assumptions of musical competence. By 1975 the Sex Pistols were leading into new fields.

These in turn were transformed as blacks reclaimed their turf: rap music, break dancing, hip-hop. Backing away from the nice-guy image of rock 'n' roll, the new style concerned itself with guns, gangs, and gangsta affectations. Misogyny ruled with big-size football jerseys, jeans worn low, and basketball sneakers. Self-consciously thug-like, no more good ol' rocker and roller, hip-hop seemed much more aware of being black but in the meantime the style was commercializing color just as Presley had commercialized being white.

This then is one accounting of the course taken by that antique musical style rock 'n' roll, now half a century later an oddity, its nostalgia tapped (entertainments like *Grease*), and in the West still seen only as a self-conscious reminder—Rockabilly Day at the Lincoln Center Out of Doors Festival.

*

In Japan, however, there are more active admirers and amateur groups (weekly rather than annual) who keep alive their version of the style. Tight jeans and black leather outfits are contrived; Presley-like gyrations are attempted. Rock 'n' roll still retains something of its original appeal and the image of the young and sexy Presley himself has never degenerated into the coarseness of his many American imitations.

In a way this is not too surprising. Japan is, after all, where the court music and dance of eighth-century Korea is still to be seen, performed by Imperial Household troupes, often at Meiji Shrine, which is right next door to the Harajuku Yoyogi Park where one can still see the music and dancing of mid-twentieth-century America, rockabilly. That these are preserved importations is apparent but, of course, the reason they are preserved is because they have at the same time been rendered Japanese.

The Japanification of anything from outside involves challenges, the successful meeting of which usually results in disregarding the integrity of the imported object. Look at the problems encountered in Japan by hip-hop and its accompanying rap. Language (lack of accentuated syllables, verbs at the end of sentences, a limited variety of word endings in Japanese) worked against it. And Japan's ignorance of hip-hop's "oppressed historical origins" meant that the message became as modified as the medium. Japanese youngsters suffer no ghetto upbringing, racial discrimination is something they often unthinkingly practice rather than suffer from, and their socio-economic plight is merely that of sometimes not being able to buy the name brands they want.

Nonetheless there is a big market for baggy denims and ill-fitted shirts. There are fake "black" youngsters who spend a fortune in the tanning salons and undergo fifty-thousand-yen dreadlock extensions. These are, however, free of the true ghetto-bred gangsta style. Consequently the content of hip-hop, the Japanese Version, is only superficially like the original. This includes the "message"—

such rapsters as King Giddra, Zeebra, K-Dub Shine, and Utamaru (all Japanese) deciding that the oppressor is merely the way things are in Japan. Hip-hop is read as a first-person statement, an expression of the singular, though rendered mainly in terms of fashion choice.

Rockabilly suffered a like sea change after its importation to Japan. Presley's celebration of poor-white pleasures answered no Japanese need, his takeover of black delivery was not even recognized, his brainless wholesomeness (at least in the early part of his career) was locally unnoticed. Indeed, he was soon confounded with the troubled teen angst of James Dean. What was retained in Japan was his overt sexuality and both his willingness to go against what passed as social norms and his ability to make this acceptable.

The Harajuku Sunday rockabilly dancers are flaunting their differences—their tattoos, their bad-boy get-ups, their gyrating pelvises—but they are doing so in an accepted fashion. They are *misemono*, putting on a show, a tried way of both affirming differences and assuring similarity. Everyone who looks at these gyrating young men knows that each holds down a steady (if often blue-collar) job, and that their "rebellion" is merely a weekly affair.

Though Japanese boys do not often have the training or the confidence to aggressively thrust their pelvises, there does exist a template that can accommodate. This is a body build that emphasizes the hips (formerly accompanied by short legs though not now thanks to changed diets) and a center of gravity that is consequently a bit lower than is common the West.

In folk dances, in Butoh dancing, the squat is a part of the choreography. This lowering of the body center both makes for more powerful thrusts and, at the same time, emphasizes the sexual nature of much Japanese folk dancing. Even the sanitized *obon* dances of late summer in Japan can still work up a sweat, and—as elsewhere in Japan—create the common impression that having a good time is hard work.

Also, this ritualistic rockabilly is a male group dance. Girls did rock and roll too in the West, but do not in Japan. And though Presley strutted his stuff all alone, his Japanese ancestors never do—it is always a group that performs. It then follows that if it is a group dance the members can appear as raunchy as they want, the assumption being that if everyone is publicly sexy, then no one is.

Group entertainments are a Japanese norm. *The Loyal Forty-seven Ronin,* that perennial traditional favorite is the Kabuki of choice because there are forty-seven of them. *Chorus Line* is the most revived of all musicals in Japan mainly because there are so many in that line. The group always reassures.

Thus, in the rockabilly exhibitions at Harajuku, though the original content may have been mildly revolutionary, the Japanese version is completely conciliatory in that so many people are apparently agreeing about whatever they are saying. In addition, emotional kick is neutralized in that we are also conscious of being nostalgic about someone else's nostalgia.

*

The original Presley message was plainly sexual. He was rebelling against repressive and hypocritical social norms, which kept good-looking boys from thrusting their pelvises in public. His jeans and black leather, with their working-man associations and their rural proletariat message, made the thrustings somehow healthy, socially acceptable.

In Japan, however, none of these messages had any meaning. Jeans were an imported fad, and black leather was an exotic material that carried the label of kinky, at least when worn by women. Early on black leather acquired a mild s/m flavor and carried not one whiff from the healthy ranch.

When the rockabilly rollers at Harajuku wear black leather they are thus sending a complicated message, one that they themselves must partially decode for their admirers. Though their sexual persona is paramount (as was Presley's) it is also augmented in interesting ways.

The Harajuku boys do not have the ability or the motivation to perform authentic pelvis thrusts, if we believe that Presely's imitation coition was authentic. Perhaps in compensation they usually, no matter the weather, appear topless. Symbol (naked flesh) becomes a sexual icon that augments that of metaphor (the pelvic thrust.) Conversely, Presley never appeared topless perhaps because this would have detracted from the impact of his thrusting bottom.

The black leather trousers are worn low so that the navel, the loins, occasionally a bit of pubic hair, sometimes the crack of the buttocks are visible. This is overt sexuality (and quite in keeping with male costuming at traditional folk festivals) but is rendered socially acceptable by the fact that everyone on the stage is doing it.

And all doing it at the same time. It is a routine, and routine famously tames. There is also the fact that these rockabilly boys, though exhibiting themselves to the Sunday crowds, are really dancing for each other. Thus we see in these photographs not only the masturbatory rigor of the solo body but also the competition, the one-on-one imitation in the cocky way they regard each other.

This living remnant of rockabilly in Japan is plainly homosocial. In being so it conforms once more to local expectations. Presley's appeal was directed toward young females (though many young males also emulated him) and he did not court approval from same-sex peers. Presley showed us an attractive young man having a good time by coming on to the audience. It's all there on the surface, for the taking, no strain. Japanese rockabillies, however, are all strain—lots of sweat, fixed smiles, frenetic movements. These are truly dances from within.

But if so, if they emerge from so deep, what then are they expressing? As we watch this group dancing together we realize that, together though they be, something further is being expressed. Their exhibition turns into what it always turns into in Japan—a competition.

Here, men compete but the way in which this is commonly done is one that is not so usual in the West. For example, when a man takes another man, a client let us say, to a Japanese hostess bar, it is understood that he is doing so in order to impress his guest—that a competition exists. Hostesses know how to make the host look great, and yet at the same time how to subtly compliment the guest—Oh, nice necktie! Making out with the hostesses is not what the transaction is about, though all of the accouterments of the place point to sexual liaison. The transaction is about levels of obligation between the males, about who gets on top, about who stays there. It is not then surprising that the liberating heterosexuality of Presley should in Japan morph into something more socially accommodating.

Another way in which Harajuku rockabilly is different from the American original and is made more Japanese is that a part of the appeal is due to both rock 'n' roll and Elvis himself being quite dead. Only in Japan is this remembered—at least remembered to the point of weekly tribute.

Though Las Vegas may have its commercialized Elvis-Look-Alike events these are not properly to be understood as tribute. If anything, they are a garish if sincere parody in which fat men with sideburns in Liberace-type drag get up and try to emulate Presley in his decline. Nothing like this exists in Japan. Here the weekly look-alikes are all muscled better than the original and are modeled upon the lean "Hound Dog" days of their idol. Nonetheless, each dancer and each fan is perfectly aware that not only is Presley dead, but that his artistic legacy is in the museum. It is this that is celebrated because Elvis Presley thus precisely fits into a Japanese category, one that is much appreciated.

To it Ivan Morris devoted an entire book, *The Nobility of Failure*, in which the man who fails is seen as somehow more noble than one who has not. The West is certainly not unfamiliar with this kind of romantic idealization but only in Japan, I think, could a whole book have been written about it.

The author naturally does not mention Elvis but he does devote a whole chapter to the somewhat Elvis-like Yukio Mishima. Both were protean, self-forming, both loved to dress up, both carried personal messages of social import, and for both sex was a part of the show, and, finally, both spectacularly fell apart.

Presley, gross, bloated, pill-popping, finally dead on the floor, satisfyingly illustrates the universal proposition that the king must die and that (Japanese proposal) it is noble for him to do so—that he and his works must vanish from the face of the earth, except for a few virtuous spots, such as Japan, where the nobility of the failure is celebrated.

*

These then are some of the ways in which rockabilly lives on in Japan. It is not gentrified, not taxidermized, but (like Gagaku and the Bugaku) kept alive by a series of transfusions (some of them listed above), which means that that it will have a longer life in this country than in that of its origin.

Perhaps. However, eighth-century court dancing is also kept alive by tradition and by governmental interest. Rockabilly has on its side no such ready money. Right now it is coasting on what the Japanese mean when they speak of the "retro-boom," but a future without the weekly rockabilly boys in Harajuku is quite conceivable.

On the other hand, one might equally well argue for a longer life. Unlike the occasional rockabilly fan in, say, New York, whose real interest is in a look he thinks cool, the Japanese rockabilly dancer has incorporated his ethos much more deeply. And he comes in but one form: the young man who weekly goes to the Harajuku Plaza, or some other urban site, and knocks himself out dancing.

The dancing is physically demanding, and dedication is required as well. Indeed, the dedication is something closer to vocation—one thinks of these young men as having a calling. The dancing comes them from deep within—very deep.

The devotion of these boys, their ability (need) to dramatize a perceived alienation (through tattoos, through navels, through being topless, through the hovering of the ghost of Elvis), their selflessness (we are a group), and their dedication—indeed, consecration—all of this records a time, a place, and a spirit.

—2004

IV

On
Film

A Definition of the Japanese Film

We are sometimes asked to define Japanese film. After our book, *The Japanese Film: Art and Industry*, appeared in 1959, Joseph Anderson and I devised a kind of answer. If, we said, the American film is often about action and if the European film is sometimes about character, then the Japanese film would be about that combination, which could be called atmosphere.

In saying this we did not mean that all Japanese films share a particular tone, or that they elicit the same emotional response. What we meant was an often-heightened sense of reality—something we called atmosphere, something that showed a person in an environment.

Before attempting to explain how Japanese filmmakers create this atmosphere, however, there are certain distinctions to be made between Japanese and Western cultures. These distinctions are important because they contribute to different attitudes toward cinema.

For example, a traditional Japanese assumption sees the individual as an integral part of his world, a part of the whole and hence an extension of this universe, which envelops and confines. A Western assumption views each individual as unique, each the center of his or her personal universe. A result is that, in much of Asia and certainly all of Japan, nature is assumed as complementary to the individual, something with which one should live in harmony. This might be contrasted with a common tradition in the West that would see nature as something to be conquered.

If this is true, then in Japan things as they are are the way things should be. Unhappy natural events are to be accepted because they exist. In the West, however, things as they are are to be denied. One must create a better world where things are as they ought to be.

One result is that the Japanese recognize a dual nature. The individual is also a social unit in a society. If one must choose between loyalty to self and loyalty to society it is often the former that is sacrificed. Western individuals, however, like to think of themselves as unique personalities, not as part of any larger unit. If it is the social persona that is sacrificed, this action can only affirm individuality.

The Japanese are limited by this attitude. They would find the average to be reassuring, the mediocre to be normal. Westerners are likewise limited, striving to exceed limitations and finding no consolation in the average or the mediocre. The Japanese finds in nature, in social duties, a sense of belonging to something larger that can sometimes affirm individuality. At the same time, it might be said that the Westerner, with only ideas of self to sustain, can more easily succumb to alienation.

In their art, including cinema, the Japanese traditionally accept things as they naturally are, and this accounts for the atmospheric realism in their film. In many Western films, however, since things as they are is not often an acceptable idea, story, plot, and action are more important than that nexus that is atmosphere.

Japanese films, consequently or not, traditionally tend to be contemplative and fairly slow. They are composed of rambling stories, built a bit like the enclosing Japanese house and its attendant garden. Western films are more tightly plotted, utilitarian, like the Western home or the American skyscraper.

The Japanese in their traditional cinema seem to realize that the only reality is there, on the surface. There is no sense of any hidden reality and little sense of conscience. These are a people who, as is often said, have no individual guilt though do have the capacity for great social shame. The West, however, refuses to believe that surface reality is the only reality. Private conscience is stressed; reality lurks inside. Consequently Westerners have little sense of social shame but an advanced awareness of private guilt. These traditional distinctions, here hopelessly generalized and simplified though they be, are all related to the matter of cinematic atmosphere and how it is constructed.

The traditional Japanese film director often creates atmosphere by limiting his locale. Though many Western films also explore restricted locales there are, I should guess, many more such films in Japan. Random examples would be Naruse's *Sounds of the Mountain* (*Yama no oto*), which takes place almost entirely in one house, and Gosho's *An Inn in Osaka* (*Osaka no yado*), which takes place in one small hotel. Ozu's *Tokyo Story* (*Tokyo monogatari*) takes us into two houses, while Kurosawa's *Red Beard* (*Akahige*), Imai's *Night Drum* (*Yoru no tsuzumi*), and Kobayashi's *Harakiri* (*Seppuku*) all take place in neighborhoods dominated by a single structure: a hospital, a samurai's house, a lord's mansion. In all these and many, many more possible examples, the chosen space—exterior or interior—is always treated as an integral, tightly controlled unit.

The use of restricted space reflects Japanese inclinations toward indirect expression. In Toyoda's *A Strange Tale from East of the River* (*Bokutokidan*) the major action takes place in one house and the director, having chosen to narrate a simple story, his attention entirely directed to oblique expression, uses the house as an extension of the woman living there. During the course of this two-hour film we come to know this house, upstairs and down. And as its presence becomes familiar so, by association, does its tenant. The increment of realistic detail within a well-defined space establishes an atmosphere, which, it can be said, in turn creates character. The woman becomes credible indirectly, through her totally believable atmosphere. This is true, to be sure, not only of Japan and its traditional film. One can think of many Western examples. I am only saying that it is more often true in Japan.

It is sometimes said that in traditional Japanese art, less means more and this is often true, even in the films. Though Akira Kurosawa is not thought by the Japanese to be particularly representative of their traditional film culture, compare his *Lower Depths* (*Donzoku*) with Jean Renoir's adaptation of the same Gorky play, *Les Bas-fonds*. Kurosawa's is made of so much less—just the boarding house, the yard outside, the sky, and the characters themselves. Renoir is interested only in his characters; close-ups begin at once. Kurosawa, on the other hand, uses few close-ups. We see his people in groups of two or three and always framed by the house itself. In a way Kurosawa shows us less but his film implies more. When this occurs the spectators, presented with less than perhaps expected, must bring more of themselves to the film, must think more, feel more. The spectator is like the camera lens—the less light there is, the more it must open up.

There are various ways for a director to restrict and consequently amplify his film. He may limit his locale, his theme, his manner of description. Kenji Mizoguchi's avowed means of creating atmosphere depended upon two limitations: he put his action far from the camera and he continued the scene for a long time. An example would be the scene on the lawn in *Ugetsu* (*Ugetsu monogatari*). The lovers are some distance away, playing on the grass. Nothing else occurs and this continues for some time. A result is that we slowly absorb the beauty of the scene and can consequently begin to feel what this might mean to that distant couple. We feel the atmosphere much as they feel it. By giving us almost nothing to look at Mizoguchi has led us to see.

The later films of Yasujiro Ozu offer particularly good examples of this Japanese talent for meaningful restriction. The camera is fixed, stationary; scenes and sequence are constructed in an identical way; there is no punctuation other than the straight cut. In an Ozu film it is impossible not to bring oneself into his milieu; the spectator is completely involved in this carefully controlled vision of a house and its family. Such involvement is unavoidable not only because Ozu creates a credible atmosphere, but also because he understands the nature of film.

The cinema's greatest strength is that it is able to perfectly record the surface of life—and nothing more. Since this is so, we should expect no more than a reflection of this surface reality. Those great close-ups of emotionally contorted faces in Western cinema (and some Eastern cinema as well) do not make us feel pain or grief or happiness. What these images convey are skin pores, mascara, nostril hair.

Since cinematic art is symbolic, however, we accept this cosmeticized monster face as a representation of human emotions. But when Ozu shows Setsuko Hara at the end of *Late Autumn*, sitting alone in the middle distance, hands folded, eyes downcast, we move nearer to a genuine feeling of sadness. Among the reasons is that Ozu does not demand our emotions and so, paradoxically, we more freely give them. More importantly, by respecting the surface of life he succeeds in suggesting the depths beneath. He allows us to feel these emotions, which the surface can only suggest. The less he shows the more we feel. In doing this, he respects not only the nature of cinema, he also respects himself and us.

The Japanese director could not respect the nature of cinema unless he also respected the nature of life itself. His aim, like that of all film directors, is complete credibility, but the traditional Japanese is better equipped than some. We have already seen that he uses the atmosphere of a place to ensure our belief in it, that he purposely restricts what he shows, and how he shows it, to ensure our participation. Now we can see the respect that such a director has for life and consequently for cinema.

Again, the example is Ozu. The typical Ozu scene begins rather briskly and the story is forwarded a shot or two. Then, at the very point where another director might end the scene, one character turns to another and remarks on the weather or simply sits and looks. The camera regards this, recording it: sound stops, movement ceases. It is a moment of silence, of repose before the next scene.

The tiny empty moments are the pores in an Ozu film through which it breathes. They define the film by their very emptiness, and its show of care and respect. Compare this, then, to the somewhat ruthless manner of an average director who might have ended the scene after the plot had been forwarded, as though it was in plot and not people where the true interest lay. In so serving his plot this average director would have missed the most meaningful portion of the scene.

Serving plot, however, is not among the strengths of the traditional Japanese film. To define plot one might look at E. M. Forster's definition. The king died and then the queen died is a story. The queen died because the king died is a plot. The story reflects simple reality. The plot comments upon that reality, ascribing motives and relating actions. Plot ought not, however, be the business of cinema, which ought to always concern itself with recording surface reality. Rather, the aim of cinematic art ought be to take life as it is and to pattern it in some way that does not do violence to its nature. Plot, on the other hand, is a pattern that does violence. It demands action and events, thus changing the nature of film as recording of a visible reality.

Traditional Japanese film often emphasizes story rather than plot. The first important Japanese film still surviving, the 1921 *Souls on the Road* by Minoru Murata and Kaoru Osanai, is composed of two interwoven stories. In their editing Murata and Osanai were not interested in contrasting thoughts and ideas, but in creating parallels of feeling and atmosphere. D. W. Griffith's *Way Down East*, made at approximately the same time, is a heavily plotted melodrama. The difference in narrative structure is reflected in the difference of these films' endings. *Way Down East* has an exciting, logical, formalized conclusion. *Souls on the Road* simply stops, with no formal conclusion at all.

The two films are roughly typical. Though Japanese cinema has probably as many unhappy formal endings as the cinema of the West has happy ones, it also has a large number of informal, or open-ended, conclusions. Happy or unhappy endings belong only to the plotted film where life is tied up into a neat package. Story, on the other, needs no such conclusion. It merely stops after a certain number of episodes.

There is a pause in the story, a pause in the lives of the characters and instead of the next episode we are given the end title.

Another difference in the Japanese traditional film is an acknowledgment that it takes time to make its full impression. Until recently the Japanese film was almost alone in recognizing this and the length of the scene, the sequence, the finished film still cause complaint in the hurried West. The famed Soviet film director Vsevolod Pudovkin once said that there was "too much unnecessary footage in Japanese films."

It should be remembered however that time is always used for a purpose: to make one feel.

There is a typical sequence in Ozu's 1949 picture, *Late Spring*, that typifies this traditional use of time. Ozu wanted to show the daughter becoming aware of the interest her father presumably has in marrying an acquaintance. Since a number of delicate feelings are involved, he did not wish to use a tool as blunt as mere dialogue. He

wanted to show rather than state. And he chose to set the scene at
a performance of the Noh drama, so the only sound is the sound of
the Noh itself. The sequence runs this way:

> Middle-shot of father and daughter watching the play
> The play itself
> Long-shot of the audience including father and daughter
> Close-up of father
> Mid-shot of one of the actors in the Noh
> Mid-shot of the other actor and the chorus
> Mid-shot of father and daughter
> The Noh play
> Mid-shot of the actors
> Long-shot of the Noh play
> The father nods politely to someone
> The daughter looks, then she too politely nods
> The acquaintance nods in return
> Daughter and father, she turns to look at him
> The acquaintance looks at the play
> The daughter, eyes downcast
> Mid-shot of father and daughter
> Close-up of daughter looking at father
> Close-up of father pleased with the play
> Close-up of daughter, sad
> Close-up of acquaintance watching the play
> Close-up of daughter, sad
> Long-shot of the audience including father and daughter
> Long-shot of the play
> Close-up of daughter, head bowed
> A tree in the wind, music of the Noh continuing

The sequence runs for about three minutes and is composed of twenty-six shots. It makes the effect that he wanted and there isn't one wasted moment. Each contributes to the emotional depth of the sequence. In the West (or in contemporary Japan), however, the sequence would probably consist of five or six shots. One or two for each character and a few for the play itself. The point, that the daughter was not happy with her widowed father apparently preparing to get married, would be made rapidly, and we would be rushed into the next sequence. By the end of the film we would probably have forgotten the entire sequence or remembered it only as a plot complication.

The sequence in *Late Spring*, however, is unforgettable. The reason is, of course, Ozu's way of showing it. He adds cut after cut just as a painter applies brush strokes, each contributing to the final impression. Ozu here edited not to contrast scenes but to compare them, to create an incremental structure in which the scenes sustain each other. In so doing he created a feeling of actuality, he forwarded his story, and he took the amount of time necessary for us to be convinced of what was happening, and so apprehend the impact of the event on the heroine. Finally, but perhaps most importantly, by creating that final image of the tree over which continued the music of the Noh, he conceived a rare conjunction of the physical world with a spiritual state.

I, here, of course, discuss only a fraction of current Japanese cinema. There is far more to be said and many exceptions to be made. For every Ozu there are dozens of Japanese directors who neither know nor care about the nature of cinema. *An Inn in Osaka* is opposed to hundreds of Japanese movies that respect reality no more than does the average California or Cinecittà production.

Furthermore, there are objectionable qualities of the Japanese film, traditional or otherwise, that I have not mentioned: the typical reliance on the overly explanatory, the shameless exploitation of sentimentality for its own sake, etc. Moreover, the virtues I have been describing have now largely vanished from the Japanese film as they are vanishing from Japanese life. There are doubtless strong economic reasons for this, but the economic explanation, whatever its strength, is never sufficient.

Japan's attitude toward its own reality has changed. In a land where nature is no longer respected, where today is seen in terms of tomorrow, the regard for truth that creates art can no longer exist and the assumption of a secure atmosphere is the first thing to go.

—*1974*

Some Notes on Life
and Death in the Japanese Film

*. . . life in its turn has evolved death. For not nature only but man's being
has its seasons, its sequence of spring and autumn, summer and winter.*
CHUANG TZU, TRANS. ARTHUR WALEY

It is problematical how accurately art can mirror such imponderables
as life and death, but it is certain that art can verify attitudes toward
them. Its history, from cave painting to cinema, gives ample indication of how people have felt about life and its certain consequence.

Since death can be conceived only as opposite of life, and since
life is necessary to give an identity to death, the ways in which death
is to be accommodated are among the surer signs of an attitude
toward life. Here cultures variously divide their means of depict-
ing death—and consequently life. There are many differences. Let us
begin with just one: the disposal of the corpse in the Japanese film.

In Ozu's *End of Summer*, the protagonist has died and we watch
an incinerator chimney as smoke appears. In Itami's *The Funeral* we
see the actual oven, the body presumably inside. In Ichikawa's *Enjo*
we gaze at the cremation itself, the flames licking the coffin.

These might be contrasted with funeral scenes in many European and American films where the body is shown at rest, hands
folded, expression serene before interment. In the Japanese example
we see a culture doing something about the remains of death. In the
Western, we see a culture doing nothing at all since degeneration of
the corpse will be accomplished without further assistance.

At the same time we know that some religious beliefs seek to
sweeten bitter death with promises of an afterlife, including one in
which the body itself is returned to its former state—and therefore

must be available. In Japan, however, such beliefs are relatively rare and the afterlife is not much featured as an attraction. Bodily remains are not important. Their shelf life is over.

Once death has occurred the usual Japanese funeral service is, to be sure, observed before the disposal of the body. But this too is distinguished by a kind of dispatch—from a Western perspective, a certain briskness. In Kurosawa's *The Bad Sleep Well*, the funeral service takes place at once. This is not simple editing. In Japan the wake can even occur on the same day as the death, the funeral following the day after. Propitious signs (lucky days, etc.) being favorable, this is even a kind of goal.

Nonetheless the corpse has at least a night of human attendance and yet, as in much else in the Japanese way of death, how domesticated it is. In several senses. Most viewers of Kurosawa's *Ikiru* do not notice (unless they are Japanese) that the room in which the wake occurs is the same room we have often seen where the hero Watanabe returns from work, where his son and daughter-in-law have their dinner. Japanese funerals occur at home.

They also occur in the temple or in the crematory itself, but the home funeral remains common. (If now difficult. Itami's *The Funeral* is very funny in its spectacle of modern Japanese forgetting the proper funerary process.) It is perhaps this homemade aspect of Japanese funeral observation (in life as in film) that indicates death in Japan is not regarded as extraordinary; it is everyday, quotidian.

That it is to be expected is indicated not only in the homemade funeral and by the prompt removal of the body, but also in the way in which preparations are marshaled. If the wake is to be tonight and the funeral tomorrow, then everything must be made ready.

In *The Funeral* we see the bereaved characters running down the list of necessities: the photo portrait, the posthumous name, the refreshments for the mourners, the envelopes of salt to keep away "evil." All of these must be produced at once. And these are ordinary family members, not funeral parlor employees.

And all of these are produced at once. The dispatch of the funerary arrangements in Japan is dazzling. It is as though death had been foreseen. And they must be complete—all that black and white bunting, the platform for the coffin, the Buddhist decorations—so complete that we do not even recognize that room in *Ikiru*.

Such economy does not suggest any lack of respect or loss of affection for the dead, however. The leave-taking is as filled with veneration and love as is that of any other culture. The face of the dead is gazed upon before the sealing of the coffin. Beloved objects are put inside; the whole is strewn with flowers.

One of the most affecting scenes in Japanese cinema occurs when the body of the dead heroine is being prepared in Naruse's *Floating Clouds*. Her inconstant lover, overcome, takes her lipstick and uses it to return to her a bloom she has lost. Let us linger on this scene. He is doing what beauticians routinely do in the funeral parlors of the West. The difference is the spirit in which it is done: in not only his repentant affection, but also his lack of any hesitation at taking a corpse in his arms, at decorating it. The Japanese approach is hands on.

In Japanese films as in Japanese life, people are, in their way, confronting the fact of death. There is little of the overwhelming confusion that so dramatizes some Western funeral scenes. Japanese people—on the screen and off—are capable of doing something about death.

Much of this capability has to do with the fact that death is both expected and accepted to a degree seemingly greater than in the West. In Ozu's *End of Summer* this is articulated when the farmers look at the crematorium smoke and mention how sad but necessary this is, that one person dies and that another is born.

An acceptance is implied in the traditional Japanese death scene whether this be on the stage, the screen, or in life itself. I am unable to think of a single scene in the Japanese film where anyone rails against death, though I can think of many Western examples, beginning with King Lear.

To be sure, no one in Japan is very happy about dying. (Unless there is an imposed reason for it such as the various "loyal" deaths in samurai films and the like.) Nonetheless, death is seen as pathos rather than tragedy. Pathetic things you get over; tragedy, you don't.

The West imbues death with a tragic dignity, which is often reflected in films. Noble and dignified death scenes abound. The viewer is expected to view these as terminal in several senses. The bereaved are supposed (in film at any rate) to remain permanently so.

Remember the criticism voiced when Agnes Varda's *Le Bonheur* suggested that her hero could find true happiness with another after the death of his devoted wife. This can be contrasted with, say, Hirokazu Kore'eda's *Maboroshi no hikari*, where the bereaved wife's finding contentment with a new husband after the death of an old is seen as a happy ending.

A further contrast might be the behavior of the dead after life. In all cultures the dead return accompanied by varied degrees of frisson. In Japan, however, the dead never return en masse to terrorize the living as in the American *Night of the Living Dead* and many other films. So unfriendly a relationship between the two is rarely imagined. Rather, the Japanese dead return on business, as it were. They have unfinished and individual accounts to settle, personal revenges or private grudges to satisfy. They are not unmotivated zombies, but rather dedicated individuals who happen not to be around any longer.

Oiwa, the unfortunate wife in *The Yotsuya Ghost Story*, both in the original Kabuki and its many screen versions, has been badly treated: poisoned, rendered hideous, stabbed, nailed to a door, set afloat. She returns to avenge herself on only the faithless husband. Variations on this theme continue. At present they galvanize the "new Japanese horror boom"—*Ring I, Ring II, The Grudge* in both Japanese and American versions, etc.

Among other things, this difference between mass and personal horror might indicate that life after death is not to be so dreaded— in Japanese film not just everyone is threatened, only the bad individuals. If you behave yourself the avenging dead will have no reason for animosity. Normal death is normal.

Similarly domesticated is the moment of dying itself. While there is just as much violent death in Japanese film as in any other cinema, even the slicings and decapitations of the period film insist upon a kind of domestic supervision, one that renders death quotidian. These samurai or *yakuza* or suicidal businessmen subscribe to a code that insists upon death as definition.

In the beloved *Chushingura*, the tale of the forty-seven loyal samurai, the mass suicide that comprises the final tableau on stage and screen is domestic, ordained, related to the household. It is the opposite of unexplained horror, it is reasoned and expected. Even compassion is dampened when it is understood that these men are merely doing their duty.

Even in so liberal a film as Masaki Kobayashi's *Harakiri*, the spectator feels sadness but no horror at the death itself; horror is felt rather at the means imposed. (The would-be suicide has sold his sword, only has a bamboo replacement, and is forced to use it to cut himself open.) Death itself is accepted.

Otherwise, death on the Japanese screen is decorous. People die in hospitals or at home, surrounded by family. They take their time. This is the theme of the compassionate *Dying at a Hospital* of Jun Ichikawa, where we simply watch this slow-motion death. In more popular films a kind of domestic production is made of it, with music, tears, and handkerchiefs.

Such an anodyne presentation is indeed so common in Japanese film that something more honest in death scenes always seems shocking. Most shocking is when this occurs in what is otherwise a world of peaceful convention, in a film such as Ozu's *There Was a Father*. Here the father has a major stroke on camera—collapse, twitching, the works. In the balanced geometry of Ozu's scene, this lurching, inchoate fact is deeply upsetting. Likewise, at the end of *Tokyo Story* the beloved mother dies of a stroke and we are not spared the struggling body, its various noises, nor the spectacle of the corpse, face covered.

Director Shohei Imamura, then an assistant on *Tokyo Story*, has said that after this painful scene had been filmed, Ozu turned to him, knowing that Imamura had recently lost his mother to just such a stroke, and asked if he had gotten it right.

This might well indicate a certain lack of empathy but it also indicates that what was most important to Ozu was the reality of subject. He had used his own father's death as the model for the stroke scene in *There Was a Father*. He was not going to gloss over the fact in any movie-like way. He was going to show it in a realistic fashion. That is, he was going to accept it.

It is just this acceptance that so distinguishes death's appearances in Japanese films. There is a noticeable lack of keening (compare with Korean films) and though there is a lot of crying there is also lots of drying of eyes and blowing of noses.

Japan makes space for death. Perhaps that is the reason it makes so much of it. Look at the drama, the poetry—death is an ordinary subject. Someone once said that Japan was as death obsessed as was ancient Egypt. Well, yes, but obsession means to be haunted, harassed, preoccupied, and Japan is none of these things. Rather, and indeed much like ancient Egypt, it celebrates death and accepts it. One would rather say that Japan is just life obsessed. It, like ancient Egypt, is so preoccupied with life that it can afford a place for death.

And this is reflected in the small facet of Japan we have been examining, its films and their representation and the attitude that they reveal toward death and life. After all, the single Japanese film most concerned with any meaning to be found in the fact of death is named *Ikiru*, the intransitive verb meaning "to live."

—2006

Buddhism and the Film

There are various ways in which to regard that anomalous object, a Buddhist cinema, but before I enumerate some of them we might first look at the aims of Buddhism itself.

In the view of the historical Buddha, Gautama, life is suffering (*dukkha* in Sanskrit). This we experience because everything is the result of ever-changing causes. Thus human existence is always in flux and transience (*anitya*, or in Japanese, *mujo*). It is therefore impossible to claim anything as belonging to a permanent self (*atman*) or to even assert that there is any such thing. There is thus no dichotomy between a subjective and an objective world. Rather, all things (including ourselves) came into existence through the conditioning of innumerable causes.

Our perplexing existence stems from these causes. If they are extinguished, however, then our confusions dissolve—a welcome event called *pratiyasamutpada* or, in Japanese, *engi*. Those who want to be freed from suffering must thus come to a clear understanding (sometimes called enlightenment) concerning suffering, impermanence, and the nonself (*anatman*). To attain this true knowledge (*prajna*), all attachment—the root of illusion—must be denied, and there are various ways (spiritual disciplines such as meditation) through which this is achieved. Only then will one find freedom (*nirvana*).

As this atrociously simplified account indicates, there would on the surface be little to connect the Buddhist faith with the cinema. This is an entertainment that is largely based upon satisfying our desire for the various attachments, which Buddhism counsels us to deny. There are, however, a few promising areas where some agreement might be detected.

Cinema, for example, is famous for destroying the sense of self. Indeed, the reason we go to the movies is to be relieved for a time of this troubling companion. We habitually seek for situations where our difficult self (a homemade and ill-fitting invention) is sloughed off—drink, drugs, sex, gambling, the silver screen, and the TV tube are all unifying activities that exclude our ideas of who we are and instead allow us to experience a cohesion we might never otherwise encounter.

Film famously accomplishes this. It has been variously called a waking dream, a mass illusion, pop propaganda, but no one has ever denied that it takes one out of oneself. This then is a promising beginning in any consideration of Buddhist claims for cinema because this absence of self is precisely the condition that Buddhism counsels. From here, then, taking this theme as the ground, sounding its drone beneath our speculations, we may begin to enumerate a few qualities.

*

I mentioned some ways in which to regard that anomalous object we are discussing. From the simplest to the more complicated, these might be films about the historical Buddha; films about Buddhist belief; films on Buddhist themes; films that incorporate Buddhist beliefs. These and their implications will inform this essay.

Films about the historical Buddha are few, though not so few as those on the historical Mohammed since there is no proscription. Buddha and Buddhism are allowed to be pictured; Islam is not. Yet there are many fewer films about Buddha than there are about the Hindu pantheon, the so-called Bollywood films, or those about the historical Christ.

One reason for this might be that the Buddha story is simply not dramatic enough. He laid down and died—which is much less sensational than being nailed to a cross. Also, he did not expire in a melodramatic welter of treachery, ill will, and recrimination. Just the opposite: the disciples gathered, there were a few speeches, and the Buddha passed on in an atmosphere of brotherhood and accord—pleasant certainly but not nearly dramatic enough to sustain a money-making movie.

An equally important reason is that the Buddha story has no political reason for any overt dramatization. Buddhism was not, originally at any rate, a proselytizing religion, though some sects certainly became so. Christianity on the other hand is. Buddhism thus does not have the propaganda needs that Christianity does. *The Ten Commandments*, *The Robe*, *The Greatest Story Ever Told*—all of these to an extent are intended to spread the good news, make new converts, or to make secure the old. Christ has so far appeared in 150 recorded screen portrayals (someone has counted them), which is more than the most enterprising of movie stars.

Compared to the various filmed lives of Christ there have been very few films starring Buddha. Those countries that might be inclined to make them (those where Hinayama—the Lesser Vehicle—Buddhism maintains) do not have the money, historical spectaculars being expensive. Those countries that have the money (lands where Mahayana—the Greater Vehicle—maintains, Japan among them) are not inclined to make them. Actually Japan tried: the 1961 *Buddha*, followed by bio-epics on Nichiren and Shinran. All, however, indicated their incapacity by failing to show much profit. The basic story is perhaps just too nondramatic to engage popular attention—even that attention that is engaged in trying to lose itself.

*

As to films about Buddhist belief, these too are relatively few when compared with those about Christianity. There have been some twenty-seven films about Joan of Arc, and there are many picturizations of various other Christian saints, nuns, monks, priests, and so on. And when such films picturing Buddhist convictions are made, the emphasis is often different from those films about Christian beliefs.

For example, in the various Korean films about Buddhist monks the emphasis is not upon exemplary lives but upon the *do*—the way—itself. In both Kwon-taek Im's 1981 *Mandala* and Yong-kyun Bae's 1989 *Why Has Bodhi-Dharma Left for the Orient?*, two exemplary films, the title of the latter taken from an unanswerable Zen *koan*, the emphasis is not upon person but process. Again in Sri Lankan films about Buddhist monks and nuns the emphasis is not upon martyrdom but upon some more peaceful manner of joining the elemental, as in Lester James Peries' *The Yellow Robe*.

In the popular Japanese pictures about Buddhist nuns, it is usually the link between religion and sexual expression that is candidly acknowledged—something that would never occur in a Christian film. That these cavorting creatures occasion no public comment is perhaps indicative of differences between Buddhist and Christian means—one remembers the uproar in America occasioned by even something as mild as Martin Scorsese's *The Last Temptation of Christ*.

Thus no film has been produced in the East that is the moral equivalent of Bresson's 1950 *The Diary of a Country Priest* or Kawalerowicz's 1961 *Mother Joan of the Angels*, and there is no reason that they should have been. Buddhist tenets do not adapt well to the narrative needs of commercial films. Only when these are enlarged and socialized in a film such as the 1956 Japanese picture *Harp of Burma*, directed by Kon Ichikawa, do they become usable.

*

Films on Buddhist themes themselves (i.e., pictures that animate known liturgical beliefs) are again more rare than like films concerning Christian themes. In the West, in the earlier days, there were many Christian propaganda pictures the burden of which could be reduced to Love Thy Neighbor, Do Not Commit Adultery, and the like. In the East the Buddhist theme-film often attaches itself to the religious-bio. Thus the Japanese movies about the militant Nichiren are theme-films: Give Your All for Buddha. The film about Shinran (being about Pure Land doctrine) is theme-reducible to Speak Up for Buddha.

However, if we enlarge our definition to include pictures that perhaps did not intend to mirror Buddhist themes but nonetheless do, then we have many more examples. As Ronald Dore has observed: "Elements of Buddhist thought are so thoroughly absorbed into Japanese culture that they no longer depend on Buddhist institutions for their perpetuation."

One such noted is the high value placed on the state of nonself. In Buddhist thought the concept of self is itself to be obliterated so that something like reality may be apprehended. In Japanese society, the idea of such an individuality is to be sacrificed so that the needs of the community may be recognized.

The desired result of this secular interpretation is what Dore has called "a fatalistic determinism emphasizing the necessity of a resigned acceptance of one's lot." The result is by no means an illumination in the Buddhist sense, but the two processes are similar.

This reference now more concerns Mahayana (Greater Vehicle Buddhism) than Hinayama (Lesser Vehicle) and it should be known that this distinction in vehicle size is made because the Mahayana, having gone geographically furthest, still thinks that it did the most peddling. Since it proceeded from India through Nepal and Tibet to China and Korea, ending—for the time being—in the Japanese archipelago, it might be well to examine just what Buddhism means, or is supposed to mean, in this furthest flung of its provinces, Japan.

One of the enduring traits of Buddhism is its ability to tailor its nature to wherever it is—consequently the differences between the various Buddhisms of Asia rival the similarities.

In Japan the religion more strongly emphasized the impact on human institutions. It became a vehicle for practical morality and was able to accompany a decided work ethic. It emphasized the importance of human relations, of family morals; it further taught a reverence for ancestors.

At the same time it learned to compromise with nationalistic tendencies—the concept *chingo-kokka*, national peace through religious discipline. Along the way it became nonrationalistic—no rationalist speculation, no grand doctrinal system, and with this an acceptance of things as they are. Consequently, there is an openness to other beliefs. In Japan there are Buddhist temples and Shinto shrines but these are not viewed as mutually incompatible—like the cathedral and mosque.

Instead, and in a very Japanese manner, the market is allocated. Shinto gets birth, coming of age, and marriage rites. Buddhism gets the much more lucrative market for death—funerals, posthumous names, grave rights, necessary and expensive ceremonies on death dates, etc.

It might be argued that such tolerance for all religions indicates a certain lack of belief in any of them but this is not an idea that readily occurs in Japan, where the major religion is perhaps neither Buddhism nor Shintoism but, rather, simply being Japanese.

*

It is from this point of view then that one might consider the last
of my suggested categories—those films that incorporate Buddhist
beliefs. These are, of course, everywhere since Buddhism is a part
of Asian culture as a whole. Such elements are included along with
chopsticks, saris, kung fu, etc., with no one being the wiser—and no
one intending to be Buddhist in the first place.

To take a homely example from Christian culture: Walking
along the street we see a ladder leaning against the wall and taking
up most of the sidewalk. It is more convenient that we walk under
it. But do we? Well, that depends upon who we think we are, but
even if we decide not to, it is not because we remember the ancient
belief that first made the question necessary—that this is a situation
analogous to the devil's sitting triumphantly under the ladder leaning against the cross upon which Christ was hung.

In this spirit of ignorant acceptance, let us then look at the
work of the Japanese film director Yasujiro Ozu. A thoroughly secular man, he would doubtless be startled to find himself an exhibit
in a talk on Buddhism, yet he belongs here. Let us consider his
style.

The camera gaze: his people often look straight into the camera lens (or so close beside it that the effect is the same) and one
could find here a paradigm to Zen Buddhism, that straight-on view,
which, even when the eyes are veiled, as in *zazen*, sees directly.

The camera shot height: that of a person on a cushion—not only
host-and-guest, but also tea master, haiku master, *zazen* practitioner.

The shot length: one that is long by other standards, which is
not controlled by the exigencies of plot, which exists as though for
itself—a paradigm is religious concentration.

The occasional awareness of a Buddhist concept: the Noh theater sequence in *Late Spring*, the coda of *Early Summer*, which the director himself called *rinne*, that Buddhist apprehension of evanescence.

The mundane: Ozu's films are filled with the ordinary, with the everyday, one of the qualities of the transcendental—that is, the religious.

In stressing these qualities I am not arguing that Ozu is overtly Buddhist but I am suggesting that he is covertly so. His means are supportive of an attitude we would call religious (though we could also call it other things as well—modernist, for example), and Buddhism is the only religion he knew anything about. Buddhist attributes are thus, unintentionally, willy-nilly, helplessly, to be found in film, often in large quantities.

*

Finally, there is a more important matter: the fact that film itself can be seen as a kind of paradigm of Buddhism since it shares so many of its properties. In a sense then the cinema may be seen as Buddhist vehicle (though a strange one) in that so many of its observations are therein inculcated.

First, and not so frivolously as it might seem, film is an illusion.

There are only shadows on the screen. Like the mere shadows in Plato's cave, conjured up, they instantly vanish; the only difference is that Plato was watching shadows of real events. At the movies we are seeing only the shadows of shadows. Both are, in Buddhist terms, illusions—*maya*. We know what the Buddha, sitting under his *bo* tree, thought of these—they were to be vanquished and he stayed up late just to do so. The leading Indian film magazine is rightly named *Cinemaya*.

Second, the Buddha observed that all life is flux, transience, and what are the movies but just this? And in a double sense: each of the images only lasts 1/24 of a second, and film itself (both nitrate and safety) only lasts a number of decades before it chemically combusts. (Tape is no less transient, and the time involved is even less; and if you think eternity is yours with DVDs you are wrong—the matrix flakes after mere decades.) Consequently film is a double reflection of life. It reveals life's surface, and it reflects life's own mode since the major mode is flux.

Third, the Buddha held that all life is suffering (*dukkha*) and that the root of this suffering is illusion. We desire that which is transient and illusionary. Therefore the root of suffering is desire. We must learn not to want. However, wanting is the stuff of life.

This the movies amply indicate. They are about nothing but desire and suffering. In this sense, Douglas Sirk is a Buddhist sage and Lana Turner a bodhisattva. And in the larger sense, a conversion to the Buddha would mean the end of cinema since this is itself a compound of desire, suffering, and illusion, and all of these are bad things.

Fourth, in the Buddhist limbo, the deluded are forced to end-lessly repeat those actions that led to their being put there in the first place. Again a parallel suggests itself. As anyone who has endured the same film twice knows, the film experience, like, I suppose, the life experience, is (except in rare cases) impossible to duplicate as experience (though not for study purposes, nor for the emotional aspirations—the need to cry, for example).

One of the ideas behind that of the *dharma* is that of *karma*—the repetition of life. And it takes many forms. The person who willingly saw *The Sound of Music* some dozens of times was, in my opinion, either undergoing a purgative or enduring something approximate to the Buddhist hell. In its infernal form, one of the most thoroughly

Buddhist films ever made—its hero forced to endure the same ordinary day over and over again—was *Groundhog Day.*

                                    *

Dharma comes from an Indian word, the original meaning of which
is law, custom, duty, justice. Its contemporary meanings are double:
the teachings of the Buddha and those various elements that combine to make up the physical world, including us.

    This is not very helpful but it is clear that Buddha did not go
to the movies and would not have approved of them if he had. They
are distracting, illusionary, transient, and they inculcate desire. Also,
they encourage opinion and self-expression, while one of the tenets
of original Buddhism is *atman,* the impossibility of just this self.

    There are no film critics in the Buddhist pantheon. In that
sense, any stressing of the connection between *dharma* and the film
is anathema and an essay called "Buddhism and the Film" adds insult
to injury.

                                              —*1993/2003*

Japanese Women in Society and in Film

Social structure marginalizes the female of the species. In all cultures women are perceived to be physically inferior to men and much more emotional. These and other false attributes are central to the role that society has prepared for women—they are to be feminine, are thought to be more like children than adults, must therefore be supervised and kept in their inferior place. Women are seen—in Simone de Beauvoir's famous term—as the second sex.

This much benefits the male. It is he who finds the well-paying job, he who independently creates the life he wants. This includes appropriating a woman (usually through marriage) and she becomes his helper and has a role in his domestic life. She cooks for him, keeps his house, sleeps with him, and bears his child. Whether she is slave, servant, or partner depends on the husband. Consequently the woman is, from childhood, subjected to propaganda that both fits her for the feminine role and indoctrinates her into supporting the male view of the inequality of the sexes.

In Japan the means are well known. Prewar Japanese society officially insisted that the roles permitted women were limited to just three: *musume, tsuma, haha*. She is her father's daughter, her husband's wife, her son's mother. All three were subservient roles—women subservient to men.

Born into a position openly regarded as inferior, Japanese women were expected to shuttle between kitchen and bed and to be cheerful with the fretful male. She was also expected to deny herself as a person and yet, somehow, to find fulfillment within her narrow social confines.

Okusan means the one inside, but by extension it means the one who cannot get out. If she tries to, then it was said that she was *onnarashikunai*. To be thus accused of being unwomanly means that she has done something to realize herself in human rather than feminine terms.

She is thus, like an unruly child, punished. She is made helpless and dependent, ward of fathers and husbands, and marriage is her job because otherwise she would be economically unemployed. Even if women attempt to make a career, the double standard continues and females are often paid less than males in the same position.

Socially, if women remain single, or work for a living, or get divorced, they are traditionally subject to varying degrees of opprobrium. True, in old age a kind of freedom is attained, but only because a woman has by then become useless.

In no other country as otherwise advanced as Japan are women still so frankly regarded as chattel. The double standard is so ingrained that it is taken for granted. Consequently, few attempts are made to conceal it. The manipulation of women for economic, social, and sexual purposes is openly displayed and its rightness is seldom officially questioned.

One would not, indeed, expect men to doubt a system so beneficial to themselves. But in Japan, more often than not, the women seem also to subscribe to the rightness of their own oppression. They submit and endure. Or they enter professions designed to entertain men where, unless vigilant, they become as predatory as the males they serve. Sincerely, cynically, or hopelessly, they collaborate.

*

This is now an acknowledged view: women in Japan are traditionally marginalized and are rendered largely powerless. And it is true enough, many women still are. At the same time, however, there are many, many exceptions to this rule, and their numbers continue to grow.

It is now common for women to take jobs, to enter professions. They may still be paid less, and they must sometimes be the one who brings the tea to the men, but many more women work than before and suffer no added discrimination because of it.

It is now also not unusual for women to refuse marriage, and—if married—to refuse to have children. This is very different from the prewar pattern where a woman was officially not considered a finished person until she married; had not earned full citizenship, as it were, until she had a child; and was even more favorably regarded if the child was male.

This is a great change and an indication of emancipation; yet, even during the times of greatest discrimination Japanese women always had the ability to fight back. They control the family's finances and decide how the money that the spouse works so hard to acquire should be spent. They also control and form the children, particularly the boys.

The lives led by Japanese women are perhaps not so hopeless as the stereotype suggests. Though Japanese society is pictured as wholly paternal, many families are in effect matriarchies, with women making the decisions rather than men. Their authoritative role is covert but nonetheless there.

This might explain the large number of Japanese women reported satisfied with their inferior position in society. They accept their place, do not regard it as a plight, and make room for themselves in the narrow confines that Japanese society affords. Foreign feminists coming to Japan are always surprised that feminism is not an active issue here, that the females they encounter prefer less confrontational means.

It is true that a full feminist revolt disrupts (as well as gives meaning to) individual life. It itself becomes something like a full-time occupation. And it is also true that Japanese in general prefer to keep confrontation at a minimum and to solve social problems through more subtle means. At the same time discrimination against women is still much in evidence and one of the reasons is that there is no organized female front against it.

*

There is one quarter of the vexed area, however, where women have been observed by men in a less self-serving manner. This occurs in Japanese literature and drama and, overwhelmingly, in the cinema. Here an extraordinary dossier has been built up of films devoted to women and their various problems and solutions.

That this should have occurred in a society so frankly male chauvinist is surprising. Films, after all, are usually made by men and financed by them.

One of the reasons for the relative candor, however, is that until recently a predominantly female cinema audience was actively promoted.

Going to the movies is traditionally one of the freedoms allowed a woman, since it was presumed that she had both the time and the inclination to do so. Thus the "woman's film" became a genre in the films—one which still continues on television. In this genre, beginning in the 1930s and still visible, there was little of the hopefully compensating elegance of women's films in the West. Rather, within its generic limitations Japanese film reflected the plight of Japanese women.

One of the reasons is that until fairly recently Japanese cinema sometimes concerned itself with a faithful delineation of aspects of Japanese life. Another reason is that any serious filmmaker is concerned not only with meticulous representation, but also with a kind of drama that must, by its nature, question the ethical rightness of things as they are. This director is drawn to situations with maximum dramatic potential. Invariably that potential is provided by strife and friction between the individual and the environment.

In Japanese women, Japanese directors discovered a protagonist. This does not mean that Japanese directors are feminist. It does, however, mean that directors seeking objectivity as well as dramatic revelation have, naturally, shown Japanese women as they are.

Of all Japanese directors it was perhaps Mikio Naruse who best understood the position of Japanese women and, consequently, the nature of their dilemma. Certainly when he wanted to delineate the close confines of life, to show the hopelessness of all attempts at escape, it was women he chose to carry his message.

Other directors have responded similarly. When Keisuke Kinoshita and Kon Ichikawa criticized Japanese social standards, it was often women who served as their protagonists. When Susumu Hani wished to show optimistic hopelessness, and when Imamura wanted to indicate doomed intransigence, they did so through stories about women. It is through women that Toyoda portrays lost innocence and thwarted bravery, and when Mizoguchi comments pessimistically upon the fruitless journeyings of all humankind, it is through the example of women that the dark nature of life is revealed.

In the performances of the actresses chosen by these directors there is, moreover, a sense of reality. Compared to the dramatic honesty of Setsuko Hara, Hideko Takamine, Sachiko Hidari, the performances of many Western screen actresses seem manipulated.

I remember speaking once with the director Shiro Toyoda. We were talking about film acting and I asked why Japanese men were usually such poor actors and why Japanese women were almost invariably so good. He said that this was only natural.

The Japanese woman, from childhood, is forced to play a role. There are only three roles—those of daughter, wife, and mother—and she graduates from one to the other. From the earliest age she learns to mask her true feelings and to counterfeit those she does not feel. One of the results is that the Japanese woman is a consummate actress. Toyoda went on to say that he could take almost any female, put her up on the screen, and she would do very well.

The paradox is striking. The most honest cinematic portrait of women occurs in a country where honesty on the part of women was not socially tolerated. To think of Japanese women in film is to remember a whole gallery of meticulously honest performances: Setsuko Hara as the daughter who does not want to graduate to wife in Yasujiro Ozu's *Late Spring*, or Hideko Takamine as widow who has nowhere to go in Naruse's *When a Woman Ascends the Stairs*, or Sachiko Hidari as the farm girl determined to get ahead in *The Insect Woman*, or Kinuyo Tanaka's spectacular fall from court lady to common whore in Kenji Mizoguchi's *The Life of Oharu*.

Meticulous though these renderings are, however, one must further question the intentions of the producers and directors of these films about Japanese women. In showing their brave unhappiness are they not further supporting social attitudes that are the cause of this unhappiness? And are they not ignoring the many changes that are occurring regarding the social position of women?

*

Today women have many more social roles than *musume, tsuma, haha*. And they can neglect this time-honored triumvirate and decide against playing daughter, wife, and mother. Many more women nowadays leave their parents and choose an independent life, working for a living. Many more positions are now open to them—a woman no longer need retreat into motherhood or into *mizushobai*—she can hope to be a doctor or a lawyer or even a politician. Things are not perfect but they are certainly better.

Here the films have not very successfully mirrored reality. One of the reasons is that entertainment more often retells difficulties than successes. This is because difficulties are thought to be more dramatic, though they are actually not.

And there have been far too many films that blame women for their recent relative independence. We are shown girls dressed up on the streets of Shibuya, or, having left the safe family, falling into the hands of unscrupulous men, or—ruined by independence—giving way to drink, drugs, and *enjo kosai* (delicately translated in the dailies as "compensated companionship").

There are, at the same time, some young directors and some recent films that reflect something like today's social reality, and that are not tragedies. Hirokazu Kore'eda's *Maboroshi no hikari* is about a young widow who becomes an independent person in her own right. Nobuhiro Suwa's *2/Duo* shows a troubled couple in which the boy wants marriage and the girl is not at all certain. Naomi Kawase's *Moe no Suzaku* shows the dissolution of the family and its effect on her heroine. Hideyuki Hirayama's *Out* carries independence to new extremes—killing and chopping up the male villain. Ryuichi Hiroki's *Vibrator* shows a classically oppressed Japanese woman and then indicates how bravery and honesty gets her out of her existential mess.

I do not want to suggest that Japanese films invariably honestly portray contemporary Japanese women, but I wish to point out that some films do and that this reflection can be trusted. Women in Japanese life are changing, growing, and so are women in some Japanese films. Neither movie heroines nor ordinary women are any longer stuck with their limited repertoire of social roles. And the more that Japanese women work to emancipate their position and realize their selves, so will rise, to a degree, the films about them—their dim but faithful reflection.

—2005

The Japanese Eroduction

Both sociologically and economically the eroduction (a Japanese portmanteau word coined from the English "erotic" and "production") is an interesting phenomenon. In the days of falling box office receipts it at least makes back its costs; in a time of empty movie theaters it plays to houses half full; and it continues to command the attention of a loyal if small audience.

One of the reasons for this is that Japan, unlike other civilized countries, has no hard-core porno houses. The eroductions are the limpest of soft-core, and though there is much breast and buttock display, though there are simulations of intercourse, none of the working parts are ever shown. A major problem is thus faced: how to sexually stimulate when the means are missing.

Japanese production must remain within certain limits and when it does not, as did certain Nikkatsu pictures, the company is sued by the Metropolitan Police and a full-scale court case follows. Imported films are no exception to this general rule and many are rendered chaotic because of scenes missing or obscured. *I Am Curious (Yellow)* had forty-one scenes blacked out. A further curiosity was the Japanese showing of the American *Woodstock*. In several of the scenes nude couples wandered in the distance. Though they remained perhaps unnoticed in other countries, in Japan the sharp eyes of the censors instantly detected this irregularity. A number of these moral guardians were equipped with small, scraping needles and painstakingly picked the emulsion from the offending parts. When the film was projected the distant strolling couples seemed consequently girdled with fireworks. Though this called attention to what the censors were presumably attempting to hide, the letter of the law had been observed and this result satisfies all censors everywhere.

In Japan, consequently, the eroduction is needed. There is otherwise small outlet for prurient interest or for simple curiosity. Though any number of illegally imported "blue" films are around, they are expensive, difficult to obtain, and dangerous to show. For the average interested moviegoer, the eroduction is all that there is.

Thus, unlike other countries where free access to pornography has resulted in a satisfied curiosity, a stilled prurience, and emptier and emptier porno houses, Japan retains its compulsive and relatively obsessed audience. There are perhaps deeper psychological reasons for this but, in any event, attendance is still good enough that the eroduction business remains a solvent one.

During the height of eroduction production, several years ago, some twenty small companies made about two hundred such pictures each year. The shooting time remains short—a week at the most, studios are seldom used (rather, actual apartments and rooms people live in), wages are low, and the cost of making such a movie can be quite reasonable.

The released film is then often triple-billed and leased to a distributing chain that owns its own theaters. There were eventually twenty such chains in Japan and the profits were divided in such a way that from the per-picture average admission price, more than one quarter goes to the original producing company, less than one quarter to the distribution company, and one half to the theater.

The division would seem unfair to a production company owning no theaters, but there are actually few such. Usually, the production company, the distribution chain, and the theater management all belong to the same corporation. The profits are therefore total and considerable.

There are over one hundred eroduction theaters in Tokyo with an average capacity of a hundred spectators a house, and they are open daily from ten in the morning until ten at night and are always at least partially filled. Given the small original budget and the moderate overhead costs, the profits are considerable.

In Japan, the eroduction is the only type of picture that retains an assured patronage. The mass audience for movies has fallen away. There still exists, however, small, isolated audiences, and among these none is more faithful than the eroduction audience.

An assured audience ensures a standardized product. It is only in times of economic disaster that different formulas are tried out and experimentation is indulged. If commercial cinema in Japan is now changing its content along with its form it is only because the assured audience has disappeared. The eroduction, however, has its own loyal audience and this has resulted in its becoming a highly codified form of entertainment. Like the sword-fight *chambara*, like the three-handkerchief women's film, all cinematic forms that enjoyed a stable audience, the eroduction is formula film.

The eroduction is thus predetermined. Since the audience knows what it is getting, it need not be informed. Consequently, the films' titles are decorative rather than descriptive. *Intercourse Before Marriage* (*Konzen kosho*); *I Can't Wait for Night* (*Yoru made matenai*); *Wriggling* (*Notauchi*)—all these tell nothing about the respective contents of the pictures, they merely make the ritual statement of intent to titillate, the ambition of all eroduction.

The length of each film is predetermined. Since each is usually meant to be shown with two others, the ideal length decided upon is 6,500 feet, or 70 minutes. Further codifications are also introduced into the structure of the film itself. In theory, directors are to aim at some kind of sex scene every five minutes. In practice, however, it has proved impossible to construct a narrative that allows this, with the result that sex scenes are sometimes fewer but often longer.

Also predetermined, though perhaps not so consciously, is the interior shape of the film. One comes to recognize the component parts—just as in the period film there is the last sword fight, in the Western, the final shoot out. In the eroduction these necessary parts would be establishing sequence, plot set-up, defiling sequence, consequences, and conclusion. The connecting tissues may vary with the story, but all of these predetermined parts are invariable.

Since the intent of the eroduction is to arouse, the establishing sequence commonly shows the beginning if not the conclusion of a sexual act. Common among these are: tipsy bar hostess being escorted home by inflamed customer; hiking girls being offered and accepting rides from plainly untrustworthy gentlemen; foreplay during which conversation establishes that this is her first time. From these and other such beginnings grow scenes that establish coming sexual union.

The plot set-up begins at once. This establishes that the drunken hostess has really fallen into the hands of a white (or yellow) slaver; that the girls are not to be shown the good time they had perhaps expected but, rather, are to be painfully raped by numbers of men; that the despoiler of the repentant ex-virgin was not really interested in those now wasted charms—rather, he was really captured by those of an as yet virgin younger sister, etc.

With such tragic complications occurring so shortly, one rightly suspects that Japanese eroductions are about something other than the joys of sexual union. The next sequence confirms this. It is all about the denigration of women. Bar hostess, good-time girls, ex-virgin—all are given a very bad time. Common are scenes where, in order to escape, women must run naked through the fields or the streets; scenes where nude or near-nude women are overtaken in muddy rice-paddies; scenes were women are blackmailed or are in other ways compelled into giving themselves to various sexual irregularities.

The consequences of such excess are depicted in following sequences. These are various and include women (never men) coming to see the error of their ways through the dangers and humiliations of unwanted pregnancy or venereal disease. A singular result (but occurring often enough to warrant comment) is that the man, having finally achieved his way, is suddenly unable to perform. This is all, somehow, her fault, rather than a consequence of his own rashness. Naturally, such failure is never seen as human or as amusing. Indeed, as entertainment, the eroduction is unique in being both risible and humorless. The failure is, rather, a sudden tragedy for which woman is to blame.

This leads directly to the concluding sequence where repentance and remorse are the emotions most often simulated. If the girl has been bad, she will now be good; if merely unfortunate, she will now be prudent; if hurt, she must simply live with the knowledge of an abortion or a ruined younger sister; if dead (as she is in a surprising number of cases), she becomes a symbol for the general dangerousness of sex.

If she is dead she has often become so as the result of the impotent sequence. Unable to otherwise express his baffled emotions, the man resorts to shooting, strangling, knifing, etc. Since, somehow, it was all the woman's fault anyway, the eroduction audience (entirely male, watching a film made entirely by males) finds that this murder is to be regarded sympathetically. It was perhaps unkind, but the hero had experienced the worst humiliation known to man, so what else was he to do? More often, however, man and woman agree to part. After such extended sexual encounters, such pleasure and such pain, the feeling is that it was somehow not worth it. They go their separate ways, sadder, wiser, and the screen darkens.

This conclusion is surprising in a film of which the announced aim is titillation. But then, like most formula films, the eroduction is of two minds about its subject. Unable (being soft-core) to dwell upon a detailed examination of the sexual act, the eroduction must sublimate and hanker after what it cannot legally have. The resulting compromises do damage to an already myopic view of the sexes. American or European pornography is kept forever on its elemental level because, free to show all, it need do nothing else. The Japanese eroduction has to do something else because it cannot show all. This limitation sometimes creates works of art. In the case of the eroduction, however, it has instead created a mythology.

The producers of the eroduction believe that they have discovered a money-making recipe. The patrons of the eroduction think that they have found a harmless and inexpensive way of killing a few hours. Both, however, are actually sharing a belief, a myth. To be completely enjoyed, a woman must be completely denigrated.

How different are the various myths suggested by the pornography of other countries. There, if an amount of sadism involved it is always plainly labeled, never suggested as the norm—something that invariably occurs in Japanese eroductions. Though the women in Western pornography may be a bit more forward than is common in Western life, her only motivation is to have and to give a good time. She is bold, even brazen, but this suits her audience. Indeed, if a man did not require that kind of woman he probably would not be sitting in a porno house.

The Japanese eroduction is very different. Woman must be denigrated and she must deserve to be. The ways in which this is shown are various, but the conclusions are identical. Often, for example, the woman has had some prior experience. Since she is no longer a virgin, she is ritually unclean and therefore deserves all that she gets. Again, however, if the woman is still a virgin, her culpability is evidenced in other ways. A simple crush or mere attraction for some young, clean-cut type suffices. He shortly vanishes from the film, his sole function having been to uncover her low, animal nature. Or a man may not even be involved. Instead, she is observed in amorous dalliance with another girl—a spectacle some men find exciting—which at once establishes her worthlessness.

One recognizes here an inverted idealism. Pornography is typically puritanical about the virgin state. Women are presumed (on specious grounds) to be better than human and the hymen is proof of this. They have emerged from the creator's hands clean, pure, factory-sealed as it were. Being human, women naturally do not long remain in this state, to the chagrin of romantically minded males. Since they are no longer pure they must then be made completely impure. Thus it is that women who naturally, humanly, warmly acknowledge their emotional needs are regarded as vicious.

Men who so acknowledge their needs are, of course, not. It is here, in this rigid belief in the double standard that the hypocrisy of the eroduction rests. The man in the throes of passion is always noble; a woman in the same situation is always ignoble.

This curiously inverted attitude is visible even in the ways in which love scenes are photographed. The woman is often completely nude and is observed as a hysterical animal. The man, on the other hand, is always at least partially clothed, appearing in the raiment of civilization. While she screams, kicks, and in general abandons herself, he remains thoughtful, calm, a dedicated craftsman.

Her focus of interest is upon the loins, both his and her own. His, however, is upon the breasts and much footage is expanded on scenes of their being caressed. This reinforces the idea that man is above it all and, since he is not directly involved in the essentials of the act, he appears disinterested, civilized, a more noble person than she. He is immune to the vagaries of undisciplined emotion (all women are latent lesbians, homosexuality is unknown among them), to the tyranny of the jaded palate (scenes of simulated fellatio are common, scenes of equally simulated cunnilingus rare), and in all ways displays that he is a much better person.

He also displays—and this is something that the eroduction people do not intend—an extraordinarily immature relationship with women. Precisely, he reenacts the mother/child relationship. Mother is cast as bad-woman; bad-woman is cast as mother. Even in those scenes where the unfortunate but culpable girl is about to be tortured, there is much breast massage indicating an ambivalent and hungry child.

If the man with the whip shows the eroduction customer as he would like to be seen, the same man kneeling in adoration before the breasts would show him as he really is. This does not, however, explain why Japanese eroductions are actually (if unconsciously) concerned with a love-hate relationship of these proportions.

The hatred takes the form of undisguised sadism. The hero has turned his neurosis into a perversion and while this may be healthier for him it offers little help. At the same time, anyone engaging in active sadism is proclaiming, among other things, a profoundly felt inadequacy. And, just as idealism is inverted in these pictures to create the universal bad-woman, so masochism is also inverted to create these torture scenes that presumably so engage the audience.

At least, it is presumed that the audience is engaged or else it wouldn't be in the theater. Yet, one might also ask if it is not merely enduring rather than enjoying such savage spectacles in an effort to extract a mite of titillation. Perhaps we are seeing the fantasies of the jaded eroduction executive rather than witnessing an anthropologically interesting attitude on the part of the eroduction-goer.

That the eroduction fills a social need, no matter how poorly, is beyond doubt. During these few decades when they have been made in any number, the audience has remained faithful. And, though the films may sometimes resemble the soft-core quickies shown on Times Square or the naughty-nudies show in Soho, the differences are apparent. The foreign films are often little comedies or small melodramas. Innocent of overtones, happy to display the allowed quotient of female flesh, they babble their way to the final reel, mindless and ephemeral. The Japanese eroduction, on the other hand, can be seen as dark, tortured, plainly of psychological import.

The eroduction-makers could complain that I delve too deeply, that their hour-long fantasies were never intended to bear the weight of investigation. And, as for torture scenes, well, you have to have some kind of plot, and you cannot have that without good, strong conflict. We make an honest living, they would tell me, because we give the public what it wants. The public always wants a cheap, safe thrill and this, they would claim, is all that the eroduction provides.

I would maintain that it provides considerably more—that it, in fact, provides an outlet for the often-stultified animosity that all men everywhere seem occasionally to feel toward women. It offers this in such flashily sadistic terms because these cannot arouse the intelligence, no matter how effectively they both arouse and exhaust the emotions. This is because they are dealing with an archetypal situation. As with most formula films, one goes to the eroduction in order to witness a common fantasy endlessly repeated.

This repetition must reassure at least some members of the audience—the fantasy is as common as it is infantile. That woman is an enemy is a sensation that many men have experienced, but it is not an idea that we usually or necessarily believe. We may occasionally cast women in this role but we usually do not long keep them there. Yet this is just what the eroduction does. With a truly compulsive insistence, it monomaniacally maintains that the nursery vision is the only one, that women are evil, that sex is their instrument, and that men are their prey.

The men are doing in the women before the women have a

chance to do them in. This is an extremely primitive view of the male-female relationship but it lurks in the mind and only this knowledge and good will can make happy relations between the sexes possible at all. This is matched by a fear within the woman herself and it is her self-knowledge and trust that completes the bridge connecting her and a man. The eroduction, however, is not concerned with happy relations. Indeed, it does not believe in them. It encourages in the spectator a rigid dichotomy of thought and offers provocation to every love-hate neurosis in the house.

Which is why the eroduction cannot afford to be altruistic or fair-minded. Every speech, every action must be compulsively related back to what is identified as woman's voracious sexual appetite. This is a world where generosity, freedom, and affection are unknown. This is the world of the solitary, the domain of the voyeur.

Naturally, the eroduction is, like all pornographic productions, masturbatory cinema. The audience is not thinking about women, it is thinking about itself. Watching the most elemental of fantasies being acted out, it is affirmed in its own infantile nature.

In Japan the eroduction seems to be habit, like smoking, drinking, biting the nails. Its gratifications are instant, meaningless, and necessary. An audience of great economic potential has been tapped. It is for this reason that films can afford to be shoddy, unerotic to an extreme, and often ludicrously inept. The economic phenomenon is firmly based on the psychological phenomenon.

The eroduction theater is, like the bar and the racetrack, essentially harmless. But at the same time the patrons of the eroduction must receive some rather strange ideas of the world they live in. The point about fantasy is that, after all, the real world is different.

—1972

Trains in Japanese Film

When the locomotive pulled into the station in Louis Lumière's *L'Arrivée d'un train*, it arrived not only at La Ciotat, but all over the world as well. In 1897, in far Japan, Osaka and Tokyo audiences were viewing the event. And as with the rest of the world, it was not only a train, but a new century that was arriving.

In Japan, as elsewhere, the locomotive with its steam, speed, and power seemed to embody the promise of progress itself. Particularly in films, hurtling engines meant the modern age and whole friezes of racing trains occupied many motion pictures. Not those, however, of Japan.

Although the movie-going Japanese were just as train-struck as everyone else, an appreciation of the phenomenon could come only after it had been domesticated. The train was thus humanized, or anthropomorphized, to a degree uncommon in films of other countries. Hurtling engines were all very well, but something more controllable was necessary if the train was to enter Japanese reality as viewed in the films.

Trains in prewar Japanese films look miniature. While it is true that Japanese trains of the period were actually smaller than those in some other countries, they were perhaps not quite so toy-like as those seen in films like Kiyohiko Ushihara's *He and Life* (*Kare to jinsei*, 1929) and Mikio Naruse's *Apart from You* (*Kimi to wakarete*, 1933), but this very tractability early fit a gentrified role. Even the locomotive became benign, as in Akira Kurosawa's *Sanshiro Sugata* (*Sugata Sanshiro*, 1943) where it blows a cinder into the heroine's eye so that she may meet the rescuing hero.

These early trains are anthropomorphic. They can express

human qualities, and they do so, right into postwar Japanese cinema. Take the films of Keisuke Kinoshita—a director said to include a train in many of his films. One remembers his *Distant Clouds* (*Toi kumo*, 1955) where the youngsters of provincial Takayama look with longing at the trains passing on their way to Tokyo. The lonely trains in Shiro Toyoda's affecting *Grass Whistle* (*Mugibue*, 1955) epitomize the aspirations and longings of adolescence. In Masahiro Shinoda's *Childhood Days* (*Shonen jidai*, 1990) trains lyrically part the two friends. Kazuo Kuroki's *Preparations for the Festival* (*Matsuri no junbi*, 1975) has the hero (as in Federico Fellini's *I Vitelloni*) going off second-class smoker to the big city. Here the toy train has turned into a *Bildungsroman.*

But Japanese directors usually do not limit the train to a single role in their films. Rather, it is given a degree of latitude somewhat like that of a noticeably talented actor. Even train-prone Kinoshita has varied uses for it. The toy train may appear—one of the most entertaining is that which carries the stripper back to her rural origins in *Carmen Comes Home* (*Karumen kokyo ni kaeru*, 1951); it is Japan's first train in color—but it has other roles as well.

In Kinoshita's *Army* (*Rikugun*, 1944) the celebrated coda puts the inducted son on board while his mother patters after him along the station platform and there is not a dry eye in the house. In his *Japanese Tragedy* (*Nihon no higeki*, 1953) the train goes even further and crushes a suicidal mother, thus plays an essential role in the picture's plot itself.

Yasujiro Ozu was as fond of trains as Kinoshita, but his uses for them were different. Although otherwise much influenced by the modernist-accented American cinema, he found no value in pounding pistons and hurtling cowcatchers. Rather, he saw in trains a device that enforced and made visible the structure of his films.

In his *I Was Born, But . . .* (*Umarete wa mita keredo*, 1932) the suburban trains (in which none of the characters ever ride) come and go, lending themselves to the creation of the many parallels within the picture. Punctual (like all Japanese trains), they offer themselves to both high and low uses: temporal geometry on the one hand and sight gags on the other.

It is their structural use that eventually most appeals to Ozu. In his *Tokyo Story* (*Tokyo monogatari*, 1953) trains appear in both opening and closing sequences, acting as frames to the story but also asserting their own structural importance. Without them none of the trips back and forth from the provinces to the capital would have been possible. Trains can also play an iconographic role. At the conclusion of *Equinox Flower* (*Higanbana*, 1958) we look at the chastened father in the train, off to meet his daughter.

The opening sequence of Ozu's *Early Spring* (*Soshun*, 1956) shows the suburban trains carrying commuters (including the hero) into the city. Later, this young man is transferred to the provinces and so a reverse journey is described. Here the train serves a metaphorical function. The hero is receiving some advice about his failing marriage—failing in part because of his transfer. The setting is by a railway bridge and, sure enough, a prescient train rolls by.

Trains are often given this metaphoric role in Japanese films. One of the most remarkable examples is in Kon Ichikawa's *The Key*, aka *Odd Obsession* (*Kagi*, 1959). The mother's young man and her daughter are making love in a hotel near the tracks, and the director deliberately intercuts their intercourse with massive close-ups of shunting freight cars. Here the metaphoric intent is so naked that the sequence can be seen as comic, which may well have been the director's intention.

An equally bold metaphor occurs in Kurosawa's *Dreams* (*Yume*, 1990) though we can here be certain that any humor is unintentional. Martin Scorsese, playing Vincent van Gogh, observes: "I drive myself like a locomotive," and Kurosawa instantly cuts to a big close-up of a locomotive massively underway. Though the engine itself does not otherwise appear in the picture, we are, during the remaining scenes, sometimes treated to its wail.

The "train picture" is another genre. Here, the train constitutes the plot itself. Without it there would be no picture at all. Surely the best example is Junya Sato's *The Bullet Train* (*Shinkansen daibakuha*, 1975). The whole film takes place on the train or at various stations and offices belonging to it. A bomb has been placed on the express, set to go off if the train slows down (opposite to most train-bomb pictures where it goes off only after a certain velocity is attained)—a plot point, almost product placement, emphasizing the bullet train's major advantage, its unusual swiftness.

Another "train picture" is Kurosawa's *High and Low* (*Tengoku to jigoku*, 1963), the second half of which is devoted to detailed bullet train sequences. Ransom money must, according to instructions from the kidnapper, be dropped from the speeding train. In the making of the film, however, it was discovered that the bullet train had sealed windows and hydraulic doors. Eventually it was decided to use a vent in the toilet window for the drop, though this necessitated a much smaller packet of ransom money than had been originally envisioned.

For many, however (myself included), the quintessential train picture, one that combines the various roles that a train can play in the movies, is Shohei Imamura's *Intentions of Murder*, aka *Unholy Desire* (*Akai satsui*, 1964), a film shot in the snowy north of Japan where train travel is often necessary as roads are frequently blocked.

It is in a railway station that the wife is first glimpsed by the man who later rapes her and then becomes her lover. It is also on a train that he finds her for a second time. Finally, it is a train that carries them off, and it is this train that becomes snowbound, necessitating a trek through the snow that ends with his death and her freedom.

The fact of the train pulls together the various strands of the story and clarifies its structure. Her house, for example, is near the tracks and the passings of the various trains marks the time. Also, trains contribute to the feeling of menace. They are shown as big and black and bulging. All of these roles eventually combine in one of the finest train sequences on film anywhere.

This is the second meeting, where the rapist follows the housewife onto the train. Imamura films the action from both inside and outside the stationary car, which is waiting at the station. She flees to the back of the train and just as she reaches the rear, the train starts to move.

These various movements (hers, his, the train's) are contrasted, then combined. Inside the moving train, he pursues her to the rear platform. The camera, now inside the car, stares at them against the background of rushing tracks. From stationary to full motion, from horizontal to vertical, from flat two dimensions to full three—the perspective of the unreeling tracks—this sequence allows its filmmaker to do just about everything that it is possible to do with a train.

In addition, though the power of the train (as machine, as symbol, as metaphor) is fully acknowledged, at the same time, all of this is harnessed to the anthropomorphic: it serves to illustrate the state of a single human being—the violated, fulfilled wife.

—*1993*

Subtitling Japanese Films

All translation is a compromise but I doubt that any translation is so thoroughly compromised as that of film dialogue subtitles. The translator is given only so much space and within it is supposed to render into writing spoken dialogue in the amount of time it takes to say it. This is impossible.

The impossibility is indicated by the necessary mechanics of this sort of translation. In order to achieve this approximation of the original, both a written transcription of the dialogue and a list of temporal speech lengths must be used. The latter is in feet: one foot means you are allowed only a word or two; six feet means something like a full sentence.

Anything longer must be broken into shorter lengths since dialogue space on the screen is restricted to two full lines at the bottom of the image—about twelve feet. Anything bulkier gets in the way of the picture.

Word count, however, depends upon who is doing the reading. The English or American translator naturally reads faster than does the Japanese film-company person checking the work. The latter often insists that the finished titles have too many words, since the rule is that you must have time to read them twice—if you are Japanese. Such rules, carefully followed, would mean that very little of the dialogue could be included in the titles.

The major problem in translating spoken dialogue into written form is not long titles but short ones. A character in the film, speaking fast, can include up to eight syllables. For example, "*Mo dekakeru-kana?*" A possible translation is "Shall we go then?" It is pushing the one-foot limit and sacrifices a nuance or two, but I would probably use it—if it were allowed. But most Japanese translators (and many films continue to be translated by Japanese with little supervision) might settle for "We go?" or even "Go?"

Getting the sense of the speech to come through in this strained form of communication is difficult enough, but even harder is duplicating the tone of the speaker. Yes, this is necessary. Here is how I attempt it.

When doing titles, I always work with an under-translator, usually a Japanese, since my written command of the language is not nearly secure enough, and I am proceeding from a written manuscript.

First, having seen the film several times, I am ready to block out the dialogue, using both the under-translation and the speech-length list. Once this preliminary fitting is done I then watch the film again, this time with my translation draft.

It is here that I must attempt to fit the dialogue to the tone used by the characters. This is usually difficult. English, for example, has nothing approximating the various levels of respect in the Japanese language, little like the difference between male and female usage, no convention for naming through position (*onii-san*, *aniki*, both terms for "elder brother"), and no custom of dropping pronouns. Yet, one can still approximate most of these effects through analogous forms.

In working with meaning and with tone, I feel that the ideal is a smooth and standard English. Consequently I am careful not to heighten. If anything, I underplay the emotion of a scene by reducing the intensity of the language—no loaded words, no convoluted phases, and on my part no emotionality at all.

This is because I feel that the translation should be invisible—it should be a convention, like the screen size, like black and white, like full color. Once you have emphasized a convention you need not keep on emphasizing it. If you do you distract the viewer from the film itself.

In the titles, any oddity, any term too heightened, as well as any error, calls attention to the written dialogue and is, I feel, a mistake. I won't even use exclamation marks. The language should enter the ear as the image enters the eye.

For this reason I attempt colloquial English but one purified of slang and conscious of the various levels of historical usage. At the same time I attempt to create a scrupulously anonymous kind of English. If I don't succeed, then I myself rend the illusion I am supposed to be assisting.

This I did when I was working on the titles for Kurosawa's *Ran* (1985). Carried away by the pageantry, I relaxed my guard and thought to intrude a bit of period color. Nothing like "'sblood" or "by my oath," of course, but I left out occasional prepositions in a way common to formal court English. Something like "I want you to go," I foolishly rendered as "I would wish you go." Not incorrect, actually forwarding the effect I wanted, but in dialogue titles completely inappropriate. The result of course was that foreign audiences thought that the titles were full of mistakes and that some Japanese had made them.

The only time I successfully impose a heightened effect is when the film itself is heightened. If it is itself artificial then my artificiality becomes a convention, which, established at the beginning, causes no distress and supports rather than destroys the illusion.

When I did the titles for *An Actor's Revenge* (*Yukinojo henge*, 1962), a film about early Kabuki, and one with a very strong and self-conscious visual style, I felt that the visual style would be able to sustain titles equally self-conscious. Finding a period analogous to that within the film, I read a lot of Congreve and Dryden and only began to work when I decided that the rhythms of Restoration drama had sufficiently penetrated. In this case my attempts were successful and they do, I think, give the English-speaking viewer an adequate support.

There are, at the same time, so many cultural differences among countries that nearly insoluble problems occur. I was doing the titles for Kurosawa's *Rhapsody in August* (*Hachigatsu no kyoshikyoku*, 1991) and the term *kappa* came up. Dictionaries still insist on "water imp" but for this film I was wary of so old-fashioned a term. Even in its adjectival form "imp" is becoming obsolete in English-speaking countries. Further, in this picture the malevolent rather than the merely mischievous attributes of the creature were being empha- sized. I settled for "water demon," which could explain the wetness and why the children were carrying on so, but I am still not satisfied. Often there is no proper approximation.

Naturally this problem works two ways and the Japanese trans- lator must equally suffer trying to do something with intransigent English. Consequently the problem is sliced through by using only dictionary definitions, regardless of intent, tone, or anything else.

One of the more spectacular examples of ignorance occurred in the Japanese dialogue titles for *Wish You Were Here*, a 1987 British film that used a certain amount of bad language. Among the result- ing anomalies was the rendering of the English term "bugger." This was a word the young heroine of the film used to excess, but only in its current sense of designating a no-good.

The puzzled Japanese, faced with "bugger," looked it up in the English-Japanese dictionary and found only one definition. From among the Japanese synonyms the translator chose *okama*, a term that usually denotes a cross-dressing passive homosexual. Japanese viewers of the film were thus baffled by the many scenes of the foul- mouthed heroine being mounted by manly, rugged, ardent men whom she addressed, bafflingly, as *okama*.

Given the difficulties of film dialogue translation, one can sympathize with even such ludicrous accommodations. And there is always the possibility that something equally appalling is awaiting you once you start your next translation job. Constriction of time and space make qualifications impossible and the error of simplification is always present. I suppose the way one ought to think of this enterprise is not with chagrin that so much gets lost, but with surprise that so much gets through.

—1991

V

*The View
from Inside*

Wasei Eigo: A Beginner's Guide

Tourists coming to Japan notice that English is written everywhere: shop signs, advertising slogans, brand names, shopping bags, T-shirts. One's first reaction is relief—here is a country where everyone knows English. Soon, however, it becomes apparent that almost no one knows English.

The first intimation occurs when the tourist reads what is written. There are many examples—here are some from the number that Andrew Horvat has collected: a fashion design company labels its products "Delirium Bravery," a polo shirt is embroidered with "Hysteric's," and a leather jacket bears "Vigorous Throw Up—Since 1973"; there is a satchel labeled "Joyful Bag," a notebook with "Campus Fecund" on the cover, and a shopping bag with the legend, "Elephant family are popular with us. Their humming makes us feel happy."

At this point the tourist must stop and ponder. If a majority of Japanese cannot understand English, why this plethora? If people cannot read what is written on a shopping bag or T-shirt then why is English written there at all? The question will remain unanswered until the foreigner realizes that this written English is not intended to communicate what is written.

The Japanese young woman walking along, say, fashionable Omotesando in Tokyo, wearing on her T-shirted breast the latest American-import obscenity, does not intend to indicate that she too is consequently obscene. Unable to read what she has chosen to have written across her bust, her message—the true message of all written English in Japan—is quite different from what the words themselves indicate.

Briefly, the Japanese use of English means we are modern, we are progressive, we are fashionable. It also means that we would like to be thought of as being cosmopolitan enough to understand English even if we don't. In other words, English has become an accessory, just as a Dior belt or an Yves Saint Laurent scarf is an accessory. Indeed these fashionable items carry much the same connotations (modern, fashionable) as does English itself.

The *Oxford Dictionary* defines *accessory* as "additional, subordinately contributive, adventitious." The Japanese use of written English is truly adventitious since English actually comes from abroad (the literal meaning of *adventitious*) and it is used in a manner both "accidental" and "casual," two further extensions of the word.

Thus the English-decorated T-shirt or shopping bag informs others, accidentally perhaps, casually certainly, that the owner aspires to cosmopolitan modernity. The foreigner, finally understanding, sees that his language—if it is English—has become, in all of its richness, merely the indication of an attitude.

Having understood this, the tourist may then think that this made-in-Japan English compounds the affront by getting it all wrong. Mistakes in grammar and spelling, mood and tone abound, solecisms and oxymorons proliferate. This Japanese-English (referred to by those perpetrating it as *wasei eigo*) is so error ridden that only an assumption of massive ignorance could clarify if not condone.

In actuality, however, the *wasei eigo* does not get it all wrong. Given its ambitions it gets it all right. The reason is that it is not a variant of English but a variant of Japanese and is intended to express thoughts that standard Japanese cannot. One reason that *wasei eigo* is not often recognized as Japanese is that it looks and sounds so much like English that it is often mistaken for that tongue. Another is that we English speakers labor under the premise that language is for direct communication.

However, language has functions other than direct communication. There is indirect communication—at which *wasei eigo* excels. There is, as well, a whole nexus of suggestions that recent Japanese-English has created. For example, English used not for meaning but for effect.

To call such a vibrant creation incorrect presumes that correctness was originally desired. Such is not the case. After all, to get English right is to restrict its powers of expression. Precisely, correct usage limits language to its ordinary ways.

Wasei eigo (or "Janglish" to use a less cumbersome if somewhat pejorative term) insists upon the extraordinary. It was indeed the urge to capture this quality that led to the invention of this variant of Japanese. What was desired was a new tongue that could suggest nuances beyond the capability of the Japanese language itself—one that could speak in confident tones and yet not be tethered by meaning, one that could convincingly babble of modernity.

The products of this lingual coupling are now so inescapable that the beginnings of a grammatical codification should be possible. Like any language Janglish is forming its own rules and though no texts have so far appeared, one may at least make the beginnings of a linguistic enquiry.

First, a simple example of the utility of English in an area where Japanese is inadequate. It is still considered rudely egotistical to use the first-person possessive. *Watakushi no jidosha* ("my car") seems to suggest that my auto somehow takes preference over your car. *Watakushitachi no jidosha* ("our car") is no better if it implies "my family's car," as it always does. If the same phrase could be used to suggest both your car and my car, then it would be all right. But Japanese nouns do not have plurals. A solution to the problem then is to use Janglish. *Mai ka* is appropriately slipped into a Japanese sentence and in the process becomes itself a kind of Japanese. At the same time its plainly foreign origins absolve it of the egotism thought to be carried in all *watakushi no* constructions.

One may now move to a consideration of other aspects of the utility of Janglish and thus perhaps account for some of the reasons for its extraordinary popularity. Below are some of the limbs of the language, arranged in no particular order, but perhaps indicating the richness of the field.

THE LAW OF EUPHONY. An example is the popular advertising slogan "Healthy and Beauty." Its "wrongness" is apparent: an adjective cannot be linked to a noun through a conjunction. But the rightness ought also be apparent. The double "y" ensures agreement, a prized quality in Japan. The two words balance as Health and Beauty never could in English and the phrase becomes symbolic of a community endeavor. A new harmony, a linguistic euphony is created.

THE EXHORTATIVE MOOD. With a fully enforced euphony, it would follow that exhortation is a necessary mood, speaking as it does of a forceful and admonishing urging. Here are some examples of it in action. "Let's Kiosk" is a phrase found on all Japan Railway kiosks all over the country. The communal exhortative is its sole message. Likewise, *Let's Sex*, the title of a popular do-it-yourself manual. In both cases, it will be noted, the assumption is nonexclusive, nonelitist, and mandatory.

From such simple examples one may proceed to the more complicated. "Go on Powerful Poshboy Spirits," a slogan seen on a surprising number of sweatshirts, indicates a powerful exhortative appeal in which we can sense the onward aspiration even if we cannot fully formulate the subject. But such considerations are, of course, beside the point of Janglish. To ask of what a powerful poshboy might consist would be to hold back, through considerations of mere meaning, the flight of the forceful phrase and in the process completely misunderstand the aims of the utterance itself.

THE IMPERATIVE VOICE. Exhortation being the usual mood, it would follow that the voice is almost always imperative. And, since the Japanese language itself tends not to use relative pronouns, this "you (understood)" voice is appropriate.

For example, on a napkin: "Hey! This your useful friend, having simple and fashionable exciting, will be active in your life. Table Mate!" Or, the all-round (T-shirt, shopping bag) stern but popular: "Smiling do!"

Recently less peremptory wording has appeared. Here adjectives take (in proper Japanese fashion) the place of verbs. And since some open-mouthed vowel sounds ("*ee*") are perceived as attractive (*kawaii* = cute) the English "y" has been used to create such urging but at the same time reassuring brand names, such as Blendy (a canned coffee beverage) and Drafty (a canned beer).

THE ASSUMPTIVE STANCE. Another way to imperatively exhort is to assume that a desired euphony has been previously enforced, that we are thus already in full agreement about everything. Here we find a number of examples.

The slogan of a local hamburger chain says: "Of course I'm so happy." This happily implies that a desired accord has already occurred because (of course) if enough people announce that each is so happy, then we will indeed all be so happy.

This assumptive stance is seen not only in the emotional ("happy") message but also in others more neutral. That title of a popular TV series, *Naruhodo za warudo* (Of Course, the World), assures that nothing need threaten nor discommode because (*naruhodo*) we know it already, and our assumptive stance protects us from unpleasant surprises.

A variation of these assumptions of assumption is the popular ploy of agreeing that repetition doubles strength. Thus, the name of a popular hair-styling foam, "Free & Free," and the title of a popular magazine column, "Talk & Talk." One is familiar with the principle as used in the TV commercial that instantly repeats itself. There is with the Janglish version the advantage that it cannot be turned off.

THE COPULATIVE SHORTCUT. Japanese can be seen as a relatively simple language—at least structurally. As one authority has said, Japanese "manages to get by without certain connections considered indispensable in English."

No relative pronouns, adjectival clauses must precede nouns, nouns are not declined and have no gender, verbs have no specific reference to person or to number, adjectives act like verbs and are so conjugated with no reference to person, number, or gender.

In addition, verbs are linked by copulas. For example: *A wa B desu*. In English we would say, "Cats are animals." In Japanese this becomes "As for cats, they are animals." It is a construction, however, that is capable of great contraction. *Watakushi wa biru desu* means not "I am beer" but "I am having beer." This capability is widely used in Janglish, hence the grammatical (and mercantile) rightness of "I Feel Coke."

THE TELESCOPIC PLOY. Just as the Japanese language itself is constantly shortening its own parts and combining them to make new words, so Janglish shows a like aptitude for creative telescoping.

Many such constructions have now entered the language proper. For example, *apato* (apartment house) and *depato* (department store). Others, now no less Japanese, have been assigned new meanings. *Sumato* (smart) means "slim," *beteran* (veteran) means "expert," and what sounds like "axel" in English (*akuseru*) has become the accelerator. Among new examples of the commercial telescopic ploy would be Rinpoo, a hair-washing product combining "rinse" with "shampoo"; and Energan, a mouthwash combining (perhaps) "energy" and "elegance."

THE JAPANESE "ARTICLE." Lest we suspect that Janglish fails to respect the integrity of the English language, we ought to examine the way in which the problem of the article is solved.

No problem exists, to be sure, in that Japanese has no article, nor any need of one. In addition, Japanese nouns are uninflected, have neither number nor gender, and there is usually no special indication of plurality. What indeed would such a streamlined tongue do with an article? The problem is that English suffers under the strain of having not one but three: two indefinite and one definite.

The manner in which Janglish solves this problem is typical. It lies in the simple assertion that there is no problem. The English definite article is used for everything and in this manner everything becomes definite.

The Concert Hall is the name of an Osaka concert hall, *The Tokyo* is the name of a magazine, The Coffee is the name of—*naruhodo*—a coffee shop.

HIGH-DEFINITION "ENGLISH." One of the ways in which Janglish can be recognized is by the high-definition gloss it puts on English itself. This is accomplished in the approved post-modern manner of unexpected couplings. Pocari Sweat, the best-selling soft drink, is already well known, but few foreign scholars have been introduced to that recent brand of toilet tissue, Idol Care.

Another method of high-definition buffing is to wed an

English import to a *hayari kotoba* (vogue word), often also English. For example, another soft drink, Fuzzy Navel, takes the navel orange (English) and staples it to a recent buzz word "fuzzy" (as in "fuzzy logic") to create a brand name that defines itself as brand new.

Such cross-cutting is popular. There is the initially startling Dog & Croissant Store, where the dog is a hot dog. There is Nervous Care, which turns out to be a product for damaged hair. And there is the impressive Cosmodemi—For Your Amenity, descriptive (it transpires) of a new air conditioner.

All of these newly minted names and phrases indicate that the cutting edge of English is in Japan. It fully fits a world where you buy only brand names, where you freely and shamelessly demand attention, where selling is called an art, and where you wear someone else's name on your underwear. And any language that can directly order you to "Visit our Rooftop Bierkeller" is going to go a long way in today's world.

—*1995*

Mizushobai: The Art of Pleasing

Visitors to Japan are impressed not only by the social order and the cultural beauty of the country but also by the quality of the service. Waiters perform with a willing alacrity unknown in other lands, bar hostesses are solicitous to a degree foreign to the rest of the world, elevator girls bow to everyone, and the geisha, as is well known, have transformed ingratiating service into a high art—the art of pleasing.

In the West one hears of the customer's being always right, though he somehow never seems to be. In Japan, on the other hand, he definitely is. Almost any request is promptly gratified and a waiter has never been known to say, sorry, but this isn't his table. Even the unruly customer is right. The bartender will accept an insult with a smile, the waitress will accommodate public rudeness with affability, and no one—from the taxi driver on up—expects a tip.

It seems, to the first-time visitor at any rate, as though the art of pleasing is for its own sake, as though one portion of the population has elected to devote itself to creating a sense of powerful well-being in the other portion, and all for no ostensible extra reward. In Japan one is treated not only to superb service but also to service with a perfectly sincere smile.

This fact has much intrigued foreign visitors and has long taken its place among the mysteries of inscrutable Japan. Actually, however, there is nothing mysterious about it. The life of service has a venerable history in Japan and the attitudes proper to it have long been codified. An understanding of how it works, and what it means, demands only that one see the phenomenon from the Japanese point of view.

Japan, a country unusually given to categorization, traditionally divides its working force into two parts. The numerically larger half comprises the professions, white and blue collar alike, and all the crafts and industries attendant upon them. This half is sometimes—and in contradistinction to the other half—characterized as *katai shobai*, or, as we might paraphrase it, "steady work."

The other half is given over to the service professions. These include those professions which, for various reasons, *katai shobai* finds unsteady—cooks, waiters, actors, musicians, most of the traditionally female professions from coffee-shop girl to geisha, and many, many more.

This kind of work is called *mizushobai*, literally "water work," implying that these occupations are fluid and formless, unstable as water itself. The two terms have further nuances as well. *Katai shobai* is considered respectable; thus, by definition *mizushobai* is considered not. The man who drops out of the company in order to open a snack bar has committed an act close to social indecency.

Given this attitude one might wonder what attractions the *mizushobai* life could have for its members. Actually, however, the attractions are considerable. Decent, hardworking Japan is so very *katai* (this time in the word's other sense of being hard and unyielding) that the rat-race, rabbit-hutch life, no matter how respectable, begins to lose its allure.

The very fluidity of the *mizushobai* life is thus one of its appeals. One works as one likes, one takes time off as one can afford to, one no longer has a big-brother company looking over one's shoulder and demanding a proper attitude, proper marriage, proper children going to proper schools. In a sense *mizushobai* is a vast ghetto, and in this context, ghetto life is attractive.

Certainly, as well, the world of the *mizushobai* offers occupation to those who, underprivileged in various ways, cannot find "proper" work, particularly women who want to work and have no other place to go. Professional women are a token minority in Japan, and even they are often expected to make the tea for the men, in itself a *mizushobai*-like undertaking.

How much more attractive the life of a bar hostess, where one can make in one evening as much as during a month in the office and all without (contrary to public opinion) having to please to the *full* extent the customer's wishes. These unmindful assumptions of the proper public, and even the occasional insult, are a small price indeed for the freedom and the monetary rewards of these professions—at least in their upper if not in their lower reaches. If one owns a lucrative bar or "snack," if one becomes a famous screen or TV entertainer, the rewards are great and any public disapproval not too difficult to bear.

In addition, the *mizushobai* professionals, like the medieval guild members who they resemble, have their own ways of being decent and taking a proper pride in their work. Tips are never demanded and are accepted only in return for extraordinary services—the porter who had had to go all the way to the station for the trunk, or the geisha who, having received four fur coats and two convertibles, decides to give in.

Mizushobai thus offers the hardworking Japanese an alternative to the big-business style of life. In this it is no different from what it has always been. The "willow world" of the Tokugawa period with its actors and wrestlers and courtesans and palanquin bearers, glimpsed in the prints of Hokusai or Hiroshige, was much the same and performed similar services.

Mizushobai remains a way out of the samurai/businessman life and, at the same time, offers the means to an often well-paying profession. The art of pleasing, with its own standards, its own integrity, is a profession in itself.

—*1981*

Some Thoughts on Car Culture in Japan

The Japanese may not have invented the wheel but they certainly went on to perfect it. Just look around. Japanese wheels abound. There is not, I think, a single country in the world, emerged or emerging, that does not have its quota. The names of Honda, Toyota, Nissan, Isuzu, Suzuki—all are known everywhere: cars from Japan.

The history of the vehicular wheel in this archipelago is long. First references are to be found in that ancient but politically correct Japanese history, the *Nihonshoki*, and in the later *Manyoshu* poetry collection. Both, fittingly, refer to methods of transportation—probably the two-wheeled ox-cart, early Chinese models having perhaps been adapted by the Japanese. But, and here we see early prowess, by their using a much more efficient Japanese-invented double-shaft yoke.

It was also the Japanese (say the Japanese) who invented the later and even more efficient *jinrikisha*, that vehicle that came into general use around the end of the nineteenth century. This improved model boasted a real Japanese internal-combustion engine—that is, it was a real Japanese who pulled it.

As is indicated in the name. *Jinriki* means man-power and *sha* means vehicle. The method was said to have been inspired by the horse-drawn carriage, which had just been introduced from abroad. Japan did not have many horses but it had lots of people and the rickshaw (as it is still called in other countries) was—after governmental permission was received in 1870—produced in quantity.

One of the reasons for the popularity was the means of public transportation that it had replaced. This was the *kago,* a palanquin born on the shoulders of two or four men, depending on the weight inside. No wheels were involved, the runners bodily carried it, and the journey was expensive to the passenger and exhausting for the carriers. The rickshaw, comfortable and cheap, was shortly so popular that it was exported to Shanghai, Hong Kong, and other South Asian cities. There it took such root that even now many think the vehicle a Chinese invention.

In the land of its birth, however, it did not last so long. After the Tokyo Earthquake of 1923, the rickshaw completely disappeared—taken over by the automobile. It made a reappearance after the defeat of 1945, however, in the form of the *rintaku*, a bike-drawn cab, also now long gone. It is presently seen in its original form only at tourist sites (Kamakura, the Asakusa Kannon Temple in Tokyo, Arashiyama in Kyoto) where one is at considerable expense pulled about by young part-time workers.

*

The first steam automobiles were imported from the United States in 1897. By 1902 two business partners, Yoshida Shintaro and Uchiyama Komanosuke, had produced a trial car with a two-cylinder, twelve-horsepower American engine. In 1904 one Torao Yamaha was manufacturing the first two-cylinder steam auto in Okayama, to be followed in 1907 by Tokyo Jidosha Seisakusho's first domestic gasoline-fueled car. In 1912 Kaishinsha, a company established by Masujiro Hashimoto, produced one named the Dattogo.

These, however, were all trial models—as was the Otomogo, created in 1920 by the Hakuyosha plant. By 1923, however, some 250 of this model had been created, the largest total production of any make in Japan during these years. This was also the year of the Tokyo Earthquake, an event that hit all industries hard.

Not only was production curtailed but imported cars, almost

entirely from the United States, soon flooded what market existed. This was encouraged by the government's purchasing of a number of Model T Fords—the auto of choice since Ford had moved into the Japanese market as early as 1903. These were remodeled into mini-busses (the popular Entaro bus), which proved the only means of public transportation within the devastated city.

Scenting a market, both Ford and General Motors established subsidiary companies in Japan by 1925. Five years later some sixteen thousand new American cars were annually running around the islands. It was not until 1933 that the native industry could even boast one thousand locally sold.

That the Japanese automobile industry was so swiftly left behind by foreign competition is to be attributed to the backwardness of Japan's industrial technology, particularly that involving machine tooling. The few companies that existed were, despite commendable early activity, all considered bad risks and few of the established financial and industrial combines (such as Mitsui and Mitsubishi) wanted to make any commitments.

The Japanese military authorities were, on the other hand, pressing for a locally made car. Actually, it was trucks they wanted and though the large combines resisted the pressure, new, small companies (Nissan, Toyota, later Isuzu) were being licensed by 1935.

After the beginning of WWII the government and the now more enthusiastic combines closed ranks and Mitsubishi Heavy Industries, Ltd., did its share in producing necessary trucks, as well as planes and weaponry. It continued even after the war was lost, encouraged by the Allied Occupation authorities who had a vested interest in getting the company back on its feet, or at least on its wheels.

After the war, production was almost entirely trucks. People either walked, took streetcars or busses, or hired the fume-emitting charcoal-fueled taxis, which were to be seen on all streets until the late 1940s. By this time, however, another war was looming (the Korean conflict), which was good economic news for everyone (except the Koreans), and Japan, taking advantage of the military procurements boom, began manufacturing passenger cars.

This was around 1952, and shortly after the government began its own policy of support/protection of the domestic auto industry. The Ministry of International Trade and Industry (MITI) provided no money but it did ensure favorable allocations of foreign currency and began to restrict vehicle imports.

As a result, by 1960 the domestic production of passenger cars increased. More companies—Fuji Heavy Industries (makers of the Subaru and the Prince), Toyo Kogyo (the Mazda), and Honda (which also made motorcycles)—climbed on board. Strategic models (Crown, Cedric, Corona, Bluebird) were designed for high-volume production and by 1965 the auto industry was here to stay.

The rate of production was enormous. In 1955 only twenty thousand cars were made and a mere two were exported. Twenty-five years later in 1980, seven million were made and nearly four million exported. This steep success continued on and on until overextended Japan's economic collapse in the 1990s.

To keep up with the number of new automobiles being sold, new methods of accommodation were sought. Roads were built, often to nowhere and over unnecessary bridges, simply to have somewhere to drive. Parking space diminished to the point where prime land found its most advantageous market as car-park property. "My Car" was pushed as a theme and it soon seemed that every man, woman, and child on the archipelago owned one.

*

It would probably be unfair to blame the automobile industry alone for the massive despoiling of the country during the latter decades of the past century and coming years of this one. There are other factors such as governmental pork-barreling, a destructive alliance between construction companies and local governments, and unbridled "development," which saw even national park land pressed into service. At the same time, however, as in many other countries, it was the coming of the automobile that heralded a wholesale destruction of the environment such as Japan had hitherto seen only in such natural disasters as earthquakes and such unnatural ones as wars.

The government attempted to cope. The horrendous traffic conditions in Tokyo (plus a level of industrial pollution so high that it is said nylon stockings ran on women's legs) was brought under control. New trains and subways took the pedestrian flow, and a system of elevated highways siphoned off much of the car glut. By 1964 (year of the Olympic Games in Tokyo) auto flow (which had often, Bangkok-like, stopped cold) was again possible.

Later, despite a runaway economy (first, running straight up, then running straight down), there was some attempt made to temper the depredations of the auto. A recall system to improve auto safety has been established. Laws now deal, in a way, with pollution. There is an emphasis upon saving fuel in the small energy-saving cars presently being pushed—partly through a steep gasoline law. The brightest hope of the nation is the darkest fear of the industry. Car business is nothing like it was in the so-called "bubble era." People cannot now afford the product.

Koichi Shimakawa, to whom I have turned for some information in these pages, maintains that "the industry will now have to make a transition from a period of simple quantitative growth to a period of qualitative improvement." And so it must. If it can.

The car has truly changed Japan's culture just as it has that of many countries. There are, however, a few differences. Family outings may be more frequent than they were, but drive-ins never caught on. Nor did the phenomenon of a lover's lane packed with parked autos—since Japan is already equipped for this purpose with the ubiquitous "love hotel." Shopping, however, is much facilitated—at least in the suburbs. In the city itself parking is usually thought too much of a problem.

The car-packed metropolises of Japan have yet to designate "carless" days, and the always unpopular alternate-driving-day plan was never even suggested, much less implemented. And there are no nondriving zones. Any street wide enough to take a car is already full of them.

At the same time there are some tokens that at least the problem is seen as a problem. Many large-city thoroughfares now have carless Sundays (10 a.m.–6 p.m.). Despite some police complaints (the rerouting problems are considerable) and also from merchants (until they discovered that more patrons than usual took advantage of the weekly Pedestrian Paradise) the custom continues and offers a few hours of respite.

*

Most inventions are intended to create advantages for those inventing them. Man-made fire cooks meat, etc. An invention such as the wheel was an attempt to mold space and time into shapes more conducive to human comfort. Few have ever argued against these inventions, which so change our environment and yet wholesale dispensation of space and time has both advantages and disadvantages.

We take the former for granted and sometimes complain (though never seriously) about the latter. The automobile is too convenient for anyone to seriously doubt its virtues. It gets, say, the child to the hospital in time to save its life. If we still had to rely on the doctor and his buggy the tyke would be dead in its bed by the time he got there. About the adverse results of mass automobilization, however, we have less to say.

Indeed, so completely has the car created our environment that we have, with scarcely a thought, shaped how and where we live according to its demands. We live in the suburbs and we drive in to work, the kids are bussed to schools, the parents shop at the mall. Without the car this suburban life would not be possible. It might not even have been necessary since the flight to the suburbs was both cause and effect of the collapsing city center.

Since everyone has a car no one rides public transport and it consequently becomes too expensive to maintain. In a city like Los Angeles, if you do not have wheels you might as well have no feet. For people with no automobiles, space stretches impossibly vast and the time taken to get anywhere is endless. At the same time, for those with wheels it is common (in Texas, I hear) to take an hour and drive a hundred miles simply to eat at a chosen restaurant.

The car has created its own space. We are all, everywhere, used to (and grateful for) the ingenious highway systems that cut through forests, cross mountains, span bays. Thruways slice up our cities, yet few complain when the needs of the auto so destroy and create such hardship.

I am thinking of Seoul, where the needs of the car have destroyed all the old sections of the city and where the carless must, at every city-center crossing, clamber down stairs to a tunnel and, on the other side, climb up from it. Likewise, in Japanese cities the carless are forced to climb high bridges that span busy highways and then descend. They are called by the more elderly "heart-attack machines." Down, up—up, down. This is a true disadvantage and yet none complain. Or if they do they are in such a minority—mere pedestrians—that their voices are not heard.

Yet, though the bane of car culture is omnipresent, the forms it takes are various. A country like Japan experiences the automobile in a manner different from some Western countries. Let us count the ways.

Though car/truck traffic is ubiquitous in this archipelago there is the difference that distances are not great. There is no question of driving an hour to dine. Big four-lane highways do run up and down the main islands but sheer geographical length is broken up and thus that temporal quality, sheer speed, is limited. In addition there are the tollbooths. Japanese highways are designed to be expensive. In most countries once the road is paid for it becomes free. Not here. Highways are perpetual money machines. The results are said to go into "upkeep."

Another difference is that in Japan the automobile has not cancelled out public transportation. Indeed Japan has one of the best public transportation systems in the world—the famous bullet trains, all sorts of inter-city "interurbans," the finest of subways and inner-city train systems, and an admirable bus system.

A major reason for this is that there are too many people for all of them to be driving at once. The equivalent of half the population of the United States is crammed into an area a little less than California. If everyone took to the road (as everyone does in, say, the United States), terminal gridlock would be nationwide.

Another reason for the excellence of Japan's public transportation system is that it is widely used. It is not given over to the poor and otherwise underprivileged, whose small numbers would eventually force it into bankruptcy. It is used because having a car can actually be an inconvenience. Car parks cost as much as hotels, police routinely tow away street parkers, insurance is high, and car taxes are higher. Consequently "My Car" is not used as much as its Western equivalent.

On the two times that it is, the effect is at once perceived. This is at New Year's and the mid-summer vacation week when all the city dwellers return to the country, the *furusato*, the hometown. Since they drive (the whole family goes; the car is a lot cheaper than train or bus), all Japan appears to be on the highway at these times.

The result is a national traffic jam of Bangkokian proportions. "Delays" up to half a day or longer are common, the whole family crammed into "My Car," fretting and bickering throughout their holidays. And no sooner do they finally, eventually, arrive at their rural destination than it is time to drive back, the dreaded "U-turn," where getting back into the city is even more traumatic than getting out of it was.

Except for these two periods of automotive excess, however, Japan is relatively free of the damage that the private car has elsewhere inflicted on public transportation. At the same time the ubiquitous auto has introduced values that have done much to degrade traditional Japanese attitudes and, I think, virtues.

*

Let me explain. Ideas of space and time inform every culture. Japanese traditional culture was noted for the way in which these ideas were used. The haiku, for example, depicts the crux between the two. To use a common example, this famous lyric of Basho:

> *An old pond: a frog jumps in—the sound of water.*

Here, in Hiroaki Sato's single-line translation, we have the conjunction. First, the spatial setting, then the temporal event. We contrast the two and appreciate—splash—their coincidence. For us to do so we must conceive them, momentarily, as opposites brought miraculously together by their correspondence.

To make this occur we must have, perhaps like Basho himself, been sitting there for some time since frogs are not continually jumping into ponds. Our assumption is that the moment is privileged. We have been sitting quietly in one place (space is empty) and suddenly the equally vacant flux in which we live (time is empty) is stamped, signed, sealed, by the extraordinary occurrence of a single sound that makes us aware for an instant of our true spatial and temporal position.

To explain in such a manner is, of course, to destroy the poem. It is about sudden apprehension, not laborious interpretation. But it does help us understand that it would not have occurred at all had Basho been in My Car. Even if he had driven to the lake and hung around a while it would not have been the same thing. In all likelihood the only frog he would have seen would have been road kill.

This is because the point of the poem is that the conjunction was not searched for. Basho was not going anyplace at the time. He was not thinking about his destination. Indeed, during the whole trip along the narrow road to the deep north getting anyplace was not the point. The journey, which came out shaped something like a circle, not the destination, was the point.

I suppose it is possible to aimlessly drive, going nowhere. There are such things as family outings in the family car and adolescent joy rides in the hot rod. I do not, however, believe that these are considered major employments of the automobile. They certainly aren't in Japan.

A result is that what occurred regularly to Basho and his contemporaries now occurs to very few. One cannot completely blame the automotive industry for this—there have been too many other changes. At the same time, however, the automobile has played its part in the redefinition of time and space, which has not only filled in most old ponds but has also made their contemplation unlikely.

*

AN ILLUSTRATIVE PARALLEL. For most of its existence Japan has been a poor country. There are few natural resources and it was early overpopulated. While there have been a wealthy few, the majority were those whom we would now find financially challenged. Indeed, so general was this situation that an entire culture rose, which, it could be argued, was based upon want.

Lots of mud and so, with help from Korea, extraordinary pottery. Lots of space but no furniture, and so the concept of *ma*. Space itself as not an absence but a presence. And an aesthetic vocabulary which stressed *l'art pauvre*. The aesthetic term *sabi* can mean not only the rusted, but also the lovingly worn, the patina given by use; *wabi* can mean the elegant loneliness of the common, the singularity of the aesthetically quotidian; and the mysterious and beautiful *yugen* can arise when the everyday meets, in some time-worn way, the eternal.

This state of affairs continued from around the sixth century to approximately the 1960s. Then Japan began to become wealthy—not just the privileged few but the common many. The era now termed "bubble" (a structure bound by definition to burst) found Japan buying everything in sight including the Rockefeller Center and the more famous golf courses. The country at large in a decade became nouveau riche and all those centuries of *maigre* beauty became beside the point.

Among signs of new affluence was the automobile. The rise of the mighty industry coincided with this extraordinary enriching of the citizens. Considerations of space, time, beauty, and life itself would never again be the same.

*

One can offer no solutions since the situation itself cannot encompass one. And of course many in Japan would not believe that one is required. Certainly any proposed solution would have to be impracticably radical. A radical solution would be to wait until the time machine is available (a mere matter of time) and then return and murder Henry Ford in his crib. This is unlikely, and is further impractical in that no such Japanese Luddites exist.

One may then, as Basho might have, adjust to things as they are. Few ponds, fewer frogs, but getting there faster, on time, efficiently, economically. At the same time one might also reflect upon the fact that the triumph of the wheel is a mixed achievement for its users.

—2002

The Window and the Mirror:
Some Thoughts on International Culture

When talking about cultural exchange one often uses the metaphor of the window, that domestic opening onto a foreign vista, which provides a view leading to understanding, appreciation, accord.

The metaphor is appropriate in a double sense. A window undoubtedly provides an educative view, and it also—by its very shape and size—a partial one. A single window is not large enough to contain another culture, and no cultural exchange can or should be total.

Culture, after all, is—*Webster*'s primary definition—the totality of socially transmitted behavior patterns, arts, beliefs, institutions, and all other productions of human work and thought. No window on the world could properly embrace all this.

This fact is widely accepted and rationalized. There is an agreement that culture is—*Webster*'s second definition—intellectual and artistic activity and the works produced by it. This is agreed upon as self-evident, that an exchange of such concepts, ideas, and information is both necessary and beneficial, and that the window is quite wide enough for this burden.

So it is, but while agreeing I would still like to point out that the resulting view remains deficient. Often what is exchanged are examples or samples deemed typical or representative. They stand for not only themselves but also for their class. They are taken out of their context, even if the context is what gave them their meaning. The view through the window sometimes ignores the integrity of what is being seen.

This is understood. That is the way windows work—otherwise doors might be the common metaphor. Information must be in some sense abstracted in order to be communicated at all. This is because, in cultural exchange, as in all other kinds of exchange, it is necessary that there be both a sender and a receiver, both sending and receiving at the same time. Again there is no major problem. But there is a certain deficiency.

The deficiency has a number of facets. One, as mentioned, is that context is sometimes ignored. Another is that senders may select not what they consider the essence of their culture but only those portions of it that they believe the receivers will be capable of understanding.

The history of cultural exchange is rich with such examples. To choose merely among those that Japan early perpetuated: It was locally agreed that foreigners could well appreciate Nikko but could not understand Ise. And, indeed, there were several reasons for such belief. Early foreign travelers sometimes admired Nikko because its architecture so reminded them of beloved Victorian bric-a-brac.

Again, when kimono were first exported to the West, it was those gaudily alive with dragons and tigers that were sent, since it was understood that the West was incapable of understanding anything more tasteful, subdued, or, indeed, typical.

To be sure, such early exchange was usually more actively commercial than intentionally cultural, and so some evaluation of the buying power of the market had to be considered. If dragons sold, then dragons were sent. Such considerations still exist.

One sees that, even now, cultural exchange carries a subtext that, if not overtly commercial, is still sometimes covertly political. For example, the cultural examples sent should not contain items of which no one approves. Indeed, those that show the sender in a politically bad light are by definition not to be transmitted.

Another facet of the problem of deficiency is that a sender unwittingly conveys only those sections of the culture that constitute his or her self-image. In this sense the window then becomes a mirror and the satisfied sender views the self-image that he wants to see. The United States posits itself upon assumptions of youth. Consequently it often sends the latest products, the newest exemplars.

It will send rock music or, if the intention is more serious, the popular Philip Glass rather than the more serious (and much older) Elliott Carter.

Through this underwriting of youth as virtue, the United States transmits a cultural projection that shows itself as it wants to be seen. So do all other countries—the difference is merely one of degree.

If the choice is, as I have indicated, that between the window and mirror, it is perhaps better then to send not isolated examples of the representative, but rather to transmit the means by which another culture may be more fairly and fully understood, since understanding is the agreed-upon aim of all cultural exchange.

(And here I use "understanding" in its dictionary sense of "comprehending the meaning of" and not in its occasional Japanese sense where "understanding" means merely "agreeing with.")

Certainly it is best to exchange the means of language itself—for the Japanese sender to encourage the study of the Japanese language, to encourage those abroad who are researching the totality of aspects of Japanese culture. Best of all would be to dispatch and to receive self-contained units of culture.

By which I mean people—Japanese who carry within themselves the context of their culture and are not overly driven by a desire to please the recipient or the need to gratify their own of idea of themselves; foreigners, equally open-minded, who want to contribute to a study of their own culture or this culture in which they will now for a time live.

The window is then stepped through and the mirror turns transparent. International cultural exchange will never be perfect but it is always perfectly possible.

—*2005*

An Alternative Way of Thought

It was in 1947 that I was first aware that Japan was offering me a way of thought different from those I had come with. It was at Engaku-ji, sitting with Dr. Daisetz Suzuki. Sitting not *seiza* in the *zendo*, but on the sofa in his study, it having been agreed (with no words at all) that I was not *zazen* material.

Every Sunday I would sit often all alone in the white-striped Allied car on the Yokosuka Express looking at the Japanese jam-packed in the cars on either side, would get off at Kita-Kamakura and, bearing gifts, call on my *sensei*.

The gifts were boxes of crackers, assorted processed cheeses, peanut clusters—things that the PX could contrive in the way of offerings. These Dr. Suzuki would receive and then disappear into the back of his house. Upon his return I would be given a cup of tea and some conversation.

I stared at my *sensei*. Given his appearance alone he would have had no recourse but to embrace Zen. With his high forehead and his fuzzy eyebrows, he looked even in old age like one of those acolytes—Jittoku, for example—who in many a scroll and screen cavorts as he sweeps the garden or baits the *roshi*. Always in kimono, always the same one, Suzuki *sensei* looked like an acolyte suddenly become a patriarch. He was the very picture of Zen.

I was the very picture of something else. Twenty-three years old, young for my age, I was at Engaku-ji waiting for something to happen to me, convinced that mere attendance would be enough. I was, in my own way, being virtuous. Benefits would accrue if I were simply there. It was like being busy for its own sake, a sound bourgeois superstition to which I unthinkingly subscribed.

Dr. Suzuki knew, of course, all about my disability. He was well practiced in talking about Zen to those who had no aptitude for it. So, wordlessly, I was moved from to the *tatami* to the sofa. While the other *deshi* sat in the lotus position in the *zendo*, I was seated comfortably with him. There he talked and I listened, hoping that some of this learning would rub off on me. In the end he gave me a definite taste for something he knew I could not eat.

For, as I sat hopefully listening, I realized that I was not understanding. It was not the fault of the language—Dr. Suzuki's English was better than my own.

Rather, it was the fault, if that is the term, of the young postulant sitting there with him on the sofa.

I knew only one way to think, that which was common back where I came from—the United States and the rest of the West. Though I was a member of the forces then occupying Japan I was beginning to detect the limitations of the way I thought.

My English-speaking Japanese teacher had already countered one of my arguments with "No, you are just being logical."

Just? Applied to logic, the diadem of Western thought? Aristotle's gift to the ages? Yet, in Japan, I was discovering that logic was not enough, and that "logical" (*ronriteki*) was a term of disparagement. Also I was being prepared for what Dr. Suzuki now disclosed.

We always talked about Zen and it became gradually evident that I was not understanding a word. Or, rather, it was the words alone that I understood. Each word, even each sentence, made sense but none of the paragraphs did. Other Zen discourses I had heard— Ruth Sasaki's, for example—were logical, rational, one thought leading plainly to the next. Dr. Suzuki's were something else.

The process seemed associative, one thing linked to another by something other than meaning. Yet, when examined, the seemingly fortuitous had become organic, and when looked at again it became inevitable. I did not apprehend the governing structure but I did grasp that I was being offered a new way of understanding. And as I listened I understood that there were modes of thought different from the one I had always known and thought unique.

This was really all that I ever learned from Dr. Suzuki, but it was of the greatest importance. I had learned to mistrust my pre-conceptions. My prior methods were not enough. I must allow for other methods of comprehension. What had once seemed necessary now seemed arbitrary. That "great ball of doubt" of which Zen speaks turned out to be myself.

I slowly became aware of this new way of regarding—new to me at any rate. Actually, it was widely known. Zen scripture is filled with examples, but so is other, Western, literature. Here is Victor Shklovsky, one of the Russian formalists: we should impart "the sen-sation of things as they are perceived and not as they are known." Here is Paul Cézanne: "Paint what you see is there, not what you know is there."

And here was Dr. Suzuki showing me through his discourse that there are ways of apprehending that depend not upon patterns of logic but upon something closer to the shape of things themselves, something that would allow me to respect their original integrity.

One Sunday, near the end, my *sensei* mildly remarked: "You are very much of this world, very much of this flesh." Then he smiled and that smile was a way of shaking an understanding head at the ways of the world.

And I understood at once—it was a kind of illumination—that I had no vocation and never would, not because anything was miss-ing but because I would never summon up the necessary discipline, not because it was impossible—nothing is impossible—but simply because it was unlikely.

A true vocation would have made it possible to see what was

actually there, not what it thought it knew was there. And this I did not have. But I had apprehended that there were alternatives to me and my habitual way of thought, that there were alternative ways through which something like reality could be apprehended.

This was Dr. Suzuki's parting gift to me and it was of inestimable value.

—2005

Foreign Thoughts on Watching the Passing of a *Matsuri* Procession

The foreigner watching a folk festival, a *matsuri*, is delighted and excited. Something familiar is being sensed, but it cannot quite be named. At the same time this viewer is vaguely disturbed. Something seems not quite right. Looking about, the foreigner decides that this is because the *matsuri* is being held in front of modern buildings, in the midst of ordinary traffic, beneath the electric wires of the contemporary Japanese city.

Traditional *omikoshi* floats are being born by naked men in the loincloths and half-coats of family from the prints of Hokusai and Hiroshige. Yet these are mixed in with the contemporary activities of everyone else. This disturbs foreigners particularly if they are trying to take pictures. They find themselves searching for angles that do not include buildings, electric wires, other people. They then realize that they want to separate the traditional *matsuri* from its contemporary background.

Why, they would then perhaps wonder, was it important to take pictures showing the festival but indicating nothing of the contemporary life in the midst of which it takes place? Then these foreigners would perhaps realize that they were thinking of the *matsuri* as something different from modern life, and that the other viewers, the Japanese, were not.

Then, perhaps, they would understand the reason why. It is because the *matsuri* is a part of everyday life, no matter if the *omikoshi* is brought out only once a year and that the young people wear their *fundoshi* and *hanten* on no other day. A *matsuri* is not something dead, to be viewing only in a folk arts museum. It is something alive to be seen every year on the streets of Japan.

Other counties have their own seasonal *matsuri* but these are often solemn, quiet, staid, historical, and in some cases dead. But to view the typical city *matsuri*—Tokyo's Asakusa Sanju, Shinagawa's Kappa, the Kanda Myojin festivals—is to see the difference. The ordinary Japanese festival is filled with contemporary life. There is shouting and pushing, exertion and exhaustion, there is a packed, disorderly throng, and there is nakedness—flesh against flesh, a sure sign of life. The Japanese *matsuri* is so different from the staid processions of Europe and America that the pondering foreigner must realize that something real and vital has, somehow, survived directly into our own times.

The gods in Western processions are carried slowly and reverently, like corpses. The god in the *omikoshi*, however, is bounced up and down like an infant—he, like all babies, likes to be tossed into the air. He is no corpse—he is an infant deity, full of life and promise. And this, the foreigner decides, is fitting because the *matsuri* signalizes not only the birth of the new year, the coming of spring, the advent of the full harvest, but also the birth of religion itself.

Those in the Western procession proceed with solemn tread; self-important, each individual is also part of a social occasion. Those in the Japanese *matsuri* weave as though drunk under their burden. And there are no individuals—each member is merged into the mass, that many-legged-and-armed creature carrying the god. Each individual has willingly submerged himself and happily becomes another pair of arms, another pair of legs. He is no longer himself, he is outside himself—one with the others, one with the god.

The *matsuri* is no civic occasion. It is an eruption of raw, chaotic life into the measured, restricted city. Watching, foreigners feel a vitality, a nearness to nature, that in their own countries seems to have been forgotten, except for the uglier manifestations—gangs, mobs, war.

It also displays an important paradox. Just as this ancient and traditional *matsuri* occurs in front of a modern, contemporary background, so the mystery of religion, its concern with death and with life, is embodied through the mundane health and high spirits of the *omikoshi* carriers. It is a ceremony where the common and the vulgar become the vehicle for the obscure and the profound. It is the yearly mating of the transient with the abstract eternal.

A thoughtful foreigner remembers something he once read. "And within the thick white and scarlet ropes, within the guard rails of black lacquer and gold, behind those fast-shut doors of gold leaf, there is a four-foot cube of pitch-blackness." The author—who was it?—was writing of the *omikoshi* and noticing its strange calm. The black and empty weight seems to stabilize the motion. The shouting, heaving men are like the waves on which rides, serene, this "cube of empty night."

The foreigner suddenly remembers. It was Yukio Mishima, in *Confessions of a Mask*. At the same time this foreigner again recalls a prior feeling, that the *matsuri* is somehow familiar to him. Then he recalls. It reminds him of childhood, that time when one does not yet know of civilization or other form of socialized order. The *omikoshi* is empty because the god is reborn every year.

The foreigner ponders the paradoxes: a traditional festival still so alive that it can take place right in the middle of contemporary city life; a strange but natural combination of vulgar activity and unearthly stillness; a coupling of flesh (that most transient of human attributes) and spirit (which alone can transcend the generations); a combination of the mundane and the sublime, the transient and timeless.

Standing on the street corner the foreigner watches the *matsuri* procession pass. The drum and the flute, the shouts and scuffling, fade into the distance; city life at once resumes as though this ancient vision had never occurred. The foreigner, turning to go, pauses to think: It is only through the mundane that the eternal can still be glimpsed.

Japan has somehow kept alive what its own acquired modern civilization has attempted to kill. Perhaps this is because it still acknowledges its own early beginnings, and displays, if only once a year, one of the most paradoxical and important of human truths. The foreigner is grateful but he does not congratulate Japan for this. It is despite official "Japan" that the *matsuri* still exists.

At this point the foreigner (myself) suddenly remembers his camera. He has taken only a few pictures. But then photographs cannot capture the spirit of the *matsuri*. Only its picturesque exterior would be there—the eternal core would still be as black as the inside of the *omikoshi* itself. One cannot carry home souvenirs from a real religious experience.

The foreigner listens. Above the growls of the passing cars, beneath the roar of the overhead jet, he hears the final distant shouts of the distant *omikoshi* bearers. They are as far away as sudden memories of childhood, but as piercing as the joy they bring, the instant apprehension of the illogical beauty of existence.

—*1985*

My View

I live in a small apartment overlooking Shinobazu Pond in Ueno.
From my eighth-floor balcony I look down at Little Lotus and its
lotus, over to the Benzaiten temple, on to Ueno Park, and (on clear
days) off to the Chichibu mountain range. It is visible today, far away,
and snow covered since it is now so cold. Winter—and it seems
just yesterday that the pond below me was filled with great green
lotus leaves and the pink budding of the flowers, the very image of
summer.

But then the seasons in Japan have a certain solidity. I have lived
in this country long enough to know—the day when it suddenly
decides to be spring, the day summer stops in its tracks and even the
light is different, the day (like today) when the mountains are visible,
the snow already there.

Like many foreigners living here I too have been amused at my
Japanese friends insisting upon their four seasons and wondering
if my country did not find four seasons odd. Amused, because all
countries in the temperate zones have four seasons and their asking
seemed to indicate that they did not know this.

But now I understand what is meant. The Japanese seasons have
a certain solidity. Summer is indubitable and there is a rainy season
to prove it. Winter is uniformly chill, like a woven garment, all of a
piece. The seasons have an integrity here that seems to make them
particular.

Why should this be, I wonder. But then, looking from my high
window out over the largest expanse of trees in this whole enormous
city, I know. It is because for so many centuries, so many generations, Japan had really only one guide. This was nature—things as

they are, as they must be. Japan accepted the constraints of the way things are.

Seasons untampered with are seasons clearly differentiated. But many other countries were not satisfied with this. They wanted man to dominate, not nature. And so forests were cut down, weather was disregarded, mountains leveled, rivers straightened—all so that men could make a profit.

Japan was not wealthy enough back then to do this. It had to make do with what nature wanted. I remember something that seemed a paradigm of this. Near my house some workers were making a wall next to a grove of trees. One of the trees had a low-hanging branch. In other countries the solution would have been to cut off the branch. In the Japan of fifty years ago these workers solved their problem by making a hole in the new wall in order to accommodate the branch.

But would they now, I wonder? It is in Japan as elsewhere much more economical to destroy than it is to accommodate. In modern Japan we now tear down old buildings because it is cheaper to raze than it is to rebuild.

Now Japan has become rich enough to join the despoilers. The country has been "developed," most of Japan's coastline has been contained, all but one of the major rivers has been straightened and dams installed, much of the native forest has been cut down, and the land is filled with great empty bridges, and long expensive highways that no one uses.

As I look out over Ueno Park, this small patch of what is left of nature in the center of Tokyo, I wonder how one can retain this naturalness in the modern world. There is no going back. You can take the concrete off the riverbank but the stream is never the same. You can replant vanished forests with cedar trees but you only increase the pollen count. Indeed you can only preserve what little you have left.

*

I get out my camera, unfold my tripod. If I frame my picture properly there is a bit of the brown pond, the dead leaves, then the last color of autumn in the surrounding trees, and over them the greenish tan of the park and above it this line of snow-covered mountains, which is so barely visible. Snap—I have taken my picture ("Nature in Ueno Park") and can show it to friends as though to prove that nature still exists in this enormous city of Tokyo. But I have done something else too.

I have preserved nature—not nature itself but by providing a simulacrum I have maintained its semblance, the shell of what once was. If this pond had been drained to make an underground parking lot, the temple turned into a boutique, and the mountains are no longer visible in the smog, my little photo would attest to what was. It would be proof.

That is what photos and movies do—they prove. I look at a photograph of the Ginza in the late Meiji era, everyone in kimono, a streetcar here or there. This is as it was. I look at a newsreel taken in the early Taisho period, and there are automobiles and fedoras and a man turns and looks straight into the lens, looks straight at me. He didn't know that he was looking into the future but I know that I am looking into the past.

But am I? Film—still pictures, moving pictures—are illusions. There are only shadows on the paper, on the screen. Like the shadows in Plato's cave, conjured up, they instantly vanish. But I can look at the picture I have taken, now a time capsule since it is already in the past. Holding it up I can compare it with this new present, which has raced up to me. But already my present is no longer there, it is past.

Looking down I see that two of the homeless have found brooms and are carefully sweeping the plaza, the steps down to the water, the paths. They are not paid for this. It is voluntary labor. Why, I wonder. Perhaps if they police their place the cops will let them stay undisturbed—but the cops do anyway. No, I think it is because working is all they know and their enforced idleness is a terrible punishment for them. So they find brooms and in the middle of the night sweep. If they were given buckets and brushes they would scrub.

My empty past has joined this meaningful present. The unfortunate homeless are putting themselves back together through meaningful meaningless work. I am looking at my handicraft, my photo, and the season majestically moves on, the leaves fall and the pond turns winter-dark.

*

It is late afternoon and the winter light is already fading. I stand in the growing dark by my window and look at all the borrowed scenery: the entire park hanging there.

And I remember that when I was sixteen or so, over sixty-five years ago, I was writing something about a park. It was to be an allegory and the protagonist, then a child, entered the park in the morning under the bright sun. Around noon he, much older, would meet a girl and they would continue their walk together, then it would rain. In the evening, still older yet, he would lose the girl in some dark path and finally come to the exit. The park was closing.

So, I suggested, this is man's life—from the bright morning opening of the park to the dark, final, twilight closing. And now it is really late afternoon for me but Ueno Park never closes and I stand at the window and look at the sight as though it is some kind of autobiography.

I have always come to Ueno. I remember the first time, in 1947, when there were still some hopefuls looking for members of their sundered families. There were hand-lettered paper posters whispering that a mother was looking for a child, or a child for a father. Now I look down and see the homeless, working away, homeless but not hopeless.

Buddhists hold that all life is suffering and that the root of this suffering is illusion. We desire that which is transient and illusionary. Therefore the root of suffering is desire. We must learn not to want. However, wanting is the stuff of life. Hence the deluded, all of us, are forced to endlessly repeat those actions that led to our being so dissatisfied in the first place. We are all endlessly sweeping, trying to tidy away or to reveal a world that is no longer here.

What then of the natural world?—of that remnant now hanging outside my window? Indeed, what then of beauty, that most impermanent of all things? I am mourning the loss of what it is natural to lose. There is an answer, however: don't mourn.

*

But this does not mean doing nothing. I look down at Shinobazu Pond, dark in the twilight, and remember a bright winter day when the residents were all out marching and protesting a plan to drain the pond and install beneath it a massive car park. They were successful. The authorities backed down and now the massive car park is being constructed under nearby Chuo-dori, causing all of the inconvenience that it would have at Shinobazu but none of the danger to nature and beauty, since neither nature nor beauty exist on Chuo-dori.

In the waning light I look at my photograph of Shinobazu, the one I took when it was still light enough to take a photo. It lies there in my hand, a perfect simulacrum of what once was. I look out over my view, over the dark lake, the darker shadow of the Benzaiten temple, behind which once shimmered the snow-covered mountains of Chichibu.

And I smile because all is well. All is as it should be.

—*2006*

Acknowledgments

I The Larger View

Intimacy and Distance: On Being a Foreigner in Japan: address, University of Milwaukee, 1993, collected in *Partial Views*, 1995, reprinted in *The Donald Richie Reader*, 2001. *Japan: A Description*: installation, Walker Art Center, Minneapolis, 1984, published in *Travel and Leisure*, republished in *The San Francisco Chronicle*, collected in *A Lateral View*, 1987/1992, reprinted in part in *The Donald Richie Reader*. *Japanese Shapes*: published in *Katachi: Japanese Patterns and Design*, 1961, and *Design and Craftsmanship in Japan*, 1963, collected in *A Lateral View*. *Japanese Rhythms*: published in *East-West*, reprinted in *Japan Society Newsletter*, collected in *A Lateral View*. *Japan— Half a Century of Change*: address, Japan Society, Boston, 1984, published in *Intersect Japan*, 1995, collected in *Partial Views*. *The Nourishing Void*: published in *Intersect Japan*, 1992, collected in *Partial Views*. *The Coming Collapse of Cultural Internationalization*: address, the Foreign Correspondents' Club of Japan, 1994, collected in *Partial Views*. *Interpretations of Japan*: published in *Japan Quarterly*, 2001. *Crossing the Border: The Japanese Example*: address, Bard College 2004, unpublished.

II Culture and Style

The Japanese Way of Seeing: address, University of Michigan, 1993, collected in *Partial Views*. *Japan: The Image Industry*: address, University of Alberta, 1996, published in *Sightlines*, 1997. *Traditional Japanese Design*: originally published as the introduction to *Traditional Japanese Design: Five Tastes* by Michael Dunn, Japan Society of New York, 2001—the essay itself was expanded and rewritten and became *A Tractate on Japanese Aesthetics*, 2007. *Signs and Symbols*: introduction to *Ji: Signs and Symbols of Japan*, 1974, collected in *A Lateral View*. *The Tongue of Fashion*: published in *Some Aspects of Japanese Popular Culture*, 1981, and the *Japan Society Newsletter*, collected in *A Lateral View. Japan the Incongruous*: originally appeared as (bilingual: English/French) the Introduction to *Tokyo Love Hello*, 2006. *Pink Box: Inside Japanese Sex Clubs*: commissioned by Joan Sinclair, 2007, unpublished.

III   On Expression
The Presentational Urge as Theater: address, Third Midwest Seminar on Japanese Literature, Theatricality, and Performance, Purdue University, 1994, collected in *Partial Views. Some Loose Pages on Japanese Narration*: written for Helmut Färber's *Festschrift*, unpublished; in collecting these notes I am much indebted to Gilberto Perez's *The Material Ghost: Films and Their Medium* (Johns Hopkins University Press, 1998) and David Bordwell's *Making Meaning: Inference and Rhetoric in the Interpretation of Cinema* (Harvard University Press, 1989). *Notes on the Noh*: appeared in *The Hudson Review*, 1966, collected in *A Lateral View. The Kyogen*: appeared in *The Oriental Economist*, 1969, reprinted in *A Guide to Kyogen*, collected in *A Lateral View. TV: The Presentational Image*: published in *Some Aspects of Japanese Culture*, collected in *A Lateral View. Outcast Samurai Dancer*: text published in book form, 2003. *Retro Dancing*: requested by Alejandro Jaimes-Larrarte, 2004, unpublished.

IV   On Film
A Definition of the Japanese Film: published in *Performance*, 1974, reprinted in *Some Aspects of Japanese Popular Culture*, collected in part in *A Lateral View. Some Notes on Life and Death in the Japanese Film*: published in *The Japan Mission Journal*, Sixtieth Anniversary Issue, 2006. *Buddhism and the Film*: originally a series of notes for an address given at the Pacific Film Archive, Berkeley, 1993, published as such in *The Donald Richie Reader*, rewritten as address, University of Pennsylvania, 2003, reworked into the present essay form, given as an address at Doshisha University, Kyoto, 2005. *Japanese Women in Society and in Film*: given as address at Showa Women's University, 2005, unpublished. *The Japanese Eroduction*: published in *Film Comment*, 1972, reprinted in *Some Aspects of Japanese Popular Culture*, collected in *A Lateral View. Trains in Japanese Film*: originally published in

Trains in Film, New York Museum of Modern Art, 1993. *Subtitling Japanese Films:* appeared in *Mangajin*, 1991, collected in *Partial Views*, and reprinted in *Throne of Blood* (Criterion DVD, 2003).

V   The View from Inside

Wasei Eigo: *A Beginner's Guide*: written in 1995, collected in *Partial Views*. Mizushobai: *The Art of Pleasing*: appeared in *The Japan Society Newsletter*, 1981, collected in *A Lateral View. Some Thoughts on Car Culture in Japan*: appeared in *Autopia*, 2002. *The Window and the Mirror: Some Thoughts on International Culture*: appeared in *The Japan Foundation Newsletter*, vol. 25, no. 3, 2005. *An Alternative Way of Thought*: appeared in *The Asiatic Society of Japan Newsletter*, 2005. *Foreign Thoughts on Watching the Passing of a* Matsuri *Procession:* commissioned by *Bungei shunju* in 1985 but never published. *My View:* appeared in Japanese in the Ghibli publication *Neppo*, 2006—this is its first English appearance.

CPSIA information can be obtained
at www.ICGtesting.com
Printed in the USA
JSHW081548100323
38691JS00004B/1